UNEQUAL TREATMENT

What You Don't Know
About How Women
Are Mistreated by
the Medical Community

EILEEN NECHAS
and
DENISE FOLEY

SIMON & SCHUSTER
New York London Toronto
Sydney Tokyo Singapore

SIMON & SCHUSTER
Rockefeller Center
1230 Avenue of the Americas
New York, New York 10020

Copyright © 1994 by Eileen Nechas and Denise Foley
All rights reserved
including the right of reproduction
in whole or in part in any form.
SIMON & SCHUSTER and colophon are
registered trademarks of Simon & Schuster Inc.
Designed by Edith Fowler
Manufactured in the United States of America

10   9   8   7   6   5   4   3   2   1

Library of Congress Cataloging-in-Publication Data

Nechas, Eileen
    Unequal treatment : what you don't know about
how women are mistreated by the medical community
/ Eileen Nechas and Denise Foley.
        p.   cm.
Includes index.
1. Women—Medical care—United States.
2. Sex discrimination against women—United States.
I. Foley, Denise. II. Title.
RA564.85.N43   1994
362.1'082—dc20   93-47632   CIP
ISBN: 0-671-79186-9

In memory of my mother, Grace Foley; my aunt, Mary Costello; and my friend, Ann Newman.

—D.F.

To my daughters, Dale and Julie Mazer.

—E.N.

CONTENTS

PART TWO
UNEQUAL TREATMENT:
CRISES IN CARE

PART THREE
SMALL VICTORIES

ACKNOWLEDGMENTS

Though there are only two names on the cover of this book, it is, in reality, the work of many people whose commitment to its message, its spirit, and its authors make them deserving of special mention.

Karen Johnson, M.D., graciously agreed to be our medical consultant despite her busy private practice and her own writing commitments. Karen read every chapter for accuracy, offering gentle criticism and guidance and, though she may not have realized it, inspired us with her own courage in taking the entire medical profession head-on.

We also offer our special thanks to Florence Haseltine, Ph.D., M.D., founder of the Society for the Advancement of Women's Health Research, and to U.S. Congresswoman Patricia Schroeder for sharing their time, expertise, and insights on an issue so close to their hearts. Thanks also goes to Tracey Lee Johnson of the society for giving us her time and her files and to Marian Banzhof of the New Jersey Women and AIDS Network, whose knowledge and insight—and her love for the forgotten women—provide the structure for the chapter on women and AIDS. We would also like to extend our heartfelt gratitude to Louise Denson, Karen Sofield, and Vivian Torres, who enabled us to put a face on the invisible woman with AIDS and whose courage will be with us as long as we live.

Elaine Eaker, Sc.D.; Sharyn Lenhart, M.D.; Gary Schoener, Tonda Hughes, Ph.D.; Jean Hamilton, M.D.; and Paula Caplan, Ph.D., not only shared their knowledge—and often their private papers—with us, but were kind enough to review particular chapters pertaining to their specialties. Thanks also to Margaret Jensvold, M.D., Helen Ginsburg, and the other women, some who preferred to be anonymous, who so willingly shared their personal stories with us, including the wonderful women in the waiting room at the Women's Center. Thanks, too, to Helen Fedele at the Women's Center, and to Sister Teresa Immaculate and Donna Franklin for their help on the poverty chapter.

A special thanks to Vicki Ratner, M.D., and Carla Harrington of the Interstitial Cystitis Association for "putting in a good word." Their last-minute assistance was invaluable in keeping this book up to date. We are also grateful to Lila Wallis, M.D., and Michelle Harrison, M.D., for giving us so much to think about and to Anne Fausto-Sterling, Ruth Hubbard, and the late Ruth Bleier for their inspiration.

This book would not be a reality if it were not for the unflagging support we received from our first editor, Sheridan Hay, for a proposal that was only half written and for the initial work done by our second editor, Gail Winston, whose suggestions gave the book its life. Thanks goes to Sheila Curry for the finishing touches.

We are also grateful to the following organizations for supplying us with pertinent data and numerous experts to contact: the College of Physicians and Surgeons of Ontario, the American Psychological Association, the Congressional Caucus for Women's Issues, the Center for Research on Women and Gender, the Society for the Advancement of Women's Health Research, the Breast Cancer Coalition, the American Cancer Society, the Centers for Disease Control and Prevention, the Office of Research on Women's Health, the National Women's Health Resource Center, the National Women's Health Network, the Jacobs Institute of Women's Health, the Institute for Research on Women's Health, the U.S. General Accounting Office, Bass and Howes, the Association of American Medical Colleges, the Association of American Colleges, the American Medical Association, the American Medical Women's Association, the American Psychiatric Association, the American Heart Association, the National Council on Alcoholism and Drug Dependence, Inc., the National Institute on Drug Abuse, the U.S. Department of Health and Human Services, the American College of Obstetricians and Gynecologists, the Center on Budget and Policy Priorities, Planned Parenthood Federation of America, the National Association for Perinatal Addiction Research and Education, the National Council of Negro Women, and the American Civil Liberties Union.

Thanks, too, to the librarians at the Medical College of Pennsylvania, the Eastern Pennsylvania Psychiatric Institute, the Lehigh Valley Hospital

Center, and the Montgomery County Public Library for their invaluable help.

On a personal note, thanks to Marjorie Stoddard for baby-sitting during the critical last minutes and to David Rosenkrantz, perhaps the only English-speaking computer expert in the Western world, for saving all those thousands of words from computer limbo.

Of course, we are forever grateful to our husbands, Jim Nechas and Ed Rogan, and our children, Dale and Julie Mazer, Jon and Sacha Nechas, and Patrick Rogan, for everything that really matters.

Introduction

HOW WOMEN
BECAME
INVISIBLE

Some ideas are not really new but keep having to be affirmed from the ground up, over and over. One of these is the apparently simple idea that women are as intrinsically human as men. . . .

—Adrienne Rich
Of Woman Born

In one of writer G. K. Chesterton's Father Brown mysteries, a successful inventor is killed and his body removed from his blood-spattered flat while four men, including a policeman, stand guard outside, noticing no one coming or going.

"God!" cries one character in dismay. "The Invisible Man!"

But Father Brown, with his penetrating insight into human psychology, quickly nabs the culprit: the neighborhood postman. Not an invisible man, he gently tells his startled companions, but "a mentally invisible man."

"Nobody ever notices postmen somehow," the little priest says thoughtfully.

When we began researching this book in 1991, our intent was to document the extent to which gender bias had infected medical research and was compromising the health and health care of women. Like many other Americans, we had been reading and hearing about the failure to include women in studies of heart disease; the under-funding of diseases, like breast cancer, that disproportionately affect women; and the drugs and medical bromides that were being dis-pensed to women although their safety and efficacy had only been

13

tested on men. Clearly, doctors were practicing men's health on women and in some cases putting women's lives in danger. Somehow, in the closed world of science and medicine women had become invisible. But why?

The more we researched the issue, the more elusive the answer became. It was not difficult to document a pattern of unequal treatment in medical research and health care; scientists have been doing it themselves for many years. Long before women's health became the stuff of headlines, researchers, both feminist and otherwise, were rooting out and recording what looked frighteningly like an epidemic of neglect. No area of health care was untouched. From psychology to oncology, from the emergency room to the family doctor's waiting room, women were being ignored from head to toe.

How, we wondered, do you ignore a group that large and visible? It seemed impossible, like ignoring an elephant in the living room. How, we asked ourselves, can the majority of Americans be considered "a special case" and half the human race be classified as a subgroup, compared, as one conservative magazine did, to Cuban Americans? Women are not a subgroup. By virtue of numbers alone, we *are* the group. We are not a minor aberration of the species *Homo sapiens.* We are not, as the poet Milton called us and medical research regards us, "a fair defect of nature." We are as fully human as men. We are, men and women, two sides of the same coin, both different and the same.

The answer, as it turns out, was rather obvious. Although we had been looking at gender bias, we kept hoping to find another explanation, something more palatable, something scientific to reduce our increasing discomfort with what we now believe to be the truth. To science, women had become invisible because in this culture within a culture women's lives have not been important enough to notice. Women are inconsequential, a passing blur, a presence that barely registers on the consciousness. Decisions on what aspect of health to study, on what research protocol to fund, even whose symptoms would be acknowledged and who would receive lifesaving treatments were being based not only on scientific merit or finely honed medical skills, but on a judgment of social worth. What is valuable to medicine is who is valuable to society, and that is white men.

Why had we resisted arriving at that conclusion? Early in our research, a high-placed official at the National Institutes of Health (NIH) had assured us, "You don't have to look any further for your answer. You're there." Though in the end we had come to accept the opinion of Jonathan Mann, head of the World Health Organization (WHO), that "living in a male-dominated society can be hazardous to your health," the truth is sometimes a bitter pill. And it is one that doctors and patients alike are having a hard time swallowing. After all, we would all like to believe that the work researchers and physicians do is based on solid scientific ground. Our lives and their livelihoods depend upon it. But we also want to believe that ground is located on some island utopia where they work protected from the prevailing winds of culture.

Of course, that is not true. The men and women who labor in the halls of science were raised in a culture that still values men's work over women's work, men's lives over women's lives, where men's lives are studied in history, political science, psychology, and medicine, and women's lives are relegated to the occasional parentheses. It is difficult for any of us to escape the inference that women are but a mere footnote to humanity and particularly difficult for those who choose to study medicine.

Historically, science, particularly medicine, has been used as a weapon against women. In the nineteenth century, science designated as "biologically inferior" any subgroup of *Homo sapiens* that differed from the norm, which was then, as now, the white male. The skulls, brains, and skeletons of women and blacks were probed and measured with intense scrutiny to prove the culturally informed thesis that their subordinate roles in society were biologically determined, that they were ordained by God and their smaller brain capacities to serve society but never to share in its full benefits. Because women's bodies differed from men's, what was natural for women was seen as unnatural. Consequently, everything from menstruation to menopause was regarded as a disease state. The health of women was viewed only in the context of reproduction. As nineteenth-century physician Rudolf Virchow, M.D., explained: "Woman is a pair of ovaries with a human being attached, whereas man is a human being furnished with a pair of testes."

Unfortunately, researchers are still looking for biological explanations for the status of women in society. Scientists probe the brains of women to determine why girls don't do as well as boys in math. They produce evidence that our "raging hormones" may pre-dispose us to cyclic madness, as if only biology can explain why there are so few women epidemiologists or why female workers make only three-quarters of what males do. In many quarters, wom-en's health is still synonymous with maternal health. The hormone question is a particularly pernicious line of inquiry, given that mil-lions of baby boom women, who helped clear the path for women to enter the workplace, will be experiencing menopause by the year 2000. Premenstrual syndrome is already a psychiatric diagnosis that suggests women are unfit for life outside the home. A new diagnosis of climacteric dysphoric disorder that applies to the emotional bed-lam women are supposed to start experiencing by the age of forty-five or fifty will simply cover quite handily the rest of our prime working lives.

Do we believe that the scientific community is made up of men whose sole purpose is to turn back the clock to a time when women "knew their place"? Do we believe that women were deliberately left out of the research that could save our lives? That would suggest that scientists are guilty of some malevolent intent, which in most cases is not so. If scientists have a hidden agenda, it is hidden even from themselves. If they are guilty of anything, it is of not acknowl-edging they may have a blind spot, that they are a product of their culture and hold its biases, which then inform the work they do. In a culture in which women are "devalued by definition," it is not hard to understand why women's lives are considered not worthy of in-vestigation. It is also not hard to imagine how a scientist might de-sign and interpret a research study that accepts this culturally imbedded view of women's lives—and not even be aware of his bias. As feminist scientist Anne Fausto-Sterling points out in her book, *The Myths of Gender,* "by definition, one cannot see one's own blind spots." It is into this particular blind spot that women simply disappear. This is how we became invisible.

But what we call *invisibility* in this book is, of course, not physi-cal reality. Women are everywhere, statistically dominating the total population and making our presence felt in other areas as well. In-stead, it is more helpful to think of women's invisibility as a vision problem, one shared by most of our major institutions and by many of us. But it is one we believe can be corrected.

To correct it, we must be willing to shake ourselves and those who hold our lives in their hands out of the comfortable stupor of the status quo. To be seen in this society, it is necessary that we be heard. Women have enormous unrealized power—as voters, as workers, as patients, as health care consumers. We need to vote with our ballots and vote with our feet, electing legislators who understand and are committed to the issue of women's health and choosing physicians who know how to practice women's health care. We need to shine a perpetual light into the dark corner where we have been hidden. We need to encode a new message into the culture: There is no place in medicine for gender bias. We are two sides of the same coin. One side is not more valuable than the other.

Part One

The Current State
of
Women's Health Care

1
WANTED

Volunteers for
Medical Research,
Women Need Not Apply

Most researchers are white, middle-aged males, and the people who fund the research are white, middle-aged males. That's their orientation. As a result, the white male remains the experimental animal of choice.

Jerry Avorn, M.D.

On Monday, June 18, 1990, in room 2322 of the Rayburn House Office Building in Washington, D.C., a House panel learned from the General Accounting Office (GAO) that more than half the population of the United States had been placed at risk of ill health because scientists had systematically excluded them from medical research studies. Women, it seems, with their monthly hormone fluctuations and their chances of becoming pregnant were considered flies in the ointment of pure research, where keeping variables to a minimum was more important than uncovering any universal truths that could benefit both sexes. So pervasive was this exclusion of females from medical research that only male laboratory rats were used for experimentation.

An incredulous Henry Waxman, the Democratic congressman from California who chaired the hearings, heard testimony from a GAO investigator that some senior-level male researchers at NIH considered policies insisting on the inclusion of women in medical studies to be political interference and without scientific merit.

It quickly became clear that although women make 60 to 70

percent of all doctor's office visits, undergo more complex procedures, more examinations, more laboratory tests, and more blood pressure checks than men; receive more prescriptions and take more medications than men; spend more time in hospitals than men; suffer more age-related disabling conditions; and, perhaps most important, pay half the taxes that foot the multibillion-dollar NIH annual budget, they were being served by a science to which they were negligible.

That June morning, the congressional panel heard example after example proving a long-standing pattern of neglect of women's health. They learned, for instance, that the NIH-sponsored five-year Physician's Health Study showed that taking one aspirin every other day could reduce the incidence of heart attacks in those studied—22,071 men and no women, even though heart disease is the number one killer of women, too. They learned that a nationally funded long-term study about health and aging included only men during its first twenty years despite the fact that two-thirds of those over age sixty-five are women. They learned that a major study showed that heavy coffee intake does not increase the risk of stroke or heart attack, at least not in the group examined—45,589 men, no women.

The list went on: Even though women are the fastest growing group afflicted with acquired immunodeficiency syndrome (AIDS), research on treatment has focused almost entirely on men. Phenylpropanolamine (PPA), the active ingredient in many over-the-counter appetite suppressants, was tested primarily on young men, although those who use these diet aids are overwhelmingly women. A finding that aspirin can help prevent migraine headaches came from studies of men, although women suffer from migraines about three times more often. Perhaps the most shocking example was the Rockefeller University project that explored the impact of obesity on the tendency for women to develop breast or endometrial cancer, which used men only.

What's more, the congressional panel learned, health issues specific to women—unique to, more prevalent, or serious to women or for which specific risk factors or interventions differ for women—have received scant attention and research funding. Indeed, until recently, only about 13 percent of the total NIH budget was spent on women's health issues—issues that have a direct and profound effect on their lives—such as breast cancer, ovarian cancer, menopause, estrogen replacement therapy, and osteoporosis.

Although the NIH has been quick to point out that the other 80-some percent of its budget is spent on studies of diseases that affect both men and women, that figure is misleading. So-called gender-neutral conditions—heart disease, depression, AIDS, and others—are experienced differently by women and men. Yet most medical studies on illnesses, treatments, and outcomes—whether minor or major, low cost or high cost, short term or long term—have been done using all-male groups. Consequently, the data gathered do virtually nothing to advance the knowledge of those diseases in women. Indeed, it has left a gap so wide and so deep that it will take decades to close.

UNCOVERING YEARS OF RESEARCH BIAS

The 1990 congressional hearings were not the first time that gender bias in medicine had been brought to the attention of the U.S. government. It happened once before, seventy years ago. At that time, women found themselves competing not only with men, but with hogs. "When women got the right to vote after World War I, the first issue they directed their attention to was the lack of money devoted to safe childbirth," says Democratic Congresswoman Patricia Schroeder, who cochairs the Congressional Caucus for Women's Issues, a bipartisan group of over 125 members of Congress dedicated to promoting women's economic and legal rights. "These new voters pointed out that more women died in childbirth than Americans had died in the First World War. What's more, they noted that the federal government spent more money on hog cholera research than on safe childbirth and prenatal care. Their onslaught worked, and more money was soon funneled into those pressing health issues. But for some reason," says Schroeder, "we were never able to get that kind of momentum going again."

Even in the early days of modern feminism, women's health was a political issue of narrow parameters. During that time, the Boston Women's Health Book Collective published its groundbreaking book, *Our Bodies Ourselves,* the feminist health collective movement was born, and the National Women's Health Network was founded by a group of women concerned about the mounting death toll from the Pill. But those groups were more concerned with reproductive matters and with how women were treated in the examining room than in how they were treated in the laboratory and the corridors of political power. Crisis oriented, they were alert to the deadly dangers of the Dalkon Shield intrauterine device, but, like everyone else, they were blind to the fundamental neglect of women and women's health issues in medical science that has had more far-reaching and equally deadly consequences. However, even if they had been aware, they simply did not have the ability to build an effective grass roots movement that could exert pressure where it was needed the most: on the U.S. government's Public Health Service and its largest funding organ, the NIH, which foots the bill for much of the major medical research done in the United States.

Ironically, it was those two agencies that cast the first dim light on their own inadequacies. In 1983, then Assistant Secretary of Health Edward N. Brandt, Jr., M.D., commissioned a Public Health Service Task Force to look into the status of women's health issues. Its 1985 report, called *The Women's Health Report of the Public Health Service Task Force on Women's Health Issues,* forced closed eyes to open when it concluded that gender bias in health care research and delivery had created significant gaps in knowledge about women's health. For the first time, both academics and government policy makers agreed that women were disadvantaged when it came to health care.

As a result of that report, in 1986, the NIH informed grant applicants that if women were not included in study populations, the NIH wanted a scientific rationale for excluding them. The NIH also wanted researchers to note and evaluate any gender differences in their study results. It was that new policy, aimed at redressing years of wrongs, that came under scrutiny in December 1989, when Schroeder; Congresswoman Olympia Snowe, a Republican from Maine; along with Henry Waxman, who chairs the House Energy and Commerce Subcommittee on Health and the Environment, asked the GAO to determine its impact on women's health research.

Six months later, it became clear that NIH's policy was, as Schroeder told her congressional colleagues, "a paper tiger." The GAO found that the agency had given nothing more than lip service to its antiexclusion policy and had continued to conduct business as usual: funding research by white men, about white men, and for white men. In his testimony before the House panel, Mark V. Nadel, the GAO's associate director for National and Public Health Issues, reported that NIH hadn't adequately explained its new policy on women to the research community, most of whom, along with many NIH insiders, didn't really understand it or what was expected of them. What's more, admitted then acting NIH director William Raub, some of those who had "received the word" demonstrated "some arrogance or indifference" toward it. Obviously, that description included those in the top echelons at the health agency. It took NIH almost three years to issue detailed implementation guidelines to its staff. The grant application booklet researchers use to draw up their funding requests had not been revised to reflect the new guidelines, so that proposals that, without explanation, excluded women were still being received, reviewed, and ultimately funded. A revised form did not appear until April 1991, over four years after the policy was first introduced.

The GAO report went on to admonish the NIH for directly undermining the goal of its policy by not considering the inclusion of women as a key factor in determining a research proposal's scientific merit, which, Nadel commented, "tends to downgrade the importance of the issue." Indeed, how important could this issue have been when NIH had no system in place to monitor the effectiveness of its policy? Or when it didn't know the number of all-male studies that were funded in the past or were currently being funded? Or when the provision that researchers analyze study results by gender had been virtually ignored, so that even if women were included in the studies, there was no way of knowing whether the diseases or the treatments for those diseases affected women differently than men? And how important could this issue have been when it only applied to extramural research—projects funded by the NIH but conducted outside the organization—and not to intramural research—projects conducted by NIH itself?

Congresswoman Schroeder was outraged. "The failure to include women in research studies is symptomatic of a larger problem—a wholesale lack of investment in women's health research," she said at the hearings. "We spend $38 billion on defense research and only $7 to $8 billion on medical research, a small fraction of which goes to women's health issues." An Institute of Medicine report found that only 1.8 percent of the NIH extramural funds were awarded to support research in obstetric and gynecology departments in 1986 and 1987. And there are only three obstetrician-gynecologists (OB-GYNs) on permanent staff at the NIH. As one of those pointed out, the NIH employs more veterinarians than it does gynecologists. So weak is the government's commitment that the giant NIH, with seventeen individual institutes under its massive umbrella—including the well-known National Cancer Institute, the National Heart, Lung and Blood Institute, as well as the lesser-known National Institute of Dental Research and the National Eye Institute—has yet to establish a separate research branch devoted to obstetrics and gynecology.

EXCUSES, EXCUSES

To the layperson, it may seem obvious that women ought to be included in any research whose outcome is likely to affect their health. But that's not the way many medical scientists look at it. They argue that women's monthly hormonal fluctuations make them too "different," complicate research, and increase costs; they worry about the risk to a fetus—and the potential liability—should a woman become pregnant during a clinical trial; and they complain that it's too hard to find enough women to make the study results valuable. Yet these same researchers who claim women's differences make them research risks will turn around and assert that women are "just like men anyway," so it's appropriate to simply draw conclusions about and dispense medical advice to women from the results of all-male studies.

From the point of view of a researcher, there's an obvious advantage to having a homogeneous sample. For one thing, it makes interpreting data much simpler. Limiting a study to white males helps eliminate some of those messy variables in an experiment, like hormonal changes, racial disparities, or the multiple debilities of age, that might need to be accounted for before conclusions can be drawn. In science, the white male has become like the white rat, that simple, easy, and abundant "experimental animal of choice." Researchers have come to consider white men the "generic humans," as if women and people of color are simply deviations from the norm. "Physical differences between males and females or between whites and people of color are unacknowledged or irrelevant in this worldview," says ethics professor Rebecca Dresser, J.D., of Case Western Reserve University Medical School.

This is a dangerous worldview. Recent studies, specifically those on cardiovascular disease, have uncovered profound differences between men and women and between races. Those studies suggest that ignoring such realities has resulted in bad science and bad medicine.

For example, excluding women *because* of their menstrual cycle makes no scientific sense. The menstrual cycle is not an anomaly. It's the part of a woman's normal physiology, and "it requires study as a separate variable pertinent to women's health," says Jean Hamilton, M.D., a former researcher at the National Institute of Mental Health (NIMH) and now a professor at Duke University. It's especially important to consider menstrual cycle effects in drug research because a woman's normal monthly hormone fluctuations can vary the effectiveness of a medication. A constant dose may be too high during the first half of the cycle but not enough later on. For instance, asthma medications are sensitive to the menstrual cycle, and some researchers believe that not accounting for that may contribute to the existing premenstrual rise in asthma deaths.

Yet when Hamilton worked at NIMH, she was warned to steer clear of investigating gender differences in drug response—not only because the topic wasn't important but because, her male supervisor told her, the differences simply didn't exist. "If there were, we'd already know about it," he told her. ("So much for the scientific method," comments Hamilton dryly.) Fortunately, Hamilton ignored his advice and did the research anyway, and he took the credit, thanking her "in a footnote, along with the secretaries."

Though it's true that including both sexes adds greatly to the cost of doing research, because it means having to increase the total sample size and, perhaps, the length of the study, it's not a legitimate reason to ignore 52 percent of the population. Calling it "too expensive" implies that studying women's health is a luxury, not a necessity. As Jean Hamilton retorts, "Too expensive compared with what?"

Besides, counters Hamilton, "including women in every clinical trial is no more needed than was blanket exclusion." There are more modest, less costly alternatives. Why not decide which diseases and drugs require the most intensive gender-related study and fund those first? This approach would help control costs and keep them at a feasible level. Or if researchers want to do a study using all men, then do the next one using all women.

Of all the rationales for excluding women, the one that is most often cited is the fear of harming a fetus. In medical science, all women are viewed as "walking wombs" whose potential for pregnancy—and presumably for litigation—make them poor, not to mention dangerous, test subjects. Never mind that the drugs and treatments being tested will ultimately be given to the same women the researchers are so afraid of harming, that phantom fetus stands in the way of including women in research that may do far more to protect them from harm. Like many of the other rationales, this one disintegrates under scrutiny. The fact is that all women are not at equal risk for pregnancy. On the contrary, there are millions of women who have had sterilization procedures or hysterectomies, and millions more who are postmenopausal, gay, or not sexually active who could qualify for a medical study. Surely, as one researcher pointed out, most female cardiac patients are not planning to get pregnant. Nor are the women who might be included in an aging study. It's as if male scientists assume that all women are unreliable when it comes to birth control, says Hamilton, or that they can't be trusted to know when they are or are not at risk for pregnancy. She recalls, for example, the time a male researcher refused to allow a woman to participate in a study even though her husband was in Europe for six months and she assured him they had a monogamous relationship.

Though concerns about birth defects have merit, that shouldn't be enough to exclude *all* women of childbearing age from medical studies. Legal scholars have argued that those conducting drug trials need only show that reasonable precautions have been taken so that the risk is negligible. "It is unrealistic to expect the potential risk to a fetus to be zero since such a standard is not required for living persons," says Hamilton. Besides, women's informed consent has been accepted for other medical procedures, such as diagnostic X rays, where there is also a potential for fetal harm.

Excluding women from studies because of recruitment difficulties is an excuse that doesn't hold water either. That's been a particularly popular reason for shutting women out of heart research, even though cardiovascular disease is the leading cause of death in women. The researchers who studied aspirin and heart disease, for example, recruited physicians over forty for their project. They claimed that because women comprised only 10 percent of that group, there wouldn't have been enough of them having heart attacks to enable the researchers to draw any scientific conclusions. Though that is true enough, underlying official excuses was a clear antiwoman attitude: One NIH official was quoted as saying he doubted whether enough women would be "interested in participating and be content to go through the hassle of taking a placebo." Other researchers have argued that because women develop heart disease ten years later than men, they can't locate enough women with the condition to achieve statistical significance in their studies. But the more likely reason cardiovascular disease has been understudied in women is that the medical community has failed miserably to recognize serious heart disease in women and, because it occurs mainly in older women, considers it not worthy of study.

The truth is, if there weren't enough middle-aged female doctors to include in the aspirin study, had the researchers thought it was important enough they could have found a similar cohort of women. There are equally large groups of female nurses, usually in the same vicinity as doctors. In fact, the researchers who did the aspirin study applied for funding for a second study on women but were turned down, which suggests there are other less politically palatable reasons women have excluded from research.

Rather than acknowledging their neglect of women as a bias, researchers seem more inclined to blame women for their failure to participate. Had more women chosen medical careers midcentury, they could have been part of the aspirin study. But whose fault is it there were so few women doctors? Historically, women weren't encouraged to enter the medical profession until the feminist boom of the mid-1970s. Whose fault is it that doctors often don't recognize heart disease in their female patients? With women excluded from most of the major risk factor and treatment research, it has been easy for doctors to overlook cardiac symptoms in this presumed low-risk population. And why was it assumed that women would be less interested in participating in a heart study than men or be more likely to find it "a hassle" to take a placebo? If women were as well informed about their heart disease risks as men are, wouldn't they have just as much incentive as men to do whatever medical investigators asked them to do? In fact, researchers have found women are far more compliant than men, especially in studies seeking to change dietary habits.

DIVVYING UP THE RESEARCH MONEY

Because it is the principal funding agency for medical research in this country, NIH has been targeted for the harshest criticism by women's health advocates, who, although acknowledging the sexism rife in the medical community, point out that it has been NIH that has been paying all the bills for years of androcentric research. Even after acknowledging the error of its ways in 1986, NIH continued to treat women as an afterthought. Women's health is studied after research on "normal" human beings—the 165-pound man of medical texts—is taken care of. Says Olympia Snowe, "The NIH's attitude has been to consider over half the population as some sort of special case."

To explain the NIH's insensitivity to women's issues, many critics cite the fact that the department is top-heavy with men who are, with few notable exceptions, in all the positions of power. "There are a lot of good men at NIH, but what they study is what is interesting to them," says Florence Haseltine, Ph.D., M.D., director of the NIH's Center for Population Research who founded the Society for the Advancement of Women's Health Research. That's not necessarily bad, Haseltine points out. "You don't want scientists studying things that don't interest them. You want somebody whose life depends on that work."

But what interests those men have largely been issues on which only *their* lives depend. "To do trials of osteoporosis with the argument that this is what keeps a lot of women in nursing homes is a very valid argument, but it isn't as compelling to the people giving out the money as their friends who are dropping dead of heart attacks in the next office," says Harvard AIDS researcher Deborah Cotton, M.D.

That is not to say that money simply flows to any male researcher who asks for it. The federal funding process is, like other government bureaucracy, more complicated than chess strategy. Competition for federal money is usually fierce, especially in tight economic times. The NIH only funds about a third of the grant proposals it receives. Grant applications are lengthy, and the review process is Darwinian. "It's like organizing D day three times a year," says cancer researcher Craig Jordan, M.D. For as much as nine months or more, a grant proposal is fed through "a massive bureaucratic machine that cuts, slices and dices applications so finely that scientists sometimes wonder what happened to their original ideas," as *The Journal of NIH Research* described the process. Each application is reviewed by so-called study sections made up of the scientist's peers (and, frequently, his or her competition), a concept that is routinely excoriated every few years as expensive and unwieldy. The study sections have also been described as "an old boys' network," populated by "everybody who has some kind of conflict of interest" and, as brash NIH watcher Daniel S. Greenberg put it, "about as exclusive as the Book-of-the-Month Club." Yet every application must pass through this gauntlet. Having a good idea is a plus, but it's only a start. Scientists must also be adept at grantsmanship. Funding often goes to the scientist who is at least as talented at selling a proposal as designing elegant research protocols. That fact explains, for instance, why federal grants for AIDS research wind up in cities like Denver and not in Newark, which is second only to New York City in numbers of AIDS cases.

Though getting funded is an uphill battle for everyone, for researchers seeking funding for women's health issues, it's an even steeper hill. The NIH review and approval process for funding works against women in several ways. The male administrators—and largely male reviewers—have enormous discretionary power over what research is funded. Like male researchers, they have their interests and their biases, which, because they are so often unacknowledged, become blind spots. Though scientists like to believe they are living and operating in an atmosphere unsullied by "outside forces," they are as prone to prejudices and politics as anyone else, perhaps more so because so many are dependent on volatile government support for their livelihoods. No matter how rigorously scientists try to be objective, writes feminist scientist Anne Fausto-Sterling in *The Myths of Gender,* they "peer through the prism of everyday culture, using the colors so separated to highlight their questions, design their experiments and interpret their results." In "everyday culture," women's lives are not seen as being as important as men's, so research on women's health issues doesn't seem as compelling—or salable. From a purely practical perspective, the wise researcher who wants to stay in the business is going to steer clear of subjects that are a tough sell.

Also, fewer women are applying for federal research grants. In 1989, 12,545 men sought funding from NIH; only 2,929 women did. Women scientists who have attempted to navigate the system have found the going tough and the climate harsh. Jean Hamilton eventually abandoned her attempts to study hormones and drugs at NIMH, pooling her money with three other women scientists to establish "a lab of our own" to carry out research they believed was important. (Hamilton also filed an administrative complaint against NIH in 1980, charging it was a hostile workplace for women scientists. The complaint was settled, but under mutually agreed upon terms, Hamilton is unable to discuss its resolution.) Geriatrician Linda Fried, M.D., now director of the $7.9 million national Women's Aging Study, recalls being turned down for a grant to study the effects of physical activity on older women because the reviewers felt "it had already been studied substantially in men."

Undeniably, NIH has put two different price tags on the health of men and women. But this kind of discrimination thrives in the private sector, too. According to the New York–based National Council for Research on Women, in 1990, less than 6 percent of all foundation dollars—$165.8 million out of $3.25 billion—were spent on programs that directly benefit women and girls. Coming after a decade of bone-scraping cuts in services that mostly affect women and children, this clearly represents a judgment of worth, not need. In fact, the council says, many nonprofit executives and fund-raisers admit that having the words *women* or *girls* in the name of an organization or as the focus of an organization's proposal is the kiss of death for successful fund-raising.

There's no doubt there is some belt-tightening going on at NIH as well. Despite a declared war on cancer, funding for the National Cancer Institute has dropped by more than 6 percent. AIDS, which has held "favored disease" status for more than half a decade, was threatened with a loss in funding at a particularly acute time, when AIDS is rising among women. The climate, as one researcher put it, is "dog-eat-dog." Pediatricians and gynecologists looking for AIDS money find themselves battling over the same small slice of the funding pie. Cancer investigators are settling into three warring camps: the molecular biologists versus the clinical researchers versus the epidemiologists.

Though some diseases, like breast cancer, are the beneficiaries of an influx of guilt money, allocated by a newly enlightened—and feminized—Congress, it's clear that federal medical research money is never going to flow like defense dollars. In an economic crunch, there's a tendency to fund those projects that promise immediate gratification, ones from researchers with long track records, going over familiar territory. "So what we're guaranteed to get," complains one breast cancer researcher, "is the status quo."

That's going to make it even tougher for women's research to catch up. There's still strong resistance at NIH and among conservative lawmakers to acknowledging, let alone financially rectifying, the long-standing pattern of sex-biased research. And there are still few women in science—fewer still with established track records—to apply for and win a piece of that shrinking pie. As critics charge, studies that include women are likely to be more expensive and more attractive to jettison if cost cutting is the order of the day. If that's the case, says Jean Hamilton, researchers will "return to the most simple homogeneous sample—white males."

A MATTER OF LIFE AND DEATH

There's a gender gap in longevity. On the average, women live almost eight years longer than men. That being the case, some scientists argue, what difference has the gender gap in research really made? There's increasing evidence that what doctors don't know about women's health may be deadly.

With faulty research to draw on, physicians are severely compromised in their abilities to diagnose and treat women's symptoms. New studies on sex differences in drug response have made prescribing some medications akin to shooting darts blindfolded. Women who are sick may not even get the same quality care as men and, in fact, may be more likely to have their heart symptoms or headaches blamed on "hypochondria," a fact that the nation's largest doctor's organization, the American Medical Association (AMA), acknowledged in a scathing 1990 report of its ethics committee.

Women may not realize it and, in fact, their doctors may not be aware that from the moment they enter the physician's examining room they are virtually uncharted territory. Diagnostic procedures and treatments in common use have never been tested in women, and recent studies have found that some may do more harm than good. For example, the exercise stress test, a noninvasive procedure used to detect heart problems, has been shown to be far less accurate in women than men but remains one of the most commonly used tests for detecting heart abnormalities in both sexes. Because so many of the major studies on cardiovascular risk and heart disease treatment have been done only on men, physicians have little choice but to treat women according to the male norm. Though this may not matter some of the time, there are times when it can be dangerous. Some experts worry, for example, that recommending a low-fat diet to women may be harmful because it lowers levels of a kind of beneficial cholesterol called high-density lipoprotein (HDL). Women naturally have higher levels of blood HDL than men, and it is believed to be responsible for protecting them from heart disease, at least premenopausally. Doctors continue to treat women for high blood pressure the same way they treat men, although some blood pressure drugs, which have been tested almost exclusively on men and shown to decrease their mortality from heart attack, have been shown to *increase* deaths among women.

Fast walking, an exercise often recommended to strengthen bones, may be fine for elderly men, but that advice given to elderly women can cause injuries to their fragile musculoskeletal systems weakened by the decline of estrogen levels following menopause.

A number of studies also have provided disturbing evidence that women frequently get second-class medical treatment. They are less likely than men to undergo kidney transplants, although women with kidney disease have slightly better survival rates than men. They are also less likely to have their lung cancers detected despite the fact that lung cancer is the leading cause of cancer deaths in both sexes. Studies have shown that even when women present with the same symptoms as men, doctors don't order the same tests that would confirm a lung cancer diagnosis. A 1987 study found that even when the exercise stress test did detect heart abnormalities in

women, only 4 percent of them—compared to 40 percent of men—
were referred for cardiac catheterization to confirm the diagnosis.

Nowhere are the biases more evident than in the field of pharmacology, the study of drugs. The underrepresentation of women in
drug trials has long-range consequences, because it ultimately affects the selection, safety, and effectiveness of treatments prescribed
by physicians. Despite the fact that 60 percent of total drugs prescribed are for women, they are virtually invisible in the testing
process. Even when women are included, the results are often not
analyzed by sex, so there's no way of knowing if the women's responses to a drug differed from the men's, according to a 1992 GAO
report. That's particularly true in the earliest phases of drug testing
during what is known as Phase I, when medications are screened for
toxicity; when appropriate dosing is determined; and when studies
of the metabolism, absorption, and elimination of the drug are conducted, and during Phase II, when effectiveness and relative safety
are established.

Testing for drug effectiveness only in men, for example, may
eliminate drugs that might have worked better on women. That
early exclusion may explain why antidepressant drugs work better in
men than women, who suffer from depression twice as often as men.
Indeed, gaps in knowledge about women and depression persist
even today in part because doctors failed to study sex as a variable in
depression research.

Doses that are optimal for men, who are generally larger than
women, may be quite different than those for women, leading to the
possibility of overmedication and serious side effects. In one case,
says Hamilton, early testing of the antidepressant bupropion (Well-
butrin) revealed a risk for seizures. Nevertheless, the drug went on
to the next stage of testing using dosages that had been established
in studies using males only. These clinical trials (Phase III) were
conducted using men and women, but it was the women who had an
excess of seizures, because the dosage, based on the studies with
men, were too high for them.

Adverse drug reactions (ADRs), in general, occur more often in
women than men, in fact twice as often, according to one study.
What's more, ADRs are most prevalent in women during their reproductive years, suggesting that sex steroid hormones may play a
role, says Hamilton. But the risk also increases for those who take

more than one drug at a time, a common practice among the elderly, who are often prescribed numerous medications. Younger women can be at risk, too, especially if they use oral contraceptives, and according to estimates, about 23 percent of U.S. women aged fifteen to forty-four do. Yet scientists are not required to study drug–hormone interactions, not even those caused by oral contraceptives or hormone replacement therapy.

That is not to say women are totally eliminated from the testing process. In fact, eventually most drugs are tested on women—after the drugs are on the market. Many of the adverse effects women experience are discovered when they take a medication that, because of rigorous testing, they believe is safe. The marketing of PPA, the main ingredient in over-the-counter diet pills, is a typical example. Although women are the greatest users of PPA by a nine-to-one ratio, the drug's safety was tested almost exclusively on males. When serious side effects were discovered—dieters were developing high blood pressure and dying of strokes—they were happening primarily to women. On top of that, women who take oral contraceptives along with their diet pills—not unlikely, since hormone-based drugs are associated with weight gain—increase their risks of serious vascular side effects, even death.

BELOW THE SURFACE

The congressional hearing of June 18, 1990, made it clear that the medical community has, by its general neglect of women's health, produced bad science and placed women's lives in peril. But the testimony, while stunning, barely skimmed the surface. There is an even larger body of evidence that much of medical science is built on a bedrock of gender bias, from the earliest studies of the human psyche to the latest research on AIDS and addictions. That evidence suggests that science is far from pure. How research is designed, funded, and interpreted, as well as how physicians and researchers are trained and treated, owes at least as much to the prevailing social order, political exigencies, and personal agendas as to scientific method. Much of that evidence comes from scientists themselves and from staid mainstream medical journals like *The Journal of the American Medical Association* and *The New England Journal of*

Medicine, where, until recently, studies revealing bias against women and people of color in the health care system were viewed as isolated, like a rare outbreak of traveler's diarrhea, rather than as the deadly epidemic they represent.

They provide the proof, as Harvard scientist Ruth Hubbard writes in her book, *The Politics of Women's Biology,* that science is "made, by and large, by a self-perpetuating group; by the chosen for the chosen." Despite the much-heralded advances women have made in the last thirty years, science, like politics and business, remains like the old neighborhood boys' club with its crudely lettered warning sign, no girls allowed. But in this case, it has served to hurt more than just our feelings.

2

MEDICAL EDUCATION

By White Men,
About White Men,
For White Men

If the female is mentioned [in the classroom] at all, it's parenthetically. Professors seem completely unaware that the information they're disseminating is based on research findings from male-only studies—as if the only patients these future doctors will be treating are men.

—*A midwestern medical student*

" 'Like most women, you won't practice. You're taking the place of a male student who *would* go out and practice medicine, but otherwise you have the qualifications so I can't reject your application.' With these words from an assistant dean, I was admitted to medical school in 1962, one of five women in a class of 120," says pediatrician Louise L. McDonald, M.D., of Foster City, California.

McDonald's experience was typical for those days. Women were not wanted in the field of medicine, and it was made perfectly clear to them. Only those with extraordinary brilliance, perseverance, and thick skin even bothered to apply. It's no accident that women's enrollment in medical schools hovered at about 5 to 8 percent of the total admitted up until the mid-1970s. It wasn't until the women's movement suggested to millions of career-minded baby boomers that a woman's place was any place she wanted to be that the numbers of women applying to medical school began a steady uphill climb. Today, more than 41 percent of those entering medical school are women, and that number is expected to increase.

On the surface, it looks as though discrimination against

women has ended. Women are in the classrooms, they're on the faculties, they are seen in administrative posts, and they work as colleagues of accepting men. But beneath the surface, the picture is different.

In truth, although medical institutions have admitted women in record numbers, once inside, many women are disappointed to find the environment still hostile to them. Indeed, classroom and clinical material are more often than not taught by white men, about white men, and for white men. The curriculum doesn't speak to women's health concerns at all, says one midwestern medical student.

Scratch a little deeper and more biases emerge. Unlike past generations, today's women medical students contend with discrimination and harassment of a more subtle nature. The impact, however, is anything but subtle. Female medical students find that their morale and confidence are often undermined and opportunities for career advancement hampered by discrimination that ranges from sexist slurs to sexual advances, from poor evaluations to outright favoritism.

The repercussions are felt well beyond the medical school experience. In their careers, whether it's in academia, research, or on medical governing boards, women find their rise to the top full of jolts and detours and, in many cases, ultimately blocked. "We no longer pound on the entry gates," says Sharyn Lenhart, M.D., of Harvard Medical School. "Instead, we bump up against glass ceilings that keep us from reaching our full potential for leadership and job satisfaction." Until women reach the highest ranks of their profession, the place where policy and decisions are made, gender discrimination will continue to permeate the halls of medicine—from lectures and clinical rotations, obtaining research grants and faculty promotions, to what's studied, who's studied, and how it's taught.

Disregard for women is still an inherent part of the American medical education system. It's not surprising that this bias is also reflected in the way many physicians treat their women patients. Although there are men supportive of this issue, their numbers are small, their voices inaudible. It will take women entering medicine in increasing numbers to make a dent in a system known for its rigidity and conservatism. "When a minority reaches about 30 percent of the group, they begin to have their own voice," says Lenhart, "and they can speak to their own minority issues." Right now, that voice is just a whisper, and gender inequities continue virtually unabated, even though women have made up 30 percent or more of entering medical school classes for the last decade.

CURRICULUM INEQUITIES

Women may be sitting in the classrooms of medical schools and populating residency programs, but what they're learning and how they're learning it is not nearly so egalitarian. Gender bias is an issue that is apparent from the moment one enters medical school, say veterans of the system. From the first textbook they open, women can't help but notice that it's the male, not the female, who's considered the norm or reference point for all courses. Women, if they are mentioned at all, are classified as the exception to the male rather than being discussed as a unique category. One third-year medical student found it disconcerting that the male was considered the standard for drug dosing in her pharmacology class—but even more disturbing that in her anatomy class, "at a lecture on the pelvis, the teacher spent forty-five minutes on the male and five minutes on the female." Psychiatrist Karen Johnson, in the course of researching a book on sexism in medical education, interviewed an anatomy instructor at a highly respected medical school who reported that her predecessor had given a three-day lecture on male genitalia and dismissed women's sexual organs with the casual comment that "men and women are basically the same." He then invited those interested in learning more about female sexual organs to study them "on their own time."

Perhaps more dramatic was another woman's experience at Georgetown University Medical School, in Washington, D.C. While a student there, Adriane Fugh-Berman, M.D., who graduated in 1988 and now practices general medicine in the nation's capital, learned the relative importance of body parts on the first day of anatomy class. Her anatomy instructor, after commenting that her group's elderly cadaver must have been a Playboy bunny, directed them to "cut off her large breasts and toss them into the 30-gallon trash can marked cadaver waste. Given that one out of nine American women will develop breast cancer in her lifetime, to treat breasts as extraneous tissue seemed an appalling waste of an educational opportunity," she says.

Women's different experience in medical school is evident during clinical rotations as well. Fugh-Berman recalls an incident that drove home that point during an emergency medicine rotation in her senior year. When asked how many students knew how to insert a central line (an intravenous line placed into a major vein under the clavicle or in the neck), most of the male students raised their hands. Not one of the women did. "For me," she says, "it was graphic proof of the inequity in teaching; the men had had the procedure taught to them, but the women had not." Fugh-Berman says that she also saw a male physician conduct an examination of a patient and then search through the group of medical students until he found a male to teach the procedure to. "This sort of discrimination was common and quite unconscious: The women just didn't register as medical students to some of the doctors."

One of the most blatant signs of women's inferior position as both students and patients is the way breast and pelvic exams have been taught. This is a basic skill that's as necessary to meet the health needs of women as reading X rays is for treating fractures. Yet teaching medical students how to do competent, sensitive, painless, and educational breast and internal examinations has virtually eluded medical educators until recently—and in many instances still does.

In their second year of training, medical students learn how to examine the entire body, including the head, neck, and abdominal areas, as well as the cardiovascular and neuromuscular systems— everything, in fact, but the breast and pelvis. Like television censors, instructors have simply excluded those body parts. Instead, many medical students learned how to do these all-important physical examinations by practicing on poor clinic patients, who were often unaware that they were being used by numerous students as human guinea pigs. "Each student would file up and do the exam that had been demonstrated first by the faculty member," says Lila Wallis, M.D., clinical professor of medicine at Cornell University Medical College. "The patient was usually in pain—after all, she had come to the clinic because she was ill. Not surprisingly, she would tighten up, and the student wouldn't know what he or she was supposed to be feeling, how much pressure to exert, or how, in fact, to detect normality from abnormality. The habit of examining a woman in pain became a cornerstone of the students' experience."

Worse yet, some students have been taught to do pelvic exams on anesthetized patients who were undergoing a surgical procedure. Even if the patient had signed a consent form, she wouldn't know what had hit her when she awoke bruised and in pain. "Aside from the dubious ethics of the whole thing," says Wallis, "it was once again a poor learning experience for the students." Perhaps that's why some gynecologists' technique for obtaining a Pap smear feels more like a jackhammer against cement than the delicate wiping of tissues it's supposed to be or why many women believe a routine internal exam is *supposed* to hurt when, in fact, it should be painless.

Because of Wallis and other concerned physicians, many medical schools have abandoned these barbaric and inadequate methods of teaching pelvic exams. They now use teaching associates, women who have been trained to be substitutes for patients and are able to guide and teach medical students—in the language patients would use—how to do an appropriate breast and internal exam without causing pain. Wallis, who organized the Teacher Associate Program at Cornell and helped other medical schools develop similar methods, admits, however, that some schools only give lip service to the program. Instead, they use women who act as living pelvic models— similar to clinic patients, in actuality—who are not trained in the process and therefore cannot teach students how best to perform the exams.

Updating the information that's taught in the classroom doesn't always occur either, at least not where women's health is concerned. The now well-documented gender gaps in basic knowledge are virtually all still present in medical school curricula despite wide media attention and the scrutiny of Congress. If medical students know that women were excluded from most major heart disease studies or that osteoporosis kills more women than breast cancer, they read it in the newspaper or saw it on television. Most medical educators are still not addressing those issues in the classroom. As Anne Moulton, M.D., of Brown University School of Medicine, points out, "Students are rarely taught to ask the question, Are the study patients similar to the patient I am treating? It bothers me that teachers don't say to their students, 'This is different in women' or 'We don't know if this is different in women.' I would like to see instructors be more honest about what is known and what is not known about women's health."

Many fear it will be years before any systemwide changes in curriculum do occur. Resistance is strong to changing the subject matter even when it's unrelated to gender. Indeed, those who have attempted to incorporate women's health issues into the current system of medical education have found it a tough sell. Moulton recently surveyed medical schools and found that only about a quarter of them offer so much as a women's health elective. Typically, these are optional courses that address health concerns unique to women or having a special impact on women, such as osteoporosis, incontinence, heart disease, breast cancer, and menopause. But as one East Coast medical student remarked, "We're only preaching to the converted. Those that need it the most—the male students—are rarely the ones filling the classroom seats." And they probably never will be unless these courses are built into the permanent structure of medical education.

Residency programs have also been slow to respond to the need for specialized training in women's health, though it's been desired by many women and even some men. One program started by Moulton, who is an assistant professor at Brown, offers a fellowship in women's health in conjunction with an internal medicine residency. For practicing physicians, there's a continuing education program on women's health offered every July at Harvard Medical School. And there have been rumblings in some medical circles of initiating a separate women's health specialty that would train doctors to treat women patients from head to toe, not just from the waist down.

DEMEANING ATTITUDES

If struggling through medical school is tough on men, it is doubly so for women. The fact is, for either sex it's an environment that's been criticized as dehumanizing, psychologically stressful, and detrimental to interpersonal as well as doctor–patient relationships. Women students, however, have to contend with the additional burdens of gender discrimination and sexual harassment.

Students say that it begins well before the first day of classes and even before the acceptance letter comes in the mail. Surveys of medical students have reported that women students first notice this attitude at the critical medical school admissions interviews, where mostly male faculty members routinely grill female applicants about marriage and family planning despite the fact that this line of questioning is illegal. One student recalled a faculty interviewer who had no qualms about letting her know that his three sons were having difficulty finding wives willing to stay home to raise the children and blaming it on the fact that so many women want to be professionals. Then he proceeded to ask her what she thought of that. On the other hand, men were rarely asked such loaded questions. Instead they were more likely to be asked about their anticipated choice of medical specialty or why they decided to become doctors.

Women in these surveys felt that they had no choice but to answer the personal questions asked of them, though they expressed fear about doing so. It's easier to discuss why you want to become a doctor, for example, or what specialty you're interested in than to explain how you plan to balance a spouse and children with school or work. Besides, no one is going to hold a student to a specialty she preferred before she even got to medical school. But the applicant has no way of knowing how her views on motherhood versus career will sit with the panel posing the questions. Putting their feelings aside, some admitted lying and simply saying what seemed most politically expedient. Or as one savvy medical student said, "I simply prepared ahead of time ways I could answer touchy questions in neutral, noninflammatory ways."

Despite equal qualifications, the weight of the interview for women applicants is reportedly greater than it is for men, yet women fare worse in their overall evaluations. "Open," "honest," but "less assertive" are the kinds of comments typically used to describe women but rarely men. The remarks are not intended to be complimentary. Indeed, those stereotypical evaluations often haunt women throughout their medical education. One survey of women residents by researchers at the UCLA School of Medicine showed that men in medicine routinely viewed female physicians as too emotional. Women who empathized with their patients were not given any recognition for their caring qualities. On the contrary, they were often criticized for them. Tears and tenderness were frowned upon and regarded as unprofessional and a sign of weakness. As one resident observed, "There's a boot camp kind of mentality in medical school."

Women also claim that they are not taken seriously regardless of the quality of their credentials. Sarah Pressman, a third-year student at Rush Medical College in Chicago, where 58 percent of her class is female, says that the faculty expects women to perform little better than average. One of her classmates, who gets consistently outstanding grades, reports that professors have expressed surprise that she, a woman, can perform so well. "These same professors," says Pressman, "seem to expect male students to make high marks."

A survey of 270 graduates of a large midwestern medical school confirmed Pressman's observations of sex discrimination by faculty and hospital physicians. Sociologist Linda Grant, Ph.D., of the University of Georgia, found that overall 34 percent of the women reported personally experiencing discrimination, and 62 percent had seen it targeted at their classmates. Students complained of invisibility and lack of attention in both classes and in the hospital setting. They claimed that instructors aimed their lectures at the men and challenged only men with tough questions. The women felt they had to work harder on clinical rotations to receive ratings (which are awarded subjectively) as good as the ones the men received. Many women also said that they got more scut work and less responsibility, which, they believe, made it difficult to demonstrate their competence.

Female residents fare no better, even though they have already earned their M.D. degrees, according to the UCLA study. On the one hand, they are expected to perform whatever clinical tasks are required with skill and dedication. On the other hand, there is still the expectation that they are there as support staff for their male colleagues, to perform the time-consuming menial tasks, such as taking dictation for a patient's chart, or to provide a cheerful atmosphere. Says medical sociologist Robert H. Coombs, Ph.D., one of the authors of the survey, "Traditionally, men do the important work, and women support them, not vice versa."

Just as disconcerting are the subtle and not so subtle forms of sexual harassment that resident women routinely experience. Comments about their physical attractiveness and grooming are everyday occurrences for many women, especially the single ones. It's not uncommon for women to be referred to as "that pretty young thing over there" or, as Pressman notes, to have their personal life be of more interest to their superiors than academic or professional achievements.

Sexual remarks, jokes, and innuendos are everywhere. One resident remarked in amazement how, even among these highly educated, professional men, it is completely acceptable to make jokes at the expense of women. "And yet," she said, "the analogous jokes about racial minorities are strictly taboo." Another woman, a third-year student at East Carolina University School of Medicine, says that during one lecture the professor inserted slides of nude women in seductive poses with himself superimposed in the shot, a joke that's apparently popular among medical school lecturers nationwide.

Surgeons are almost unanimously singled out by women as the worst offenders, with general surgeons ranking highest among all the specialties for sexually harassing women or undermining their ability. Laura Denenberg, a third-year student at UCLA School of Medicine who is leaning toward pediatrics, says that during her rotation in surgery, the general surgeons often made lewd comments about women's breasts and even went through the charts ahead of time to identify younger patients. "Flip comments about breasts don't always bother me," Denenberg admitted, "but in that setting, a breast clinic where the women had come because of possible cancer, it was particularly insensitive and degrading."

That surgery is viewed as a profession strictly for men, not women, is constantly reinforced. Surgeons make it clear that they don't think women are aggressive enough or have the physical and emotional stamina to become successful surgeons. Any display of emotion is proof positive that women are out of place in the macho world of the operating room. Third-year student Sarah Pressman says that she was evaluated by surgeons as too sensitive, but "I considered them maladjusted, because they were uncomfortable with emotional displays," she says. Another student who expressed an interest in surgery reported to Linda Grant that she was undermined by a staff surgeon in front of nurses and a patient with the comment, "I've never known a woman who was a decent surgeon, but I guess we have to give you a crack at it."

Women's discriminatory experiences do not go unnoticed by

their male peers. Indeed, most male medical students admit witnessing them, but they also seem to miss a lot. Not surprisingly, male students in Grant's study had less trouble recognizing the blatant or overt types of discrimination, but they had considerably more difficulty noticing the subtle or covert types. Curiously, grades and class standing had an effect on the men's ability to see discrimination targeted at their female classmates. The higher their grades, the better their vision, especially for the harder-to-detect subtle kinds of discrimination. Men with the lowest grades were the least likely to notice the problems women encountered, perhaps because they were too busy blaming their own poor performances on reverse discrimination.

Those on the receiving end of discrimination or harassment must decide how—or whether—to respond. It's not an easy decision, as many have discovered through trial and error. Women who squirm or speak out are labeled prissy, prudish, or too sensitive, and so they struggle for just the right combination between being a good sport and being assertive. As one student put it, "If I'm too pleasant and congenial, they think I'm frivolous, but if I speak out, I'm an hysterical bitch."

What they rarely do, however, is confront the problem directly or even indirectly through their institution's formal complaint channels. Surprisingly, many are unaware of remedies available at their own institutions, or they have little confidence that any action will be taken. Apparently, many who have complained have not been satisfied with the results. Besides, students worry that there will be some kind of professional retaliation for whistle-blowing, and so more often than not, they adopt a grin-and-bear-it attitude. "That fear is quite justified," says Lenhart, who chairs the subcommittee on gender equity at the American Medical Women's Association. "The faculty evaluates the students subjectively, and they have a tremendous impact on the students' career and training opportunities," she says. "I know of women who have changed their specialties rather than deal with discrimination problems. And I've seen women who have lowered their own career expectations or begun to doubt themselves for the same reason. It's easy to see how women students can be intimidated into silence."

INVISIBLE AT THE TOP

Alice Hamilton, M.D., the first woman member of the Harvard Medical School faculty, was appointed in 1919. She was prohibited from participating in academic processions and was even denied faculty football tickets. Though Harvard teachers of both sexes are permitted those two perks today, it's obvious from the latest statistics that in most medical schools the glass ceiling is still firmly in place. Women are virtually invisible in higher faculty positions. According to the Association of American Medical Colleges (AAMC), 31 percent of men who teach in medical school are full professors (the highest faculty rank), while only 9.6 percent of female teachers reach that rank. Where are all the women? Clustered at the bottom of the ladder: Nearly half are assistant professors (the second lowest rank) while only 35 percent of the men hold that title. And there are more women (17.4 percent) than men (7 percent) holding the lowest rank—instructor.

For those desiring to climb to the top of the ladder—chairing academic departments, for example, or becoming deans of medical schools—the opportunities are rarer still. There were eighty-seven women chairing medical school departments in 1991—under 4 percent of all such positions—and that was including sixteen women serving in an acting or interim capacity. And out of 126 medical schools, there is only one headed by a woman dean: Nancy Gary, M.D., of the Defense Department's Uniformed Services University of the Health Sciences, in Bethesda, Maryland. Says geriatrics researcher Linda Fried, M.D., of Johns Hopkins Medical School, "Academic medicine is male culture—very firmly entrenched male culture."

Medical governing boards are likewise male dominated. When the American Board of Medical Specialties surveyed its twenty-three member boards to find out how many women were on their current governing bodies, they found very few, just 6 percent, and eight of the twenty-three boards had no women members at all. And those figures aren't likely to improve significantly. More than half of those on the surveyed boards admitted that they had made no special efforts to recruit women members. Even the American College of Obstetricians and Gynecologists, whose members treat only women, has never had more than two women in its top seventeen offices at any one time in its forty-one-year history.

Gaining a foothold in these virtually all-male ivory towers has been close to impossible for women. For academic medicine, in particular, the consequences can be far-reaching. If current trends continue, the majority of the medical students during the next twenty years are likely to be women. In practical terms, that means that unless those in academic medicine are willing to recruit exceptional women into their fold, they may find themselves short on exceptional researchers in general. The result? The quality of academic research is bound to deteriorate.

Although many women gravitate toward research fields, they are often discouraged by their male superiors in subtle discriminatory ways, so subtle, in fact, that it may at first escape conscious attention. For example, women are routinely left out of formal and informal networks of peers, reminiscent of the old boys' clubs that are so prevalent in other male-dominated professions. In one case, several women fellows were excluded from consideration for a new fellowship grant because their department head only told the men in their group about it. Another woman noted that she was always included in talks about who was going to take night call, but when informal discussions turned to the best way to set up a private practice, she was noticeably excluded.

To undermine women doctors further, superiors may knowingly schedule important meetings at the end of the day when a woman's family responsibilities, such as picking up a child from day care, begin. Just becoming pregnant, says Lenhart, "is often seen as an act of disservice to the department and a sign of limited commitment to the profession."

Raising a family while holding down a demanding academic and research schedule, no matter how adept a woman is at juggling both, can still be used against her and often is. One woman, an associate professor at a major medical school, was overlooked for a coveted teaching award in favor of a male peer. Although she had successfully combined raising her large family with her teaching and publishing responsibilities, she was nevertheless perceived as more of a female role model than an accomplished teacher and scientist. Her male colleague was given the award because the awards committee believed he had published far more than the woman had. It wasn't until after the award had been presented that someone actually checked the number of research papers each had published and found that hers doubled his. She was sabotaged by the preconceived notion that because she was a mother, she couldn't possibly have done as much work as her male co-worker.

With attitudes about male and female roles stuck somewhere in the 1950s, it's no wonder that family and child care responsibilities continue to be at the root of women's slow career progress in both hospital and academic medicine. Men rarely have to contend with these situations, let alone the personal role conflicts that they engender. That's because medical education from start to finish has been developed with men's lives in mind, assuming as the decision makers did when almost all students were male that everyone has a wife or mother at home to take care of the domestic side of life. They choose to ignore the changing demographics of their institutions and conduct business as usual, turning a blind eye toward women struggling to balance their professional and personal lives. Consequently, virtually no provisions have been made for maternity leave or day care. Nor does the medical profession make any allowances for women's heavier domestic responsibilities despite equally heavy medical duties. Even in the rare instances where scheduling concessions are permitted, women risk being labeled as less competent or less committed.

Though other male-dominated fields, such as law, may have similar discriminatory practices, the study of medicine is in a class by itself because of its extraordinary time commitments. Law school, for example, takes three years, after which time the graduate is out and free to take time off for motherhood if she chooses. On the other hand, medical education takes a minimum of seven years (four in medical school and another three or more in a residency program), which also happen to coincide with a woman's prime reproductive years. During that time, the student is required to work irregular or long hours and often around the clock, hardly conducive to starting a family or caring for one. Yet that is not taken into consideration by the men charged with scheduling and making other policies.

To get around work–family conflicts, women may choose a nontraditional career path (such as part-time work), but if they do, they'll find it almost impossible to meet the requirements for promotion. That's because in many institutions the time between getting hired and getting promoted is not adjusted for those working less than full time. For faculty members, it often comes down to a choice between family and career responsibilities because institutional policies are so rigid. Says Carola Eisenberg, M.D., of Harvard Medical School, "The playing field is hardly level if only superwomen, rather than most women, can satisfy the needs of their families and meet their professional goals."

Women also find themselves at a disadvantage when it comes to aligning themselves with influential role models or mentors, the importance of which can't be overestimated. Women lucky enough to find a mentor publish more often in peer review medical journals, have more time to devote to research, and feel more confident of their capabilities than those without them. Mentors can also show newcomers the ropes. They can introduce them to the values, customs, resources, and major players in their profession, all important for career advancement. For women, same-sex mentors are particularly valuable for moral support and showing how career and family responsibilities can be combined. Yet most must go it alone simply because of the scarcity of women in senior or administrative positions. In fact, as some women have found out, they may be the only woman in a division or department.

However, medicine is poised for a change. Even Sharyn Lenhart believes "critical mass is coming." More than 40 percent of new medical recruits are women. But the most important figure may be this one: Sixty percent of the patients doctors see are women. In any medical practice, women are the best customers who not only decide who provides their own health care but make that decision for their families as well. Medicine is beginning to recognize that women's health is more than a political and social issue. It's also a financial one, too. Women are increasingly looking for health care that recognizes their unique needs and looking to other women to provide it.

The proposed women's health specialty, which proponents envision as a branch of medicine like pediatrics, has been greeted with fear by many physicians who believe it will cut into everything from the business of gynecology to the business of family medicine. Others envision a master's level curriculum that will turn out gynecologists, family practitioners, even cardiologists, who are in tune with women's health needs. Whatever final form it takes, it's clear that a change is mandated: Medicine has a stake in meeting the vast consumer demand women represent.

Otherwise, warns Pittsburgh psychiatrist and feminist Michelle Harrison, M.D., other professions are going to step in to fill the void. "Most care women need can be given by nonphysicians," she told a group of clinicians at the First Annual Congress on Women's Health in June 1993. "Physician's assistants, nurse-practitioners, advanced nursing practitioners, midwives, are all stepping in now to provide primary care. Unless we begin to incorporate their skills—listening and caring and knowing about things like nutrition—into the primary care of women, we're going to lose it."

Part Two

Unequal Treatment:
Crises in Care

3

BROKEN HEARTS

Women's

Silent Killer

Some physicians routinely trivialize women and, in particular, minimize their cardiovascular symptoms. Often, doctors decide that women's problems are all in their heads, closing the door to careful examination and accurate diagnosis. This can literally cause the deaths of some women.

—Marianne Legato, M.D.

Helen J. Ginsburg, a Denver mother of two and a successful sculptor whose work has been exhibited by the New England Fine Arts Institute, considers herself lucky to be alive. Because she is a woman, her long-time family doctor never looked for the heart disease that came close to killing her, despite the overwhelming evidence he had to overlook.

For more than thirty years, her family physician dismissed a cholesterol level that hovered near 400—more than twice the healthy level—with a few simple bromides such as "eat fewer eggs" or "cut out quiche Lorraine." There was never a suggestion that she might be at risk for coronary heart disease. Meanwhile her condition, a genetic disorder that caused her liver to produce excessive amounts of cholesterol, went undetected and untreated.

Over the years, cholesterol kept building up. It accumulated in the tendons of her legs, causing excruciating pain and finally requiring surgical removal of the deposits. Rather than diagnosing her serious condition as a heart attack in the making, the doctors were puzzled by what they saw. Although the substance resembled chicken fat, they didn't suspect that it was, in fact, cholesterol deposits, and so they didn't connect it to the high level of cholesterol in her blood.

Meanwhile, what was accumulating in her tendons was also collecting in her coronary arteries. She complained to her family doctor about being overwhelmingly tired—"like someone who was ninety"—especially when she biked or swam. "He just brushed it off with the explanation that I had a tendency to overdo," she says. "Then he'd say I was fine and to just take it easy."

Helen's cholesterol count was treated in the same cavalier way, and so she didn't worry about that either. "My doctor never gave me the impression that a high cholesterol was a very serious thing," she says. By the time it was discovered, she was a walking time bomb, a hike or a swim away from a deadly heart attack. But because she looked so healthy—she exercised, ate right, and stayed slim—even her new doctor, a lipid specialist, thought her problem could be handled with medication. It wasn't until she mentioned the exhaustion to him plus a strange new symptom of tightness in her throat that the doctor suggested she have an exercise treadmill test.

Helen still had no idea how desperately ill she was. Neither did the cardiologist to whom she was immediately referred. "He asked about my diet, my lifestyle, and it was all right on, so he had trouble believing I could have a serious heart condition," she says. But the treadmill test told a different story. Helen did so poorly that at first the doctors thought the equipment had malfunctioned.

Realizing it hadn't, her cardiologist scheduled a cardiac catheterization, and the graveness of her situation became immediately evident. Her coronary arteries were almost completely blocked, including the left main artery, the one doctors refer to as the widow maker or, in her case, the widower maker. So, at the age of fifty-two, Helen Ginsburg underwent a quintuple bypass operation. She was in surgery and on life-support systems for six hours while doctors tried to correct the mistake of a lifetime.

It is hard to say who was more surprised by her condition, her doctors or Helen Ginsburg herself. They all had been living with a deadly misconception about women and heart disease. "I thought only men got heart disease," says Helen. "I never thought it could happen to me. And my family doctor kept telling me I was fine, so I put my faith in him. It almost killed me."

Helen Ginsburg is far from alone in thinking that only men get heart disease. It's not called the silent epidemic for nothing. Indeed, one survey of women over fifty found that only 15 percent knew that their number one killer was heart disease. And why should they? Until a few years ago, the medical establishment itself believed coronary heart disease to be a man's affliction. With their physicians leading the way, women bought into this myth, too. To this day, most women still don't know the facts, and neither do many of their doctors.

Coronary heart disease has been the leading cause of death in women since 1908, although a glance at the scientific literature would suggest it is a more recent phenomenon. Indeed, women until very recently were excluded from almost all studies on heart disease, so that compared to men, what is known about the risk factors, diagnosis, and treatment of women with heart problems is still in its infancy. It never seemed to matter to the medical and research establishments that half of the 520,000 people who die from heart attacks each year are women. The central concern seemed to be whose life mattered more.

This colossal oversight on the part of doctors, scientists, and U.S. governmental health agencies has created a mad scramble to make up for lost time. Women are now being courted for new studies with nearly the same determination with which they were once excluded, thanks in part to the recent intense scrutiny by the trade and popular presses and government regulations that say they must. It's a start, but even the experts acknowledge that it will be decades before doctors know as much about women's hearts as they know about men's. In the meantime, women continue to be placed at undue risk while the research community plays catch-up.

The truth is, coronary artery disease is different in women than men, from the initial symptoms and the age they get them to how they respond to treatment. And that's not necessarily common knowledge among all doctors let alone women themselves, who operate under the long-lived myth that they are somehow protected for life. As myths go, this one is a killer. One in nine women in the forty-five to fifty-four age group already has some symptoms of cardiovascular disease. And although it's quite uncommon for younger women to die of a heart attack, they are not completely immune. More than 6,200 women under the age of fifty-five die of heart attacks each year; 23,000 under age sixty-five. For African-American women, the outlook is far worse. Between the ages of thirty-five and seventy-four, the death rate from heart attack is about twice that of white women and three times that of women of other races.

Women *seem* to be protected by their female hormones—while they last—although no one knows why. That protection rapidly disintegrates after menopause, however, with women growing ever more vulnerable as their age increases and their estrogen decreases. Yet there is very little data evaluating the impact of hormone replacement therapy on heart disease risk. As cardiologist Pamela S. Douglas, M.D., of Boston's Beth Israel Hospital says, "Perhaps that's because estrogen replacement therapy is not an option in male patients with coronary artery disease."

What current research has uncovered will be of no comfort to women and only points out the gap in knowledge between the sexes. Recommendations for prevention of heart disease, for example, remain the same regardless of sex despite differences in several key risk factors. There are fewer diagnostic tests done on women than men, so that when heart disease is finally discovered, women are far sicker and more debilitated than their male counterparts. Women are less likely to be referred for cardiac catheterizations than men with the same symptoms, even though early diagnosis is crucial to survival. Women who suffer a heart attack are not given the new lifesaving clot-dissolving drugs as often as men who have heart attacks, which may explain, in part, why women are twice as likely as men to die within the first few weeks after a heart attack. More women die after coronary bypass surgery than men do if they manage to get the operation at all.

By all accounts, women with heart disease have been shamefully neglected by the medical community and by scientific research simply because they are women. Part of the reason for that neglect was the discrepancy between the ages that men and women start dying from heart disease. The incidence and death rates have always been higher in younger men who are in the prime of their lives. Because doctors used to believe that hardening of the arteries (the cause of coronary heart disease) was a natural consequence of aging, research tended to focus on those who were getting sick "prematurely," namely, middle-aged white men. Women, on average, get heart disease ten years later in life, and it isn't until they reach their sixties and seventies that their incidence of the illness approaches that of men's.

Researchers argued that research studies that included women would take too long and require too many people to achieve meaningful results, conditions that never seemed to limit the studies on men.

THE RISK FACTOR KNOWLEDGE GAP

Because of the gender gap in heart disease knowledge, doctors have no way of knowing whether the advice they give their female patients is as beneficial to them as it is to their male patients. Yet, for the most part, it's the only game in town, a game where women are likely to be the decided losers. That's particularly evident in the area of risk factor reduction, the key to preventing heart disease in the first place. Indeed, the most comprehensive study on that subject, the fifteen-year, multimillion-dollar project called the Multiple Risk Factor Intervention Trial, ironically known as MR FIT, was conducted on 13,000 men and no women. Even the director of the National Heart, Lung and Blood Institute, Claude Lenfant, whose department funded the research, acknowledged that if the study were to be launched today, it would be more appropriately dubbed "Mr. and Mrs. Fit."

Although conventional wisdom might dictate that reducing blood pressure, cholesterol, and dietary fat, the most common risk factors for heart disease, is sound advice for anyone, that's based more on guesswork than on facts. Now, a closer examination of the existing—though limited—research on women is beginning to question these long-held assumptions, and the results emerging are more baffling than enlightening.

For doctors treating women with high blood pressure, for example, treating a woman just like a man may prove deadly, according to a group of New York City internists who reviewed current treatment recommendations. One study, for example, found that death rates decreased significantly for white men, black men, and black women who had taken blood pressure medications—an expected outcome. Unexpected, however, was that white women had a slight *increase* in mortality when they took the same drugs. Most disturbing was that the women whose blood pressures started out the highest had the greatest death rate of all despite the fact that they had the most success in lowering their blood pressure of any group studied. In another experiment, women fared even worse. Those taking antihypertensive drugs had a 26 percent *increase* in mortality, whereas men taking the same drugs had a 15 percent reduction.

Nobody knows why white women responded so differently to treatment, nor have subsequent studies resolved the many questions those results raise. In the meantime, doctors and their unwitting female patients remain as much in the dark as ever, and women continue to be treated with medications whose value to them is questionable.

The dearth of meaningful information about women and high blood pressure might be understandable, even excusable, if this condition were a rare occurrence in women. But that's hardly the case. More than a quarter of all women suffer from hypertension, and the percentage rises dramatically as women age, according to the American Heart Association. Half of those over age fifty-five have it, whereas two-thirds over age sixty-five do. For black women, it's an astonishing 83 percent. In fact, in this age group, women are more likely to develop high blood pressure than men. Yet these numbers haven't made much of an impression on those doing the research. Some of the newest antihypertensive medications on the market were still tested exclusively on white men, so it's yet to be determined whether their effect on women—black or white—will ultimately be good, bad, or deadly.

Similar confusion has emerged over the importance of cholesterol levels—yet another case of what's sauce for the gander is curdling for the goose. Although a high cholesterol level is not uncommon to women—more than 60 percent of white women and 54 percent of black women have blood cholesterol levels of 200 milligrams per deciliter or higher—it now appears that the risks associated with it are different for women than they are for men. Those risks have to do with the levels of HDL (high-density lipoprotein cholesterol—the good kind that carries cholesterol out of the body) versus LDL (low-density lipoprotein cholesterol—the bad kind that clogs arteries), which together make up the total cholesterol in the body.

In men, either a high LDL or a low HDL represents potent risk factors for the development of heart disease. In women, however, high LDL levels are not nearly as sensitive a risk factor, whereas a low HDL is extraordinarily so. In other words, decreasing LDLs does not seem to offer the same risk reduction for women as it does for men. An Israeli study clearly pointed that out. Researchers found that a high total cholesterol (indicating a high LDL level) had no adverse effect in women as long as they had a high enough HDL level—more than 23 percent of the total, which is not uncommon for women, whose HDL levels are generally higher than men's.

It's believed that this higher HDL cholesterol is one of the reasons for women's lower rate of heart disease. Indeed, a woman's HDL level is like a crystal ball in helping to predict the future health of her heart. The higher it is, the less likely she is to ever have heart disease, and the lower it is, the more likely. So it makes sense that maintaining a high HDL cholesterol would be of paramount importance. Yet there is evidence that the use of some antihypertensive medications, including diuretics and beta-blockers, increases total cholesterol and lowers the heart-protecting HDL cholesterol. What's not known with any certainty is how HDL and LDL levels are affected when women, in particular, are given these antihypertensive drugs. Apparently no one thought it important enough to find out. When a study did bother to check out gender differences, only *total* cholesterol was measured, and although the levels did increase in both men and women, the researchers who conducted the study never bothered to record specific information about HDL and LDL levels.

Diet, too, can affect the levels of good and bad cholesterol in the body, so not surprisingly, men and women alike have been encouraged to adopt the lower-fat, lower-cholesterol heart-healthy diet recommended by the American Heart Association. Apparently, however, decreasing daily intake of cholesterol and fatty foods may not have the same health-promoting potential for women as it does for men because it decreases cholesterol across the board, including the protective HDL type.

Two studies done exclusively on women pinpoint the problem with the heart-healthy diet. Researchers found that when they altered women's diets from the typical American high-fat fare to the lower-fat plan, their LDL levels fell by almost a third in both cases, but their protective HDL levels decreased, too, by a substantial 16 and 20 percent. Meanwhile, two similar studies in men showed a drop in LDL cholesterol of 24 and 26 percent, while there was either little or no change in their HDL cholesterol. For some reason the results of these studies have received scant attention from the medical establishment.

"Right now, we know that women who have *very* high LDL levels have the same risk of heart disease as men with very high levels," says professor and researcher John Crouse III, M.D., who studies the relationship between gender, diet, and heart disease risk. "And for them, a heart-healthy diet is recommended, just as it is for men." But for average women, a diet that decreases both LDL *and* HDL cholesterol may actually be harmful. There just hasn't been enough research on women to know for sure what it all really means in terms of risk, he says.

Doctors also can't say with any certainty whether women should take an aspirin every other day to help prevent heart attacks as they recommend to their male patients. How can they when the most comprehensive study on the subject—the five-year Physicians' Health Study—was done on 22,071 men (all physicians) and no women? In that study, men who took one regular strength aspirin tablet on alternate days had a 44 percent reduction in their risk of a first heart attack. Based on that study, it was recommended that men take low-dose aspirin for prevention of heart attacks. No recommendation was made for what women should do to prevent a similar fate.

In hindsight, the decision to exclude women from that study seems like blatant sexism and the researchers' excuse for excluding them—that there were too few women physicians at that time to ensure a large enough sample—weak at best. If women doctors were in short supply, women nurses certainly weren't. Indeed, that's just who researchers did call upon in their attempt to make up for this stunning gender gap—a group of 87,000 nurses who had been tapped for a long-term project to examine women's health practices *back in 1976,* long before the physicians' aspirin study was even conceived. Using this readily available source of women subjects, researchers from Harvard Medical School examined the effect of aspirin on the nurses' risk of a first heart attack by questioning them about their use of aspirin over a period of 6 years. From that data, the researchers were able to determine that those who took one to six regular aspirin per week had a 30 percent reduced risk of a first heart attack.

As encouraging as that sounds, however, no one is recommending that women routinely dose themselves with aspirin. That's because the nurses' study had several major drawbacks, enough for the experts to recognize that the results are simply not as conclusive as the better-designed physicians' study. In that experiment, doctors were randomly placed into two groups; one group took a fixed dose of aspirin and the other group a placebo. A controlled clinical trial such as this is always preferred because it gives researchers a basis for comparison and is more objective.

The nurses' study, on the other hand, relied on memory, which may or may not be accurate over time, to determine how many aspirin were taken. Indeed, the nurses told the researchers that they took their aspirin sporadically for the most part, usually for headaches or other body pain. Less than 10 percent reported taking aspirin on a regular basis with the idea of preventing a heart attack. What's needed for conclusive evidence is a study on women similar to the one done on men, although none is planned. Until there is, doctors who may be considering aspirin for their women patients or women who may be inclined to do a little self-dosing have been advised to do so with caution. This simple over-the-counter painkiller can also cause adverse side effects, such as bleeding ulcers. Helen Ginsburg's doctors, for example, decided that the benefit of taking one baby aspirin a day clearly outweighed any risks associated with the drug.

THE GENDER GAP IN DIAGNOSIS AND TREATMENT

Getting an accurate and timely diagnosis and then the appropriate treatment for heart disease is also tricky business when the patient is a woman. Even the AMA acknowledges that the lack of research conducted on women has left doctors without a set of diagnostic guidelines geared specifically to their women patients. Not that guidelines would aid in diagnosis anyway. It's hard to pinpoint an illness when you are simply not looking for it. Like Helen Ginsburg's doctor, they do not suspect heart disease because they have not internalized the message that it's a disease of women as much as it is of men. Doctors are more inclined to blame heart symptoms in women on something else—usually a woman's emotions—than what it really is, whereas a man's similar symptoms would prompt an immediate diagnostic workup.

Indeed, one study found that women had their symptoms attributed to emotional rather than physical causes three times more often than men. Even more disturbing was that men who had abnormal heart test results were still twice as likely to have their complaints believed than women who had the same abnormal results.

Dr. Marianne J. Legato, author of *The Female Heart,* recalls one woman, a brilliant and aggressive banker, who saw three different physicians for the debilitating heart palpitations she was experiencing. All of them knew she had rapid heart beats, but they brushed her off, telling her that the condition wouldn't kill her and that she would just have to learn to accept it. For years she lived in fear of these attacks, knowing that she would be unable to work that day if she had one. She even avoided plane trips because of it. "It turned out after a careful examination, that this woman had an extra pathway in her heart over which these very rapid rhythms were traveling," says Legato. "It was an easily curable condition, and today she's very active and without symptoms."

Chest pain, in particular, is a symptom that has been historically discounted when women experience it. But at least the experts have a somewhat plausible explanation for their past disregard of this potentially serious complaint. They blame it on misleading data from the famed Framingham Heart Study. Women in that ongoing study who were diagnosed with angina (the chest pain associated with clogged arteries) had a much better outcome than their male counterparts did. The women had far fewer heart attacks and far fewer sudden deaths, and they lived longer. These data led to the widespread perception that angina simply wasn't a serious problem in women. That information became part of the women and heart disease mythology.

The basic flaw with the Framingham observations is that too many young women were diagnosed with angina, no doubt incorrectly, explains professor Philip Greenland, M.D., of Northwestern University School of Medicine. "Their chest pain, more than likely, was caused by something other than clogged arteries—peptic ulcer, for example, or heartburn or gall bladder disease, all of which can mimic angina." Recently, researchers examined the data from Framingham again, looking at the diagnosis of angina in women over sixty, the age group in which coronary artery disease becomes more prevalent. They found that angina in this group was just as lethal in women as it was in men.

What's not generally known by most doctors is that women who have coronary artery disease and the corresponding angina may experience different symptoms than their male counterparts, symptoms that doctors call atypical. Because doctors are trained to recognize typical symptoms—in other words, men's symptoms— such as chest tightness or pain in the left arm, women's symptoms may go unrecognized for what they are. Helen Ginsburg experienced an unusual tightness in the base of her throat between her collarbones when she biked or swam. Because she, too, had been schooled in the typical angina symptoms, she didn't realize that her strange discomfort was a sign that her heart was being starved for oxygen.

A woman who is able to describe her chest pain in the same terminology as a man may still be dismissed with advice to "take it easy" or reduce her stress load. "We frequently see many women who have been told that their chest pain was nothing, and no tests were done," says Legato. One forty-six-year-old doctor's wife had her chest pain dismissed by her husband's colleague to whom she had been referred. This doctor told her that there was nothing wrong with her that a trip away for the weekend with her husband wouldn't cure. "He'll give you what you need, and your symptoms will disappear," she was told. She had a heart attack a month later.

Even if tests are done, however, there is no guarantee that the most appropriate one will be chosen, that a correct diagnosis will be made, or referral for further testing will be recommended. The electrocardiogram stress test (also called the exercise treadmill test), one of the most common noninvasive procedures done to detect coronary abnormalities, is notoriously inaccurate in women, yet it is still routinely administered. A better choice is the thallium or nuclear stress test (same as the stress test but combined with nuclear imaging of the heart to detect clogged arteries), which is considerably more accurate, giving far fewer false-positive results in women.

Nevertheless, an abnormal stress test is still more likely to be ignored if the patient is a woman. Cardiac catheterization (a moderately invasive procedure that lets doctors see inside the heart without surgery) is performed ten times more often in men than in women even when both have abnormal nuclear stress test results, according to researchers from the Albert Einstein College of Medicine in the Bronx. Even when a woman is sicker than a man, when her angina symptoms are more severe and disabling, women are still referred for cardiac catheterization only half as often as men. Doctors themselves blame this failure on the persistent belief that angina in women is benign.

This misperception is likely to persist as long as women are not referred for the diagnostic tests that can prove it wrong. Part of the problem is that women are still not enrolled in the kinds of studies that determine the value of diagnostic tests and therapies. It's a Catch-22 of sorts; women continue to be excluded from those important clinical trials *because* they have not had the necessary diagnostic tests, such as cardiac catheterizations, required for study eligibility. But if women are not referred for these diagnostic tests in the first place, then they can't be included in studies that examine their value.

With this kind of runaround, it's not surprising that by the time women get diagnosed accurately, they are often far sicker and older with poorer outcomes even when they get treatment. Perhaps that's why women who have heart attacks are twice as likely as men to die within the first few weeks. Or why half die within a year after a heart attack compared to a third of men. Or why, as one study from Cedars-Sinai Medical Center in Los Angeles pointed out, twice as many women as men die after having coronary bypass surgery. In that report, researchers acknowledged that women were indeed referred for bypass surgery later in the course of their illness than men were and that that probably played a part in the women's increased risk of death following surgery.

That same study also noted, curiously, that patients who came from families with a history of heart disease actually had a *lower* rate of death following the surgery regardless of gender. The reason? Patients with a strong family history of heart disease probably had their complaints of chest pain taken more seriously by their doctors and were referred for bypass surgery earlier in the course of their illness, when the procedure was less risky.

Yet, even if they want it, women are less likely to have the option of undergoing a coronary bypass operation, which, all things considered, is still an overwhelmingly successful treatment for coronary artery disease. One study found that men were twice as likely to have the procedure as women while they were hospitalized for their coronary heart disease. But according to the American Heart Association, the numbers are more skewed than that; in 1989, for example, almost three-quarters of the 368,000 bypass operations done were performed on men.

The numbers are hardly more favorable for the newer and less invasive procedure commonly known as balloon angioplasty. In this treatment, a deflated balloon is threaded to the heart through an artery in the leg or arm. When it reaches the heart, it is inserted into the narrowed coronary artery and then inflated, compressing the blockage material and widening the artery. In 1989, more than twice as many men as women underwent angioplasty. Though death or complications from this procedure are relatively low, when a problem does crop up, it is nevertheless more likely to happen with a female patient. A woman is 30 percent more likely than a man to suffer a tear in the artery wall, for example, although why that happens is still a mystery. At least doctors no longer use a one-size-fits-all balloon designed with men's larger vessels in mind. Doctors finally learned that women's smaller coronary arteries needed correspondingly smaller balloons.

That women are treated less aggressively for their heart disease than men has also been apparent in the use of the new clot busters—drugs that when given within a few hours of a heart attack can actually stop it in progress and greatly improve the chances for survival. Yet far fewer women than men received these lifesaving drugs. When they do, however, they are more likely to experience bleeding problems, possibly because women are administered the same standard dose as men, which, with their generally smaller bodies, may just be too much of a good thing.

Of all the areas in which women's health has been neglected, heart disease is the one that has drawn the most attention. For whatever reason, altruistic or pragmatic, the medical community has, at least, acknowledged and made attempts to fill in the many blanks about women and their hearts. Dozens of medical journal articles have brought the inequities to light, and the media have brought them to the public's attention. However, that interest needs to be maintained over the long haul, because that's what it will take for the gender gap in heart disease prevention, diagnosis, and treatment to close. As it does, women will need to be vigilant in matters of the heart.

Helen Ginsburg regrets now that she allowed the reassurances of her doctor to drown out the warnings she was getting from her body. "I have since learned that we really have to be responsible for ourselves," she says.

In fact, after her surgery, Helen put herself on a strict exercise regimen to gain back her strength. "I had to," she explains. "Neither of my doctors had prescribed heart rehab for me. Yet a fellow I knew who had had a slight heart attack was sent right away to a physical therapy session. Is that because he's a man or because they thought I already knew how to take care of myself?"

Fourteen months after her surgery, Helen, her husband, and son took a four-mile hike high into the Colorado mountains, something Helen believes did her heart good in more ways than one. She explains, "When we got back, my new doctor was there and I told him what I had done and how proud I was of myself. He said, 'Great,' but he called me later. He said he didn't want to say anything in front of everyone there and told me that if I had asked him if it was all right to hike, he would have said no, it was too soon and I wouldn't make it."

Helen smiles. "Then he said, 'So congratulations. I was wrong.' "

4

BREAST
CANCER

The

Invisible

Epidemic

They fund what they fear. They do not fear breast cancer and they do not fear you.

—U.S. Congresswoman Patricia Schroeder

The day-long hearing was billed as an opportunity for some of the leading lights of breast cancer research to do some wishful thinking. If more money were available, what would they do with it?

They had come to Washington, to the Federal Ballroom of the Quality Hotel Capitol Hill, this cold February morning in 1992 at the invitation of the research task force of the Breast Cancer Coalition. The neophyte organization, a collection of 140 national breast cancer and women's health groups, had been created a year earlier as an "advocacy group"—read political force—to focus attention on the growing epidemic of breast cancer in the United States. The researchers who took their places behind hand-printed name cards were a distinguished group, a who's who in breast cancer research from such prestigious institutions as Harvard, Yale, the University of Southern California, Georgetown University, and NIH.

The ballroom quickly filled with members of the coalition, the press, and women with breast cancer. And, of course, as is the case wherever doctors gather, there were the pharmaceutical sales reps.

One, wearing a three-piece ash gray suit, sat down in a chair

71

along the wall and surveyed the small room into which roughly 100 people had been shoehorned. His company, he explained, makes products used both in AIDS and breast cancer research. He'd been to plenty of these conferences on AIDS. "And I'll tell you," he said, "at a meeting like this on AIDS, the security would have been a nightmare. There would be people spilling into the streets. There would be police everywhere. And that's the difference between AIDS and breast cancer."

It's not the only difference, but it is one of the most illustrative. Even researchers who claim it is unfair to make comparisons between breast cancer and AIDS inevitably do. "Breast cancer has gotten about 12 percent the amount of funding AIDS has gotten in basic research," says Susan Love, M.D., the breast surgeon who is chair of the coalition's research task force.

In fact, one set of ghoulish government statistics pulled together by the GAO found that the United States sinks a total of $15,268 into research for every AIDS death compared to $2,788 for every breast cancer death. Yet roughly twice as many people die of breast cancer each year as die of AIDS.

There are many reasons for the dramatic difference in the funding of these two deadly diseases. For one, AIDS is contagious. When it debuted in the early eighties as the "gay cancer," it represented a specter as frightening and mysterious as the plague must have been in the Middle Ages. But another reason may be that, at least for now, most AIDS victims are men; almost all breast cancer victims are women. The medical research community has traditionally responded with more vigor to diseases that afflict more men than women.

But what may be even more important, AIDS has been politicized. The AIDS epidemic has spawned a loud, if not massive, grass roots activist network that numbers among its members dozens of high-profile Hollywood performers, including Elizabeth Taylor. Many believe that the great strides scientists have made in AIDS research are due, at least in part, to the squeaking wheel effect. The noise made by gay groups and others such as the AIDS Coalition to Unleash Power (ACT UP) may have led to increased AIDS research funding, which was more than a billion dollars in fiscal 1993, nearly as much as is spent on research on *all* cancers.

What this has taught researchers, clinicians, and breast cancer victims is that body count alone is not persuasive enough to squeeze money out of the Congress. Says one activist, "What we've learned from AIDS is that it all comes down to how much stink you make."

The "stink" being made by the Breast Cancer Coalition has been far more genteel than the guerrilla theater practiced by ACT UP. A letter-writing campaign called Do the Write Thing elicited half a million letters from breast cancer survivors and, poignantly, from the loved ones of women who didn't survive asking Congress for an additional $50 million in research money. Members of the coalition hand-delivered those letters to the Capitol on a sunny October morning in 1991.

During a rally on the Capitol lawn, two congresswomen made it clear that breast cancer had historically been shortchanged when funding time rolled around because appropriations are decided upon by people without breasts, a fact of political life that has not changed appreciably. Congresswoman Mary Rose Oakar, a Democrat from Ohio, told the women she had led a congressional hearing on the disease eight years before "and no one was interested except women with breast cancer." Colorado Congresswoman Patricia Schroeder warned the women that it was still a struggle to bring breast cancer to the attention of the male-dominated Congress.

LOSING BATTLES, LOSING THE WAR

AIDS is the most conspicuous example of the role fear can play in the amount of attention paid—and money thrown at—a disease. A frightening disease, it is in reality a relatively difficult infection to transmit. But the AIDS epidemic has triggered the kind of runaway public terror that demands political action. Today, more than a decade after the epidemic began, through the work of thousands of well-funded researchers, science knows what causes AIDS and, theoretically, how to prevent it. Though a vaccine and a cure remain elusive, it is a remarkable testament to the power of fear—and political persuasion—that we have learned so much about a disease that was unknown in this country before 1981.

In contrast, very little is known about breast cancer, a disease first described over 3,500 years ago in Egypt. Though the link between hormones and breast cancer has been known for over 100 years, "I'm not sure we're any closer to understanding the relation-ship today," grimly noted researcher Kay Dickersin, Ph.D., of the University of Maryland School of Medicine, in her opening remarks to the task force.

Indeed, the scientific knowledge about breast cancer is full of large—and deadly—gaps. In December 1991, the GAO issued a re-port that presented a dismal picture of this country's progress against breast cancer. It is a war, the report said, "we do not seem to be winning."

Though it's widely trumpeted that more women survive breast cancer than they did twenty years ago, the survival rates actually show a very small improvement. These days, 77 percent of breast cancer patients live five years or more and 63 percent are still alive ten years after diagnosis. In 1970, the five-year survival rate was 68 percent. But the incidence rate—the number of women diagnosed each year—has gone up 1.8 percent a year, 28 percent between the years 1974 and 1986. In 1960, a woman had a one in twenty lifetime risk of developing breast cancer. In 1992, the number had increased to one in nine with many researchers warning it would rise even further.

Some of that increase can be attributed to better detection and to the greater number of older women in the population. In fact, the largest rise has been in women over fifty, a not unexpected develop-ment because cancer is often a disease of aging. But many experts believe both those factors account for only a small percentage of the increased incidence. What has been most alarming—and baffling—is the 15 percent rise in breast cancer among women between twenty-five and forty-four, women of childbearing years, women in the prime of their lives and careers. Cancer has become the leading cause of death for women between thirty-five and fifty. Though more women die of lung cancer, more women get breast cancer, the most common malignancy in the premenopausal age group. A 1993 study done at Mount Sinai School of Medicine in New York pro-vided a horrifying clue to this riddle: The newest risk factor may be the food baby boomers ate growing up, food contaminated by the pesticide dichlorodiphenyltrichloroethane (DDT), which, though banned in this country in 1972, is stored in body fat for decades.

The GAO report, which had few hopeful things to say, ended on an equally pessimistic note. Twenty years after the war on cancer was declared by then President Richard Nixon, the GAO said, "The expectation is that the coming year will see more women stricken with the disease and more women dying from it than two decades ago."

Some critics have questioned whether it is fair or accurate to call breast cancer an epidemic, a term usually reserved for contagious diseases, and to liken it to AIDS. After all, AIDS is a death sentence; with breast cancer there is always hope. Both the American Cancer Society and the Breast Cancer Coalition recently have come under fire for using what some critics call "scare tactics," manufacturing risk figures that are misleading. Those alleged scare tactics, a 1992 *New York Times* article claimed, have panicked women into needlessly taking harmful drugs or having their healthy breasts removed. It is true that the one-in-nine risk is more metaphor than any one woman's own personal risk. Though most women interpret the figure to mean that out of every nine women, one woman will develop breast cancer, it actually represents the cumulative possibility that a woman will develop breast cancer sometime between birth and age eighty-five. In fact, at age forty, the average woman's risk of getting breast cancer is 1 in 1,200, which, though low, is still greater than her chance of being killed in a car crash. For a fifty-year-old woman, the risk rises to 1 in 590. For a sixty-year-old, it's 1 in 420.

But Susan Love disagrees that breast cancer groups are conjuring up statistics to scare women. The message women are getting now, she says, is closer to the truth than the one they got before. "Until now we've oversimplified things to the point where we make it sound like we've got all the answers, that if you do your breast self-exam, have yearly mammograms, you'll find your cancer early and you'll be cured. I've had a lot of women who come into my office and they're really angry. They did everything we told them to do and lo and behold, they've got cancer. They feel betrayed, like they were lied to. And you know what? They were in a way."

They weren't deliberate lies, more like wishful thinking "and the realization that if we told them the real thing, they'd be too depressed to get a mammogram," says Love.

But one important result of those lies is that breast cancer has been robbed of the fear factor, that powerful mobilizer of public opinion and political influence, that pry bar that opens the funding coffers. "The truth is," says Love, "until women start to realize that what we have to fight breast cancer isn't good enough, we're never going to get enough research money to change things. The Breast Cancer Coalition believes that the facts ought to make all women fear for their lives."

What are those facts that should be frightening women? For one, the causes of breast cancer are just as mysterious and elusive as a cure for AIDS. The best known risk factors for breast cancer—a family history, late childbearing, obesity, certain types of fibrocystic breast disease—account for only 30 percent of all breast cancers. The only known risk factor for the remaining 70 percent is "being a woman," says Love.

Nothing is known about how to prevent breast cancer, and the only "cure" remains surgery, sometimes alone, sometimes followed by radiation, chemotherapy, or hormone therapy. Each has its own horrific side effects—mutilation, hair loss, sterility—and sometimes even death from another cancer. The GAO report also noted ominously, "in spite of many successes, a large proportion of cancer therapy is unsuccessful." A "cure" doesn't automatically occur at the end of treatment. In the language of cancer, cure is an ambiguous term. What it means to a woman with breast cancer is that if she survives five years after diagnosis, she has a fairly good chance of making it to ten, perhaps even living long enough to die of something else.

But with breast cancer, there are no sure things. Even if her cancer is caught early, when it is small, there is still no way to tell if it has spread to other organs of the body to explode later, like a time bomb, in her other breast, her liver, her bones, her lungs. In fact, a woman who learns after surgery that she is "node negative," meaning that her lymph nodes show no signs of malignancy, still has no reason to celebrate. An estimated 30 percent of all node-negative breast cancers recur. And there are no clear-cut prognostic factors that will tell her physician whether she is at high risk for the kind of breast cancer that migrates. Though breast cancer, unlike AIDS, is not an automatic death sentence, a woman who is diagnosed may have to wait with trepidation for five, even ten years to learn if she is one of the lucky ones, the 63 percent, whose cancer is just a bad memory.

One oncologist ominously put it into perspective: "Curable

cancer is curable, and most breast cancer is not curable. We just haven't waited long enough until it returns."

NO EARLY WARNINGS

The most effective armament in the breast cancer arsenal remains early detection, but even that is a weapon of relatively small caliber. Breast self-examination is of limited usefulness in detecting malignancies in early stages. A 1993 analysis of worldwide data also showed that mammography, which is recommended every one or two years for women under fifty and yearly for those over fifty, doesn't prevent deaths in younger women.

The largely unfounded fears that radiation will cause cancer may prevent many women from having a mammogram. But, says Yale University cancer researcher Janet Henrich, M.D., "the biggest danger of mammography isn't radiation; it's false reassurance."

Mammography doesn't prevent or cure the disease, and it isn't foolproof. There is a 20 percent false-negative rate, that is, a 20 percent chance of having a mammogram that misses a budding tumor, with even the best mammography. And the level is probably higher because a woman's chances of getting the best mammography can vary dramatically.

Mammography units and the personnel who run them have been, until recently, largely unregulated despite the fact that it is well known that the benefits of mammography depend very strongly on the quality both of the screening machine and the radiologic technologist. It requires special training both to do and to interpret a mammogram. "Mammography is one of the most subtle and difficult applications of X-ray imaging," says R. Edward Hendrick, Ph.D., chief of the division of radiological sciences at the University of Colorado Health Sciences Center.

There is certainly no shortage of mammography machines. The GAO report noted that currently there are so many on the market if every woman followed the national screening guidelines, there would still be machines that could remain unplugged. But there is a shortage of competent technicians. Many of those machines may be in offices where the technologist has not been properly trained or worse, where "it could be the office receptionist pushing those buttons," as a spokesperson for the American College of Radiology told *Time* magazine.

The news is worse for younger women whose cancers, by many accounts, may be more aggressive. Most experts agree that mammograms are less accurate in younger women because their dense breast tissue can hide small tumors from the X ray. Other types of screening technology, such as magnetic resonance imaging, may be more accurate but too expensive for most women—at about $1,000 a shot—and simply inaccessible to many others in nonurban areas.

Still, mammography is far from worthless. According to one study, which examined the results of screening under ideal conditions, widespread use of mammography could reduce breast cancer deaths by 30 percent by detecting tumors early. Despite that, few women get regular mammograms. A survey of women forty and older conducted by the Jacobs Institute of Women's Health found that only 31 percent have regular mammograms. The reason most gave for not having regular screenings? Their doctors never recommended it. In fact, when a group of physicians was surveyed by the American Cancer Society, only 37 percent said they advised patients to have regular mammograms. And it's not because they don't care. Most of the doctors said they disagreed with the screening guidelines because mammography was too expensive and too unreliable.

Though more and more states are now requiring third-party payment for mammography and the costs of the screenings are going down in some places, reliability remains a question, particularly for younger women. Many breast cancer activists question why better screening is not available, why what is state of the art in the nineties is essentially what was state of the art more than a decade ago. One answer, perhaps the hardest to bear, is that breast cancer has, until now, been "the invisible epidemic" as one women's health advocate put it, allowed to advance virtually unchecked for twenty years because almost all of its victims are women.

Among many breast cancer activists, there is the nagging notion that if one in nine men got breast cancer, the money would flow, not trickle, into research. And, as in other women's health issues, with NIH, Congress, and science itself dominated by men, few wonder why relatively little attention has been paid to a disease that strikes only 1,000 men a year. Says Schroeder, "When you have a male-dominated group of researchers, they are more worried about prostate cancer than breast cancer."

Roger S. Powell was sitting in on the task force hearings in his role as program director of the Diagnostic Imaging Research Branch of the National Cancer Institute. A friendly, garrulous man who attends breast cancer support group meetings in his off-hours, Powell concurs with Schroeder's assessment. "It's *absolutely* true," he says. "I've been in this for a long time, and I have always felt that if women were in charge of it, there would be something better for breast cancer diagnosis than mammography. There would be more attention paid to what's important."

But what has been important to the research community—and to the lawmakers funding it—clearly has not been women's health. "There has been a tendency, until recently, to think of breast cancer and a lot of women's health issues as a woman's 'thing' and not important to us," says Devra Lee Davis, Ph.D., of the National Research Council and a leading authority on environmental causes of cancer.

If it is unfair to compare breast cancer to AIDS, perhaps the better comparison is to heart disease, the number one killer of middle-aged men and older women. It's a parallel Cynthia Pearson likes to draw because it points up quite clearly the way in which gender determines how a disease is viewed and fought. "In the late fifties to the mid-sixties, our country became incredibly conscious of the fact that men were dying or becoming disabled at a very early age by heart disease and stroke," says Pearson, who is the executive director of the National Women's Health Network and a member of the Breast Cancer Coalition. "Heart disease became a big issue, got a lot of funding, the American Heart Association got really active on it, and it's a big success. Heart disease rates have been dropping for thirty years."

But, Pearson points out, just as the research failed to see that women also died of heart disease—albeit later in life—it failed to notice another epidemic in its early stages. In the last twenty of those thirty years, as research was cutting into the male death rate for heart disease, the rate of breast cancer grew. In the last ten of those thirty years, it grew even faster. "Today," says Pearson, "it is just barely being seen as the same kind of premature killer and disabler of women. It took an extra twenty years to see breast cancer in the light that we so easily and quickly saw heart disease. More than that, I don't think we've responded with equivalent emphasis to the high proportion of breast cancer in women as we did to the high incidence of heart disease in men thirty years ago." And the reason, she says bluntly, is sexism.

"Who counts? Who is the group in this society with the most power? It's middle-class white men, men in their fifties at the peak of their earning potential, at the peak of their attractiveness, and at the peak of power in their careers. It's the age of the men who run the country, the CEOs [chief executive officers], the legislators, the judges. And heart disease was important because it affected those people. As breast cancer has grown, it couldn't even be seen even though it's women of that exact same age who were getting it. If we had been able to see clearly and see men and women as equally important, we would have woken up to this at least ten years ago and probably closer to twenty."

As it is, the belated focus on breast cancer comes at a time when funding for the National Cancer Institute has dwindled. Although the NIH budget has grown some 27 percent since 1980, appropriations for National Cancer Institute have dropped 6 percent and clinical cancer research, which takes experimental treatments to actual patients and has been shown to increase survival rates, has lost 33 percent, according to Martin Abeloff, M.D., clinical director of the Johns Hopkins Oncology Center, who testified to the sorry state of cancer funding before a Senate committee.

Breast cancer is a particularly troublesome and expensive disease to study. For one thing, researchers believe it is many diseases, not one. The unknowns are many, leading researchers down a dozen different trails, not all of which are adequately funded. As often happens in lean times, the ones that are funded tend to be the "safest" ones, those that show the greatest promise of turning up a positive result, those that appear "doable," says Ruth Sager, Ph.D., chief of the division of cancer genetics at the Dana-Farber Cancer Institute in Boston. They're like Hollywood's new sure thing, the movie sequel. Built on what is already known about breast cancer, they leave many of the new, more radical ideas, which would be funded in more prosperous times, to languish in the minds and files of discouraged investigators. "Try and get funding for a fishing expedition," says Marc Lippman, M.D., director of Georgetown's Lombardi Cancer Center. "You can't do it."

Breast cancer research is also plagued by certain fundamental problems. There are no known biological markers—telltale genes or enzymes or other substances in blood or urine, for example—that would identify a woman likely to get breast cancer or one whose cancer was aggressive or potentially lethal. The discovery of biological markers would help clinicians tailor treatments so a woman with a more indolent cancer would not have to undergo the ravages of chemotherapy or radiation. Their lack is felt in research as well, particularly in studies examining potential preventive measures. Without a biological marker that can be used to measure the effect of a given therapy or intervention, prevention studies need to follow women for at least a decade until their breast cancers could reasonably be expected to appear, making most prevention studies astronomically expensive.

Researchers can't even effectively grow breast cancer tumor cells in culture or in laboratory animals to test therapies outside the human body. "Colon cancer cells will grow in the nude mouse. Lung cancer samples will grow in the nude mouse. Any old sample will grow. Very few breast cancers will do that," says Ruth Sager. "Those are two very fundamental problems. Can you get funded for that? No."

One area that has been only weakly addressed has been prevention, an area of research, along with the psychosocial sciences, that historically has been marginalized. Vaccines, cures, and magic bullets are the glamour and goals of much of science. Though dazzling and dramatic as such breakthroughs are, it's safe to say that given a choice of being cured of breast cancer and never getting it in the first place, most women would choose the latter. However, medical research rarely takes direction from its subjects. In fact, in the area of prevention, it's not clear from whom it is taking direction.

On the surface, prevention appears to be a high-priority item. In his 1991 National Cancer Institute Bypass Budget Request, National Cancer Institute Director Samuel Broder told President George Bush, "ultimately the real gains in reducing cancer incidences and mortality will come from prevention." There certainly is an economic advantage to funding prevention research. By one estimate, if only 10 percent of breast cancer could be prevented, $500 million a year in treatment costs would be saved.

In reality, prevention is paid more lip service than real attention. Cancer prevention and control is a lower percentage of the National Cancer Institute total funding than it was in 1984, when a distinguished group of scientists and health officials unveiled the Year 2000 Plan and its goal of cutting cancer deaths in half by the turn of the century. Then, it was 6.1 percent of the more than $1 billion budget. In 1990, under the highly competitive conditions of research funding, prevention represented 4.9 percent of a $1.6 billion total appropriations.

Among those proposals falling victim to the competition was a $107 million ten-year study that would have examined the effect of a low-fat diet on breast cancer. Researchers have long been intrigued by the plethora of studies that show that the highest breast cancer rates in the world occur in countries with the diets richest in fat. Adding to the intrigue: When Japanese women, who have among the lowest breast cancer rates in the world, immigrate to the United States, within a generation or two they become Americanized, developing breast cancer at rates equal to other American women. There is also strong evidence that dietary fat as well as obesity may increase the levels of circulating estrogen, long believed to be a precipitating factor in breast cancer.

The association appears so strong that Maureen Henderson, M.D., head of the cancer prevention research program at the Fred Hutchinson Cancer Research Center in Seattle, undertook an NIH-funded three-year pilot project to determine if through intensive education and counseling, women could reduce their fat intake to a mere 20 percent of the calories they consumed. Her guiding theory: "We can prevent a disease without knowing what is causing it." The study was successful. The women were able to maintain their diets throughout the course of the trial and beyond, a virtual miracle considering the average American diet derives nearly 40 percent of its calories from fat. But when she approached NIH to conduct the longer study, she was turned down despite the fact that her proposal was considered of scientific merit.

Asked why she believes her "meritorious" proposal went unfunded, Henderson hesitates for a few minutes. "There is," she says

finally in her clipped British accent, "a bias against prevention research and there is a bias against both behavioral and dietary research, so when you put the two of them together . . . But really, I'd
have to say it all comes down to money. If it had been cheap, there
would have been no hesitation. Once it gets expensive, everybody
raises all of the old arguments they've had in the past."

Many of those "old arguments" are, in fact, legitimate scientific
questions about a study of dietary fat and breast cancer. A number of
large and well-respected studies, such as the Harvard Nurse's Study,
have found no connection between the amount of fat a woman con-
sumes and her risk of getting breast cancer. A number of fine scientists consider the fat inquiry simply a dead end. Those objections
were certainly raised about Henderson's proposal.

But legitimate scientific objections don't always shoot down a
study. One prevention study that has come under fire is the $60 mil-
lion five-year tamoxifen study, which was launched in April 1992 to
learn whether the antiestrogen drug tamoxifen would prevent breast
cancer in healthy but high-risk women. Studies have found that tamoxifen, which is used in the treatment of advanced breast cancer
mainly in postmenopausal women, significantly improved the
chance of a woman living ten years after diagnosis. However, wom-
en's groups and some doctors think the study is too risky. For all its
potential benefits, tamoxifen may also increase a woman's chances
of developing endometrial or other cancers. "I don't think we know
enough about tamoxifen and what it does endocrinologically in premenopausal women and that really is a bit scary," says Susan Love.

What has irked many women, though, is the suspicion that
Henderson's proposal was sunk not by legitimate scientific concerns
but hoary sexist ones. They point to the fact that some of Henderson's colleagues admitted they were skeptical that women could be
taught to change their diets to prevent breast cancer. After all, some
scientists argued, after more than thirty years of trying, no one had
been able to find a way to convince men to change their diets to prevent heart disease.

Henderson, testifying before the House subcommittee on
health and the environment in June 1990, explained why extrapolat-
ing from data on dietary studies on men to one on women made no
sense: "There is a great deal of disbelief amongst my colleagues in

the general scientific community that because men were unable to change their diets when we tried to change diets to prevent heart disease, that women also cannot change their diets," she acknowledged to the subcommittee, which was learning to its dismay that morning how little the health community really knew about women. "That is an illogical belief because the way we have been able to get women to reduce the fat in their diet was by changing their buying [and] cooking habits. And it's in that way you can make major changes. To make them at the table is virtually impossible, and of course, men are faced with making that decision. So it's logical to see that women can do it more easily, but that has not occurred to my colleagues."

What did occur to one—Stanford University medical school chief David Korn—was that Henderson's study would be relying on self-reported dietary information, in many cases from elderly women, since there is no objective way to measure fat intake outside a laboratory. "How accurate would their dietary memory be?" asked Korn, then chair of the National Cancer Advisory Board. "Where would half of them be—nursing homes with various kinds of senility and forgetfulness."

The quote so incensed Cindy Pearson that she filed it within easy reach in case she had to make a point. "This," she fumes, "is sexism pure and simple because they have done these dietary interventions in men for decades. They have relied on diaries or asking people to recall what they ate afterward and they were willing to accept it from them. Why not from women?"

Indeed. And, you might ask, would there have been so great an objection to a long-term, multimillion prevention study had it been on men and heart disease? In fact, there have been at least two, both of even greater magnitude than Henderson's study. For example, there was the $117 million fifteen-year MR FIT, designed to test whether reducing blood pressure, cholesterol, and cigarette smoking would lower the rate of heart disease among 13,000 men, and the Coronary Primary Prevention Trial, which studied the effects of lowering cholesterol in 4,000 men, conducted over fifteen years at a cost of $142 million. If they were not "too expensive," why is a $107 million breast cancer study?

WINNING THE BATTLE

Though activists have little trouble making more than a prima facie case for the role sexism plays in the underfunding of breast cancer research, most believe that moral arguments for boosting that funding won't be as effective as down-and-dirty politicking. Women are going to have to fight for their lives.

It was nearly 5 P.M., after eight hours of testimony, when Harvey Kushner stood up to address the breast cancer researchers seated around the conference table at that Capitol Hill motel. If not a familiar face, his was a familiar name to all of them. Kushner's wife, Rose, was the doyenne of breast cancer activists, who is credited with starting the first and one of the largest breast cancer networks in the country—now called the National Alliance of Breast Cancer Organizations—which began as a hot line in her home. Though she won her battle to change the way women with breast cancer were treated, Rose Kushner lost her battle with breast cancer several years ago. Her husband has taken up the cause.

"Across the hall there's another meeting," began Kushner, as heads swiveled in his direction. "Across the street in another hotel there's another meeting. And in each of those meetings there's a group of people talking about a different issue and the need for money . . . Down the street from here are 600 people, men and women, mostly men. These other people at these other hotels are going to be in their offices on Capitol Hill demanding their rights and they're going to get them."

There's a $40 million railroad museum in New Jersey, he told them, and $2.5 billion in West Virginia that wasn't there three years before because someone lobbied for it. The only way to get the millions needed for breast cancer research every year is to demand it, he said. "We've got to get our money before the Railroad Museum does."

Kushner stopped to acknowledge applause, then renewed his effort. "Go after them," he urged. "Have workshops where you teach women how to become politically active on the breast cancer issue so the next time we march on Washington we don't bring half a million letters, we bring a million. We don't have a few hundred women, we have a few hundred thousand women. *Then* you'll get every penny you need for breast cancer research. Because that's the way the system works."

By the end of 1992, the widely touted Year of the Woman, it was clear that breast cancer activists had learned that lesson well. As a result of the coalition's letter-writing campaign and some persistent lobbying of individual lawmakers, a Congress that was about to become feminized allocated more than $400 million for breast cancer research—three times more than the previous year's budget and more than was budgeted for any other kind of cancer. Obviously, there were others besides women who were now afraid.

5

WOMEN
WITH AIDS

The Forgotten Victims

This is a society that is perfectly willing to let young black men kill each other in the ghetto. Is it a big surprise that no one cares about young black women with HIV [human immunodeficiency virus]?

—*Deborah Cotton,M.D.*

In 1981, the federal Centers for Disease Control (CDC) began to tally the mounting cases of a strange new disease that seemed to be afflicting only gay men. It insidiously attacked and destroyed their immune systems, leaving them vulnerable to a host of rare infections and diseases, such as *pneumocystis carinii* pneumonia, which few doctors had ever seen, and Kaposi's sarcoma, a cancer usually found only in elderly Mediterranean and African men. In 1981, the CDC also received a report of one woman with the new disease, which was then being called *gay-related infectious disease.*

In 1982, eighteen researchers from nine institutions across the country published a small study in *The Annals of Internal Medicine.* They had found five more women with the gay disease, which they now called *community-acquired cellular immunodeficiency.* Four of the women were users of intravenous drugs; one was a bisexual who included among her male partners a heroin addict with a depressed immune system. Even the dry, beclouding jargon of a medical journal could not disguise the obvious alarm of the researchers who speculated that this new disease was infectious, passed somehow from person to person through intravenous drug use and sex—and not just homosexual sex, as was thought. Clearly convinced their warning needed to be heard, they repeated it twice in six pages, as dramatically as science can sound: "The extension of this outbreak to women has important implications concerning the cause, pathogenesis and mode of transmission of this new syndrome, and should alert the medical community to consider the spread of this outbreak to new populations."

But no one heard. No one heard that year or for many years to come. And the gay disease, which came to be known as acquired immunodeficiency syndrome—AIDS—slowly ate its way through those new populations, women and their children, hidden and quiet and savage, like an army of termites through a wooden house.

No one heard. Certainly not Louise Denson. In 1981, Louise Denson, one of eleven children of a Virginia sharecropper, was sitting in Niantic Prison in Connecticut awaiting trial for check forgery, which was one of the ways—along with prostitution and selling drugs—that she fed her fifteen-year heroin habit. The cell was dark, and she was sick, cold, and wet. "But I wanted to be there," she remembers. "I said, 'God, here I am in jail and I feel safe here.' I knew then I had to change." In 1981, Louise Denson started to get clean. She entered a drug rehabilitation center and came to grips with her troubled life—as an abused child, a fourth-grade dropout, a runaway, a teenaged mother, an addict. She got her high school equivalency diploma. She made peace with her three children, two of whom had been taken from her and adopted by relatives. She fell in love and got married. Though the marriage didn't work out—she left her husband the day she learned he was shooting up drugs—Louise Denson stayed straight. She was hired as a health educator at a residential drug treatment program in New Brunswick, New Jersey, teaching recovering addicts about AIDS. She was nearly fifty, and yet she felt as though her life had just begun.

It was a feeling that was to be short-lived. As part of her job, Louise took clients to the clinic to be tested for HIV. "A lot of the clients would ask me if I had been tested and I didn't feel comfortable telling them no. Three years ago, I took a group of clients to get tested and I got tested myself." She pauses, looking down at her newly manicured burgundy nails. "I was the only one who came back positive."

She didn't believe it at first. She asked to be tested again.

Maybe, she thought, the results were wrong. "Deep down in my heart I knew it was possible," she says. "But I really didn't think it could be me. I had gotten my life together. I hadn't used since 1981. It was like somebody else's problem."

AIDS has always been somebody else's problem. First it was gays, then intravenous (IV) drug users, people who were social outcasts long before a plague singled them out. It was a disease that most Americans could file away with starvation in Somalia and bomb blasts in Beirut—something horrifying, something tragic, something that was happening to somebody else.

Categorizing AIDS—as a gay disease, as an infection endemic to only certain communities—may have tamed some anxieties, but when practiced by scientists as well as the lay public, it also allowed the epidemic to spread wildly through an unwary and defenseless population. Even after it was clear that AIDS was transmitted sexually—and sexually transmitted diseases are never limited to one sex—scientists failed to see the next logical turn it would take, failed to see the direction in which the dominoes were tumbling. Women in ever increasing numbers were using IV drugs. Women were having sex with men who used IV drugs, with men who had sex with men. Women were trading sex for drugs. African women, who had been living with the disease longer, were being infected at the same rate as African men. Yet women were a risk group that no one ever mentioned, no one seemed to see.

By the time the AIDS epidemic was a decade old, 5 women had become more than 20,000 women. By 1993, some 35,000 women had been diagnosed with AIDS, which had become the fifth leading cause of death among women of reproductive age, the leading cause of death among young black women in the drug-infested neighborhoods of New York and New Jersey. Between 1984 and 1991, the percentage of women with AIDS doubled. Between 1991 and 1992 the numbers had increased by another third. By the time the epidemic was little more than ten years old, women were the fastest-growing group of people infected with HIV, which causes AIDS. According to one set of figures, in 1993 an estimated 200,000 to 300,000 women were HIV infected, and one day they will die of AIDS.

Louise Denson often wonders how many of them were like she was, thinking AIDS was something that happened to somebody else, not realizing that they *were* that somebody else. "Sometimes I get mad at the government because I think they could have done something," she says, her gentle face reflecting hurt rather than anger. "They knew women could get AIDS and they didn't tell anyone. They still haven't told anyone. I mean, I knew people were dying, but I didn't know *I* could catch it. I thought it was people shooting up and gays. Why didn't they tell us?"

Would it have been different, Louise Denson sometimes wonders, if someone had seen and heard—and told?

THE INVISIBLE VICTIMS

"Despite the rather startling statistics," says Howard Minkoff, M.D., an AIDS researcher from the State University of New York Health Science Center in Brooklyn, "the study of AIDS in women remains a rather nascent science. What we know about AIDS we have learned from men, and they differ from women not only in gender but in race, in risk groups, and in socioeconomic status."

Though AIDS is genderless, the entire system set up to track, research, and treat the disease, from clinical trials to drug protocols to AIDS education and support programs, is clearly gendered. It was designed for men, specifically gay men, who, as Minkoff points out, are different from other risk groups by more than sexual preference. Largely though not exclusively white, gays tend to be well educated and middle to upper middle class. They have very little in common with women and IV drug users other than the disease that is taking their lives.

Unlike the gay men, most women with AIDS are either African-American or Hispanic. Most of them are young and poor, and many are single mothers. More than half contracted the virus through drug use, a third through heterosexual sex, official figures that may be misleading because they fail to recognize that female drug users often trade sex for drugs. They are the traditionally disempowered, living in the dark, unvisited corners of American society. Not even their growing presence in the AIDS epidemic could draw them into the light.

They were rarely recruited for the clinical investigations into AIDS. In one unpublished report by Harvard AIDS researcher

Deborah Cotton, M.D., M.P.H., as of 1990 only 801 women out of a total 12,084 subjects were enrolled in the government's extensive AIDS Clinical Trial Group studies. That's only 6 percent of the study populations, yet women make up 12 percent of all people with AIDS in this country. The trials were clearly set up without the demographics of the women in mind. Women of childbearing years, the prime risk group for AIDS, were excluded unless they could prove they were using adequate contraception, which translated into the Pill or an intrauterine device (IUD). At the time, nothing was known about any effects of oral contraception on HIV infection, but IUD users are at higher risk of developing pelvic infections that are more aggressive and even deadly in HIV-positive women. Most of the HIV-infected women in the country were and continue to be poor minority women in the Bronx, New York, and Newark, New Jersey, but those weren't the sites chosen for research studies. And no effort was made to provide transportation or child care, without which the women, who could not afford baby-sitters and bus fare, simply could not participate.

Like heart disease, AIDS has been studied primarily in men, and research findings simply extrapolated to women. Just as the hearts of men and women are different, so, too, are many of their other organs. Virtually nothing is known about the risk factors and unique manifestations of the disease in women. It was only in 1992 that women started being enrolled in so-called spectrum-of-disease and natural history studies that chart how the disease ravages the body. It may be many years before researchers know if there are any hormonal influences on the AIDS virus, what effects HIV has on specific gynecological conditions, and whether men and women manifest the disease differently, all issues suggested by the experiences of clinicians who work with HIV-infected women.

Studies of the drug azidothymidine (AZT) were done almost exclusively in white men, and their findings applied to women and minorities. Though the antiviral drug has been used to treat AIDS since 1987, it wasn't until late 1991 that the National Institute of Allergy and Infectious Diseases (NIAID), the principal federal funding agency for AIDS research, announced for the first time that early treatment with the drug increased survival time in women and minority groups. This new information did not come from any new studies, however, but rather from two three-year-old NIAID-funded clinical trials that had included some women and minorities. The researchers simply went back and reanalyzed their data, teasing out existing—albeit ignored—information along gender and racial lines.

As has been the case in other diseases, women also have been excluded from research on new drug treatments for AIDS, a fact that alarms physicians who have no choice but to prescribe these untested drugs to their female HIV-infected patients. "When you're dealing with a disease that is fatal and for which one's primary therapy has failed, the only hope for new therapy is through research," says Howard Minkoff. "I think it is rather daunting to know that access is completely cut off based on gender."

AIDS has even been defined by the medical experiences of men, specifically the 5,000 men, mostly white, gay, and bisexual, who are taking part in a natural history study called the Multicenter AIDS Cohort Study, or MACS. Technically, someone who is infected with the AIDS virus cannot be diagnosed "officially" with AIDS until he or she contracts one of the conditions included in the AIDS case definition established by the CDC. Although HIV infection often has its own symptoms, it doesn't become the end-stage disease of AIDS until it meets the definition. Until January 1993, that official definition contained twenty-three forms of cancer and opportunistic infections known to be associated with AIDS—in these 5,000 gay and bisexual men.

Because of its origins, the definition ignored the anatomical differences between the sexes. Though recent studies indicate men and women get many of the same AIDS-defining diseases, women have different body parts that are attacked by HIV. Many experience gynecological symptoms, vaginal yeast infections, for example, which are not going to be detected in studies limited to men no matter what their sexual orientation. AIDS activists and some clinicians believe this has delayed the diagnosis and treatment of HIV-infected women. "Keeping gynecological symptoms out of the definition does two things," says Mardge Cohen, M.D, an internist who has been caring for women and children with AIDS at Chicago's Cook County Hospital since 1988. "One, it doesn't encourage common providers who are taking care of people with HIV to look for those conditions, and two, it doesn't alert providers who are taking care of women who have these conditions to think about testing them for HIV."

Howard Minkoff adds one more consequence: Women who see their gynecologists with refractory and recurrent yeast infections, precancerous changes in cervical tissue (cervical dysplasia), and pelvic inflammatory disease are receiving standard screenings and treatments that are effective in normal women but which clinical experience has shown may not work if a woman is HIV infected. There is some evidence, for example, that the Pap smear used to detect cancerous changes in cervical cells may miss those changes in HIV-infected women, who are more likely to develop a more virulent case of cervical cancer. There is also some evidence that conditions such as pelvic inflammatory disease, genital ulcer disease, and some sexually transmitted diseases are exacerbated by HIV and harder to treat. If a physician isn't familiar with these manifestations of HIV or worse, doesn't know or suspect a patient is infected, offering tests and treatments that don't work—and, perhaps, missing the diagnosis of a fatal illness at the same time—is not good medicine.

For many years, the CDC resisted considerable public pressure to add any more diseases to the list. One official claimed it would be "too cumbersome." After all, the CDC argued, the definition was meant to be used only to keep track of the spread of AIDS, which, many activists argued in return, it wasn't doing because the disease in women wasn't recognized and studied. But in January 1993, after a year of public clamor and private wrangling, the CDC changed its definition to include one female-specific condition—invasive cervical cancer—and added an immune system marker that it believed would allow more women and IV drug users to be counted. Doctors can now diagnose AIDS based on the blood levels of disease-fighting T cells, which are destroyed by the AIDS virus. If a woman's T cells have dropped to under 200 per cubic millimeter of blood (between 800 and 1,200 is normal), she is considered to have AIDS even if she has not yet contracted any of the opportunistic conditions still included in the definition.

Though many AIDS activists and clinicians applaud the change, others feel that irreparable damage has already been done. Many of the women who are likely to be identified by the new definition may have already missed the opportunity for early treatment because they were previously undiagnosed or misdiagnosed. Others have already died. In one CDC study, 48 percent of the women whose death certificates listed them as having HIV or AIDS died of conditions not in the definition. And as one AIDS activist put it, they were "dead, but not disabled," referring to the difficulty many HIV-infected women have had getting federal disability benefits. Many of these undiagnosed women may have spent the last months of their lives battling to get AIDS-related benefits from the Social Security Administration which, in the past, relied heavily on the CDC definition to determine eligibility.

The revised definition also relies on a test, called a Cd-4 test, that was proven unreliable when studied in the Multicenter AIDS Cohort Study group. T-cell counts also are not the best indicator of health. A woman whose T-cell count is 400 can be quite sick, whereas one whose count has dropped below 200 may be relatively healthy.

But perhaps the most egregious damage done by the gender-insensitive definition was contributing to the widespread myth—believed by doctors and women alike—that women weren't dying of AIDS. This, many critics suggest, has created an even more horrific public health nightmare. It meant that women didn't know they could contract the disease and so never altered risky behavior which, in many cases, meant having sexual relations with their husbands. It also meant they didn't know they were at risk for spreading the disease.

In one study of pregnant women who were HIV positive, only 22 percent knew they were at high risk although they lived in communities where there was a high rate of heterosexual transmission of the disease. By one estimate, of the 200,000 to 300,000 women in the United States who are believed to be HIV infected, about two-thirds of them don't yet know. Those women may unwittingly be spreading the disease to their children. Most AIDS clinicians can tell dozens of poignant stories of how they had to inform women of their HIV infection after detecting the virus during prenatal tests or diagnosing AIDS in a hospitalized child.

Paula Schuman, M.D., a specialist in infectious diseases at Wayne State University School of Medicine in Detroit, recalled one patient, the mother of five, who didn't learn of her infection until her oldest child, a seven-year-old, was hospitalized with *Pneumocystis carinii* pneumonia. The entire family was tested. Along with the mother and the seven-year-old, a six-year-old daughter was found to be infected. "She has since died," Schuman told a roomful of AIDS clinicians at the First Annual Congress on Women's Health, held in Washington, D.C., in June 1993. Because AIDS has a lengthy symptom-free latency period, it's not unusual for a woman to live unaware of her HIV infection for seven years or more, which is a long time to be harboring and, perhaps, spreading an infectious disease. "And seven years is not the oldest child in which we've had to make this diagnosis of perinatally acquired HIV," said Schuman. "Actually, the oldest was ten."

Because women weren't seen as potential victims, even AIDS education efforts, the warning messages to avoid needle sharing and unsafe sex, were aimed at men, as if they were the only ones who ever used drugs, had anal sex, or slept with at-risk partners. AIDS was not yet seen as a heterosexual disease despite the increasing evidence that it was inching up in the same population disproportionately affected by other sexually transmitted diseases: young minority women. Few health professionals seemed to make the connection that drug addicts, predominantly male, had sex lives and that their partners were usually women. Even when there was concern about the spread of the disease among heterosexuals, it wasn't heterosexual women who were warned to avoid men in high-risk groups. It was men, and they were cautioned to stay away from prostitutes.

The term *safe sex* itself is gender specific. Those two words usually appear in the same sentence as the word *condom*. Louise Denson, who gives risk reduction workshops for women, says she often asks herself, "Why am I standing here teaching women how to use a condom? They don't have anything to put a condom on." It's the rare AIDS prevention brochure or TV commercial that is directed at women, who don't need free condoms as much as they need help in convincing their partners to use them. "A lot of these women get beaten for suggesting to their partner that he use a condom," says Louise. And they are at great risk of contracting AIDS from a male partner, who may be unconcerned about spreading it. In one study, researchers found that only 62 percent of heterosexual HIV-infected men used condoms during sex. (Men do tend to be more conscientious about condoms when they're the ones at risk. Condom use rises to 88 percent when healthy men whose partners are HIV infected are surveyed.)

Though the U.S. Food and Drug Administration (FDA) approved a female condom, doctors and patients have been "uniformly unenthusiastic" about it, said one doctor. Called Reality, the new female condom looks something like a baggie or a miniature windsock. But aesthetics aren't what's likely to doom it. Not only does it not stay in place, it has a high failure rate—25 percent of women become pregnant in the first year—and there's no scientific evidence that it prevents the transmission of HIV.

Even when women were given messages, they were often not the right ones. Vivian Torres recalls the advice she got from a jailhouse doctor the day in 1988 she learned she was infected. A heroin addict and prostitute, she was serving time in Camden County Jail for drug dealing when she decided to get tested. She knew drug addicts died of AIDS. "But I didn't know how they got it," she says. A month after her test, she was taken to see the doctor again. "That's when he told me I had AIDS," Vivian says. "He said, 'You've got six months to live. Whatever you know how to do best when you're on the street, go out and do it. Enjoy.' And when I got out, I did exactly what he told me to do. Sometimes I wonder how many people *I* infected because I followed his advice."

Karen Sofield might have been diagnosed earlier—might not have contracted AIDS at all—if more attention had been paid to the spread of the epidemic through the heterosexual population. In 1984, Karen Sofield was a single mother in her mid-twenties and working as a chemical operator in a large New Jersey pharmaceutical firm. There she met a man whom she describes as "the first totally sober man I ever dated. When he told me he didn't drink, I was thrilled," says Karen, who came from a family background of alcoholism. It was primarily a sexual relationship—"We were both lonely," she explains—but they never used condoms. What she didn't know then was that he was doing drugs. "Even if I had known, I don't think I would have thought I could be infected with AIDS," Karen says. "In 1984, I don't remember thinking women got AIDS."

The relationship didn't last long. The Christmas he gave her an electric teakettle she didn't need and she gave him a handmade pot he didn't like made them both realize they had nothing in common.

But about a year after they broke up, she lost her job. Then the symptoms started. She began having chronic diarrhea and peculiar skin rashes. Her hair—"which used to be long and beautiful," she says ruefully, running her hand through the golden brown curls that lie in wisps around her head—began shedding in clumps. For four years, she went from doctor to doctor, only to be assured that she was suffering from stress. But her symptoms never went away. She even sought out a feminist physician. "She treated my diarrhea with a bottle of Metamucil," says Karen. "She told me I had irritable bowel syndrome."

Then, in 1988, she got a phone call from a friend of her former lover. "She told me she was calling from his funeral," remembers Karen. "She never said he had it, but she told me to get myself tested for AIDS." Karen, who had never used drugs and had been celibate for four years, was first stunned, then terrified. She begged her mother, a lab technician, to test her for HIV. The test came back positive. "She waited four days to tell me," says Karen. "We never talk about what went on in those four days."

She made a second appointment with the feminist doctor but not to get treated. "I told her all I came for was to tell her I had AIDS and maybe she should ask the women who come in with the same symptoms if they've been sexually active in the last ten years. I said maybe you should think to test them for HIV." The doctor, she says, just stared at her, dumbfounded. Karen paid her thirty-five dollars and left.

Sitting on a couch in her airy, antique-filled apartment overlooking a park in suburban Newark, Karen Sofield unconsciously tugs the legs of her jeans to meet her black Converse high-tops, covering the fungal rash that speckles her legs. In 1992, she says, in what she calculates was the ninth year she lived with HIV, she had a bout with *Pneumocystis carinii* pneumonia. "Now I have full-blown AIDS," she says and snickers. "Full-blown. I hate that expression. You expect me to explode at any minute!" She erupts with a husky laugh.

But for four of those nine years, Karen Sofield says, she lived in blithe ignorance—and without early treatment—all because no one thought to ask her about her sex life. "I was in my twenties, single, and in my younger days, I was really sexy. Why didn't anyone ask?" Her face, pale, scrubbed, and makeupless, flashes with anger. "God forbid I got married and had children. Then I would have been a bad person because I infected my children. I've seen that. Women are made to feel like lepers when they can't keep their disease to themselves. Should I have been made to feel guilty because I had infected my husband and children? I didn't know I had the AIDS virus. No one diagnosed me."

She's sure now that no one thought to test her because "I'm not in any category they've heard of. I'm white. I'm a woman. I don't have needles hanging out of my arm and I'm not surrounded by homosexual men. But I had made love with a man who did drugs and he gave me AIDS. Why," she says again, "didn't anybody ask?"

WOMEN AS RISK FACTORS

When Karen Sofield contracted AIDS, no one seemed concerned about who was giving the disease to women. In fact, in the earliest days of the epidemic, the few research studies on women focused on them not as victims of the disease but as risk factors to others, as "vectors and vessels." Most of those studies were done on pregnant women and prostitutes, spurred by widespread fears that women were going to spread the epidemic like colds through a nursery school.

"The interest was solely in men and babies," says Margaret Somerville, director of Montreal's McGill University Centre for Medicine, Ethics and Law. "Women were the cyphers in the middle who passed the virus from the men to the babies."

Women were indeed "cyphers" whose own health was ignored—and, in some cases, put in jeopardy—to protect others, including their unborn children. For example, U.S. Public Health Service guidelines in use in 1991 recommended that pregnant women not be given preventive drug treatment for *Pneumocystis carinii* pneumonia because of the potential danger to their fetuses. "Which basically means you say to your pregnant patient, 'Miss Jones, there's a 10 percent chance you're going to get a lethal infection that I can prevent, but we're not going to discuss it,' " says Howard Minkoff. "I think it's good news that obstetricians are not honoring that proviso."

And there is the study known as ACTG 076, launched in 1991, which is an attempt to determine whether AZT might prevent the transmission of the virus from mother to child. On its face, the trial seems dictated by noble motives: to prevent babies from contracting AIDS. But the ethics and the benefits of the study to both mothers and babies are questionable. Only about 20 percent of babies born to HIV-infected mothers contract the disease, so the drug, which is highly toxic, will be given to many healthy fetuses and newborns. What's more, the drug is being given to healthy, although HIV-infected, women, who run the risk of developing resistance to it. Taken over long periods of time, AZT tends to stop halting the spread of the virus.

By enrolling pregnant women, ACTG 076 appears to be breaking some medical ground. Pregnant women, indeed, women of childbearing years, are rarely if ever included in clinical trials because of concern for fetal well-being. The truth, however, is that ACTG 076 reflects the widely held view of women as organic baby carriages, as "walking wombs." Harvard's Deborah Cotton echoes other critics when she suggests that this exception shows the medical community is far more concerned about fetal well-being than it is about the health of women.

"Women have not been included in trials until all of a sudden people want to look at whether a drug will interrupt fetal transmission. All of a sudden it's fine to include women," she points out. "You have to ask yourself why."

Originally a pediatric study designed as a drug trial for babies born to HIV-infected mothers, ACTG 076 took its current prenatal form when pediatric researchers decided it might be more efficacious if the drug "was on board when [the babies are] born," says Cotton. "They'll deny that now, but I heard them say things like that. But nowhere in this equation were people thinking whether this was good for the woman or not."

In fact, that attitude has orchestrated much of the research on women and AIDS. Even when the WHO adopted as its theme Women and AIDS for its World AIDS Day in 1990, women remained invisible as victims. Instead, they were viewed only in their roles as caretakers and mothers and then not sympathetically. "To WHO officials, the biggest problem was if all these women get AIDS, who's going to take care of all the other people with AIDS?" says Margaret Somerville. "And all those babies—10 million of them—will be orphans! The attitude was, How dare these women get sick? The whole program focused on what was happening to other people because women were getting AIDS, not what was happening to the women."

The prostitution studies are another case in point. In 1988, the CDC completed a two-year multicenter study of the potential risks posed by female prostitutes to the heterosexual community. As part of that project, sociologist Carole Campbell, Ph.D., interviewed women in a brothel outside Las Vegas, Nevada, where prostitution is legal. Campbell, who teaches at California State University, says it was clear from the start that prostitutes, though not an impressively large subgroup, had been identified as a risk to the heterosexual community, "meaning," she says pointedly, "to men." She recalls sensing a strong bias among CDC officials against seeing women as victims of the disease though she and her colleagues quickly realized "it was the women who were at risk."

She says at one point it was suggested that all prostitutes be required to undergo mandatory testing for HIV, which would assure customers the prostitutes were "safe" but offered no similar assurance to the women about their customers. "It was clear what—and who—was important," Campbell says.

But the focus on prostitutes again sent the wrong message both to the public and the medical community. Subsequent transmission studies have found that rather than being risk factors to men, it is women who are at greatest risk of contracting AIDS through heterosexual sex. Magic Johnson's well-publicized case notwithstanding, female-to-male transmission of the AIDS virus is, in the language of medical researchers, "less efficient." In fact, according to one study, a woman is nearly eighteen times more likely to contract AIDS from a male sexual partner than he from her. As of April 1991, only about 4 percent of all AIDS cases reported to the CDC were attributed to heterosexual contact, and 70 percent of those cases occurred among women.

Researchers are now paying attention to who is giving AIDS to women if only because the face of the AIDS epidemic has changed. The cases of infected women are expected to equal those of men by the year 2000 because the gay disease is now becoming a predominantly heterosexual disease, as it is in Central Africa. Brown University AIDS researcher Charles Carpenter, M.D., believes his experience in the tiny state of Rhode Island presages the direction the epidemic is taking. In 1989, he says, he was seeing few women with AIDS, and almost all of those were IV drug users. By 1993, the numbers of women had risen and almost all of them had contracted the disease through heterosexual sex.

"In certain parts of this country, we already have the heterosexual pattern where the ratio of male-to-female cases is about one to one, and this includes the South Bronx, Newark, and parts of Miami," says Carpenter. In fact, he says, the heterosexual epidemic can be tracked on an ordinary map. On the East Coast, it's moving, like a slow and ominous convoy, along the Interstate 95 corridor.

THE WHO OF THE EPIDEMIC

To Paula Schuman, all the bickering over the AIDS definition, all the esoteric harping on yeast infections and cervical dysplasia, have obscured the real reason women have been invisible in the AIDS epidemic: because they were invisible long before they contracted the disease. They are, in the newest social parlance, the underclass.

"One has to realize that the women we take care of are experiencing their lives in the context of chronic disease, poverty, social oppression, economic oppression, and on top of all this AIDS has sealed their fate," Schuman said.

What has made AIDS different from other diseases is that it is where many of the classic *isms*—racism, sexism, and classism—come together, as Harlem Hospital's Janet Mitchell, M.D., wrote in an article in the debut issue of *The Journal of Women's Health* in 1992. Since the early days of the epidemic, Mitchell pointed out, the controversy over AIDS "had more to do with *who* was infected than the *science* of infection." It was easy to disregard a disease that was cutting a swath through a despised minority—gays. Later, homophobia was simply eclipsed by a different brand of prejudice. Most of the women who are HIV infected and who are at risk of infection fall into the category of "other." They are poor minority women with little access to good health care and no political clout to influence how medical research money is spent. And to many unsympathetic Americans, what happens to these women is simply the natural consequence of the way they choose to live, the "wages of sin."

Women with AIDS are often victimized three times: first by a disease that will eventually kill them; then by their second-class social and economic status that bars them from medical research and health care; and finally by the stigma of AIDS, which is viewed as "a condign punishment for hedonism," as one doctor put it. They are, Howard Minkoff says, "seriously disenfranchised and medically disadvantaged."

But the way in which these women, traditionally underserved by medicine, have been neglected in the AIDS epidemic at times has seemed far from unconscious or benign. For example, in 1989, a group of researchers at Brown University's AIDS program wanted to find out how doctors decided which of their patients would receive AZT, then the only frontline drug available that could prolong their lives. The researchers interviewed 880 men and women being treated for HIV at nine health services nationwide. They asked the patients ninety-two basic questions about themselves and their care, including their race, what symptoms they had, if they were insured, if they used IV drugs or were homosexual. They then cross-referenced their responses with the answer the patients gave to the question, Has your doctor ever suggested you take AZT?

What the researchers found was that white male patients with health insurance were 50 percent more likely to be given AZT than minority patients, drug users, and those who were uninsured. But they were nearly three times more likely to get the drug than any of the women in the study. Why were gender and, to a lesser extent, race such important factors in clinical decision making? The researchers toyed with a number of possible explanations for this wide discrepancy, including: The doctors were practicing a form of social Darwinism along with medicine, deciding who would get the drug based on the perceived "social worth" of their patients. On that value scale, women, who are also disproportionately represented among minority, drug-using, and uninsured groups, weren't seen as "worthy" of treatment that might keep them alive longer.

The callousness of this attitude is even more striking when you consider that at the time of the study, many clinicians believed that AIDS was more deadly to women than to men. While men were living for years with AIDS, women were dying within a month of diagnosis. Some researchers suspected it was because more men got Kaposi's sarcoma, a slow-growing cancer, and women were getting diseases likely to kill them more quickly. But they were wrong. "Contrary to published reports early on that women had a more rapid course of HIV, with decent treatment women do as well as men, maybe better," says Charles Carpenter. "What those early studies reflected was poor access to health care."

For the women who are at highest risk of HIV infection, health care is as much of a luxury as a Cancun vacation. Most don't have private insurance, and public insurance—Medicaid—limits them to seeking care at clinics, often outside their neighborhoods, where two- to six-hour waits to see a doctor are not unusual. A single mother may not be able to find or pay a baby-sitter so she can sit in a crowded waiting room for a doctor to treat her recurrent yeast infection, her chronic bronchitis and, if she's fortunate, know enough about her symptoms to test her for HIV.

But having Medicaid doesn't automatically guarantee a woman access to health care either. For example, in Michigan, HIV-infected women on Medicaid still use medical services less often than men. It's not that they're healthier, but caring for their own health may fall far down on a priority list that is topped by survival issues, such as feeding their children, keeping a roof over their heads, and, quite often, caring for partners or children who also have AIDS. Consequently, many of these women are sicker when they finally seek medical care.

Those same factors that keep women from getting health care also have kept them from entering clinical trials, where their disease could not only be studied but treated. There is evidence, however, that some of that has changed. As of 1992, the percentage of women in NIAID-funded AIDS clinical studies had risen to 23 percent from a little more than 6 percent two years before. The study population also reflect a fairly accurate picture of women with AIDS: Most are women of color, and about 26 percent have a history of drug use. How NIAID has accomplished this in barely two years is an example of how the demographics of AIDS has challenged—and is changing—some fundamentals of biomedical research.

For one thing, researchers applying for funding get extra points for their ability to recruit minorities and women. NIAID has even launched a study to determine why some sites are more successful than others at recruiting women. But, perhaps most important, NIAID has been listening: to AIDS clinicians, AIDS activists, and women with AIDS. It appointed a Women's Health Committee for its clinical trials group. It funded sixteen community-based programs for HIV clinical trials, going where the patients are rather than expecting them to travel for care outside their neighborhoods, and funneling money to health professionals like Cook County's Mardge Cohen who understand the social and medical needs of HIV-infected women. Most trials now provide on-site child care, transportation, meals, and an army of social workers to help participants in the study with their other problems. Some programs offer full medical care above and beyond what is necessary for the study, and others schedule joint appointments for mothers and children so women will not have to make extra trips to the clinic. NIAID also took the bold step of recognizing that women's bodies are different from men's and sought out OB-GYN expertise in designing the trials. A number of new studies are looking at cervical dysplasia, and still others are planned for other gynecological conditions, such as pelvic inflammatory disease and genital ulcer disease.

Though these institutional changes are welcome, they are unpardonably late in coming. They are also unlikely to alter the lives of the 35,000 women with AIDS and the hundreds of thousands of other women who are currently HIV infected. They are the women no one heard or saw or warned, women like Karen Sofield and Louise Denson. They are paying the ultimate price of being invisible for so long. They are paying with their lives.

Karen Sofield often wishes someone could see her on the bad days, when she is overcome by the imminence of death, when she feels betrayed. "Sometimes the fear is so strong that it grips me," she says softly. "It's like somebody has ripped into my gut. My life has been shattered all because I decided to make love to a man, all because no one warned me that if I did that, I could get AIDS. When those days come, I'm down on my knees praying that I can forget this pain. It's so strong. The fear of dying, the fear of leaving everything you know, including your child, is too much. Sometimes I can't take it. Sometimes, when nobody's around, I can't stop crying. And I'm right down to my knees, begging for my life."

Louise Denson has those days, too. She admits she sometimes rails at God for letting AIDS happen to her when she had finally gotten her life together. She is bitter about the government's deadly decade of silence. On the bad days, she thinks of all the things she wanted to do with the second half of her life and now can't do. She wonders if it would have been different if she had only known.

On better days, she comforts herself with her own small plan for immortality. It came to her the day she saw the AIDS quilt spread out on a gymnasium floor, a still pool of colors, shapes, and names stitched, she could feel with compassion and love. If she was ignored in life, she thought, here was a way to be remembered in death.

"I began to see it as a way to make sure that we're *never* forgotten," she says. "A friend of mine has already told me she's going to make my panel. I told her I know what I want on it." Louise Denson smiles. "I want a big butterfly, and I want it to say 'Free at last.' "

6

THE AGING
WOMAN

Facing

Double Jeopardy

A woman's fundamental value to society has been her ability to reproduce, and the assumption is that once she can no longer reproduce she's useless. It's the double jeopardy of being old and being female.

—*Bonnie Strickland, Ph.D.*

Patricia Schroeder refers to it disparagingly as "the rest room excuse" because it was a rest room that kept women out of one of the first major federally funded studies aimed at learning what was "normal" in the aging process of humans.

In 1958, when William W. Peter, M.D., and Nathan W. Shock, M.D., launched what was to be known as the Baltimore Longitudinal Study of Aging (BLSA), the only facility available to them on their shoestring budget was a single room at the Baltimore City Hospitals with one rest room, which also was used by elderly men patients in the ward. To ask women to share a toilet with men seemed a problem so insurmountable that the researchers felt they had to exclude women from the project.

Ten years later, the BLSA had a change in fortune. The researchers acquired better facilities for their study participants, who were required to stay two nights every two years to undergo tests. Now they had rest rooms for both sexes. But women still weren't enrolled. There was a new excuse: Though they had enough money to include a separate toilet for women, they didn't have enough money to include women.

In fact, women weren't recruited for the BLSA until twenty years after it started. Today, there are 441 women in the study, which has followed the lives of some 1,800 participants. Unfortunately, most of them aren't very old. Only about 100 of the women are over forty, which may be the reason why, when BLSA published the results of its first two decades, the only reference made to women was a seven-line explanation of why, for twenty years, there were no women. However, there is no explanation for why the 400-page 2-pound, doorstop-sized report that contains no information on women's aging is called "Normal Human Aging."

For indeed, to exclude women from a study on normal aging is scientifically inexcusable, like studying Alzheimer's disease in twenty-year-olds. It's simply the wrong population. After all, aging is something women do, on the average, about seven years longer than men. Although women make up a little over half of the general population, they are two-thirds of the elderly population. They are nearly all of the old-old, the people over eighty-five. By the twenty-first century, the United States will have a record number of centenarians, and almost all of them will be women.

The problems of old age, as former National Institute of Aging Director Robert Butler has said, are largely "the problems of women." As a woman ages, she is far more likely than a man to be alone, poor, and impaired. Studies have shown that a woman's celebrated seven-year longevity edge is no blessing. Though women do live longer than men, their "active life expectancy"—how long they will remain healthy and independent—is about the same as a man's. According to one study reported in *The New England Journal of Medicine,* a woman sixty-five to sixty-nine has a modest advantage over a man; a woman in the older age groups has no advantage at all. The last few years of her life are spent, as the language of geriatricians grimly describes it, in "predeath morbidity."

Though American culture reviles rather than reveres the aged of either sex, a woman faces greater discrimination, largely because of economic, social, and medical realities. She faces the double jeopardy posed by living in a society riddled by both sexism and ageism. To be a woman is to be of little value; to be an old woman is to be valueless.

The graying of the population has brought into sharp relief the tremendous gaps in knowledge about the health of the older woman. Just as no one saw the urgency of including women is a study of normal human aging, older women were and continue to be underrepresented in studies of diseases that afflict them the most, including heart disease. The elderly are missing in studies of drug efficacy despite the fact that they take more drugs than everyone else. Some conditions, such as osteoporosis, diabetes, and incontinence, are largely the diseases of elderly women and largely understudied. Menopause, which every woman who reaches her sixth decade experiences one way or another, has routinely been mythologized and medicalized, but until recently, studies have been poorly done and rife with biased attitudes.

One reason for this, of course, is that it has often been social value that determines the direction of medical research. There is even some disturbing evidence that it orchestrates who receives the best care as well. Older women are at highest risk of developing breast cancer, the most likely to benefit from mammograms, yet they are the group least likely to have mammograms recommended by their doctors. At an international conference held in Washington, D.C., in February 1992, cancer specialists expressed concern that older patients, particularly those with more than one disease, were not getting the same kind of lifesaving treatment younger patients received, even if it was clear that the older people would benefit by it. There have been a number of studies that found that older women were denied appropriate treatment. In one study of ovarian cancer, researchers found that the disease was most lethal in the over-sixty-five age group and suspected that it was no coincidence that women in that age group were far less likely to be referred for aggressive chemotherapy. In a breast cancer study, older women didn't receive aggressive care when their cancer was localized and the women were vigorous, otherwise healthy, and even, by female standards, young—only sixty-five. Rather than basing their treatment of their elderly patients on established medical practice, "physicians are making these decisions based on their own judgments," says the author of another study, Paul Carbone, M.D., director of the University of Wisconsin's Comprehensive Cancer Center. Obviously, the elderly woman's needs and her prognosis do not determine what care she receives. Instead, that decision is based on whether her physician believes her life is *worth* saving.

There are signs that the plight of the older woman is finally being noticed. The Woman's Aging Study, a $7.9 million, seven-year exploration of disability among aged women, is one of a number of new research endeavors aimed at rectifying the gender inequities of the past. It is also a sign of the times. Not only has there been a new focus on women's health at NIH, the numbers have simply gotten too big to ignore. By the turn of the century, more than 21 million women will reach menopause. That's more than four times the number who became menopausal at the dawn of the twentieth century, when fewer women survived to old age. As people are living longer, the specter of nursing home populations numbering 5.3 million and the elderly disabled numbering some 13.8 million has shaken geriatricians and government experts who realize that the current health care infrastructure will simply buckle under the weight of the increase in numbers of the elderly.

To the cynical, this new attention to one of society's least visible entities—the old woman—is an example of the politics of fear. "The major initiatives to put money into menopause and research on aging is motivated by a particular cultural myth—fear of the 'aged hag,' " says Patricia Kauvert, Ph.D., a leading menopause researcher and medical anthropologist from the University of Manitoba in Canada. "She's the woman with the hip fracture in hospital, the body that will not die whose need for care will destroy us all."

In fact, in a press release announcing the start of the Women's Aging Study, then Health and Human Services Secretary Louis W. Sullivan, M.D., stressed equally the suffering of the elderly population and that of the taxpayers who will foot part of the bill for their care through Medicare and Medicaid. Though it may be sexist, the fear of "the aged hag" is not unfounded. The federal government's largest health care expenditure is for Medicare, which pays for most health care costs incurred by older Americans. A 1991 study funded by the National Institute on Aging predicted that Medicare costs could almost double by the year 2020, mounting to $212 billion compared to $71 billion spent in 1987. One reason for the dramatic increase is a carefully watched demographic trend: the rise in the number of old-old people, mostly women, who will make up an estimated 19 percent of the population by the year 2040. These over-eighty-fives are the fastest growing segment of the population and also the most vulnerable to disease and disability. Their care alone could cost as much as $57.4 billion.

STUDYING OLDER WOMEN

But geriatrics experts aren't quibbling about what has motivated this new interest in the elderly. They just welcome the attention. Geriatrics is a relatively new field that has been little respected and poorly funded, leading to broad gaps in medical knowledge about the aged and, in particular, aged women.

Harvard geriatrician Jerry Avorn, M.D., says it has been an uphill battle to draw attention to medical problems that represent such a major medical and financial burden they ought to have drawn attention to themselves. "Look, for example, at the burden of incontinence, which tends to be more of a woman's disease than a man's disease," says Avorn, who is on staff at Boston's Brigham and Women's Hospital. "Whether it be in terms of sickness or hospital days or nursing home hospitalization or dollars, incontinence is way, way up there. Yet we struggled for years trying to persuade people that this was something that a Harvard doctor should actually be studying."

But it wasn't until March 1992 that incontinence, previously regarded as an embarrassment, achieved "diseasehood." That month, the U.S. Public Health Service issued guidelines for detecting and treating urinary incontinence and urged doctors and other health professionals to be more aggressive about diagnosing and treating the condition, which afflicts 10 million Americans, most of them elderly women, and costs the nation an estimated $10 billion a year.

Another illness that should have been noticed long ago is osteoporosis, a crippling, disfiguring bone-thinning disease. More than 20 million American women have it, most of them postmenopausal, and one out of every two are at risk of developing fractures that can lead to disability and even death. An estimated 50,000 people die every year as a result of complications of osteoporosis, which is more than die of breast cancer or AIDS. Like incontinence, osteoporosis is an expensive condition to ignore. One hip fracture costs a minimum of $30,000, according to the National Osteoporosis

Foundation. The disease itself is a "budget buster" in the words of one study, resulting in roughly $10 billion in health care costs annually. But it is projected to cost some $62 billion by 2020 as the bulk of the baby boomers gain a new sobriquet: senior citizens.

Like incontinence, until fairly recently, osteoporosis was not considered a disease. Instead, it was looked upon as a normal and unalterable part of aging—and doctors couldn't cure aging. That misdiagnosis clearly set back research and may have cost some women their health or their lives. A Gallup poll done in 1991 that questioned women aged forty-four to fifty-five found that very few knew the risks and consequences of osteoporosis. Only one in four were able to identify any consequences, and only 18 percent knew hip fractures were a result of the disease. Similar surveys of physicians find their knowledge isn't more extensive. In fact, in one study of a large family practice program in Ohio, 74 percent of the 243 women over forty surveyed had two or more risk factors for osteoporosis, but only 10 percent were identified by their doctors and only 19 percent of that small group received any counseling.

Despite its profound impact on women's lives, as well as on society, there has been no real push to boost funding for osteoporosis research until recently. In 1991, NIH was spending about $20 million on osteoporosis research, which most experts say is not enough. "When you're spending $20 million on a disease that affects conservatively 25 million Americans, that's not a huge amount of money," says Barbara Kaplan, Ph.D., vice president of the National Osteoporosis Foundation.

Although there is a treatment for postmenopausal osteoporosis, it is controversial. Hormone replacement therapy (HRT) has been approved as a treatment for osteoporosis for many years. HRT comes in two basic forms: estrogen alone and estrogen combined with progestin, another sex hormone. Though similar to the oral contraceptive, the dosage of HRT is lower. Usually given as a preventative, because estrogen can prevent bone loss, it is also a fairly effective treatment that modestly increases bone mass in women who already have osteoporosis. However, HRT has its share of side effects, from bleeding to cancer, and there is sharp disagreement in the medical community about its safety. There is also the fear that with this magic bullet to cure osteoporosis, there will be less emphasis on its natural preventatives, including a high calcium intake and exercise throughout the life span. "We'd like to be at the point where we had more choices," says Kaplan.

Most experts believe that the best way to "treat" osteoporosis is to prevent it. But, as with most other diseases, there is little money available for prevention studies, which tend to be more difficult, time-consuming, and expensive to do because they so often involve convincing people to make lifestyle changes that pay off in ways that can be measured much later.

There is also no money available for early detection, which studies conducted by the National Osteoporosis Foundation found could save millions in treatment dollars. Bone mass measurement, usually done by noninvasive dual-photon or dual-X-ray absorptiometry, is still not reimbursable, says Kaplan. Yet it is effective at detecting osteoporosis at a stage when it is still symptomless, and more conservative, less expensive treatment can save bone and prevent fractures that are painful, disabling, and costly.

But not only has osteoporosis research been poorly funded, some of it may have been poorly done. Largely a disease of old age, osteoporosis has rarely been studied in older populations. "It is either not studied or when it does get studied, it gets studied in younger women for whom the basic disease process may be totally different," says Harvard's Jerry Avorn. "Osteoporosis is a case study in the Harvard Medical School curriculum, but the irony is that it is osteoporosis in a fifty-year-old. While interesting, that's not osteoporosis in America. But they just couldn't bring themselves to have their students learn about osteoporosis in the age group in which it is most clinically important—the elderly."

There is a glimmer of hope, however, that some of these omissions are being rectified. Acknowledging there are "major gaps in medical knowledge" of osteoporosis in the elderly, the National Institute on Aging in December 1991 announced an attempt to redress three wrongs—the lack of research on osteoporosis, the lack of attention to prevention, and the lack of research on the disease in people over sixty-five—by launching the STOP/IT program. STOP/IT, a catchy acronym for the more cumbersome Sites Testing Osteoporosis Prevention/Intervention Treatments, includes 1,300 women and men sixty-five and older in a program testing therapies ranging from physical exercise to HRT to determine which are the most promising. The study, which is being conducted at five sites across the United States, will run for five years. Osteo-porosis is also included as part of the $625 million Women's Health Initiative, a fifteen-year study of a grab bag of older women's health problems that will involve some 140,000 subjects, reportedly the largest single research project ever undertaken by NIH.

DRUGS AND THE ELDERLY

But there is one area where no one seems to be budging, and that is the issue of drug testing among the elderly. Although the FDA has a proposal for guidelines to guard against age bias, it has never been made official. The FDA has asked pharmaceutical com-panies to make sure there is good age representation in premarket testing of drugs and to break down their data according to age groups. But there's no documentation that this has occurred. "I have not been impressed that it has made much of a difference," says Avorn, whose area of clinical research interest is drugs and the el-derly. "If anything, it has allowed everyone to say, 'It used to be a problem, but it's solved now,' which is worse than if no one had no-ticed it in the first place. Now that it's 'fixed,' no one sees the need to fix it."

But there may be a pressing need to fix it. The elderly are one of the largest consumers of both prescription and over-the-counter drugs. Though they're only 11 percent of the population, they buy a quarter of all the drugs sold in the United States. Yet little is known about how drugs affect the elderly, except that it is often quite differ-ent from how they affect younger people. Take drug side effects, for example. A drug that makes a forty-year-old agitated may make an elderly person feel lethargic. A clinician prescribing drugs to an el-derly patient may have trouble recognizing drug side effects or the symptoms of overdose if they're not included, because of lack of data, in package inserts or drug manuals. Older people also have a threefold greater risk of having an adverse drug reaction than a younger person, a risk compounded by their use of multiple medica-tions. The average older American takes more than fourteen differ-ent drugs, which is double the total national average. Women seem to be at greater risk than men for adverse drug reaction, though no one knows why.

There is also evidence that studies of drugs tested on only male or younger subjects may not be extrapolatable to women or older people. Some experts believe that the lack of elderly people, particularly women, in drug testing has already had some deadly consequences. Assuming that old people are just like young people or that women are just like men "is just not a safe assumption," says Jerry Avorn. Recent studies have certainly provided some shocking proof of that, including one that found that an antihypertensive drug that worked equally well in bringing down blood pressure in men and women had an unanticipated side effect in the women: More of them died.

What these knowledge gaps in drug efficacy often mean for the clinician treating elderly patients is that each case becomes an experiment. This may be especially true for cardiologists, whose female patients tend to be older. Not only have older women been ignored in studies of heart disease, they've been left out of studies of lifesaving treatments. Harvard researcher Nananda Col, M.D., reviewed hundreds of trials of heart attack medications, going back to 1960, and she found that older women were "grossly, grossly underrepresented."

"When you think where the disease burden lies, it's among elderly people," says Col. "The burden is greater the older you get, and the older you get, there's an increasingly high representation of women, because women live longer than men. The evidence also suggests that when women do have a heart attack, it is more often fatal. This is the disease that should be addressed in the drug trials, but it is not."

Instead, most of the studies were done on that research animal of choice, the white middle-aged male, in part because he is less "complicated" than an elderly woman. Though hormones are out of the picture, an older woman is more likely be suffering from one or more other conditions in addition to her heart disease, something researchers call comorbidity. Researchers like to eliminate any factor that might make interpretation of their data more difficult. In a drug trial, it's easy to see how much more troublesome it might be to determine how a heart medication worked on a seventy-year-old suffering from both heart disease and kidney disease than if the subjects were all forty-year-old men who only had heart disease. If the forty-year-old dies a month after taking the drug, chances are the cause of death was heart attack, which suggests to the researcher that the drug may not be effective. If the seventy-year-old dies, the researcher has to determine what killed her—a heart attack, her kidneys, or some undiagnosed ailment—before any assessment of the drug can begin.

But research studies are more than abstract mathematical exercises that come to neat and satisfying conclusions. Their results have to be applied to living people. Comorbidity "certainly complicates matters," says Col, "but, unfortunately, that's real life."

And in real life, the elderly woman has become the victim of the quest for "elegance" in research design. "These studies tend to oversimplify reality," says Col. "While it may be easier to show efficacy in the younger male group, then you have the problem of not being able to easily transfer your results to the clinic. You have to make some major assumptions. You have to assume that this forty-year-old man is equivalent in some way to a seventy-year-old woman. You know that this drug works on a forty-year-old who has a heart attack but no other disease. How does that help you in deciding whether that drug is going to be effective in this seventy-year-old woman, who is more likely to be your patient?"

MENOPAUSE: THE BITCH IS BACK

There is at least one aspect of older women's lives that has not been ignored. Indeed, there is an amazing body of work on menopause, which is defined as the absence of menstrual bleeding for a year and represents the end of a woman's reproductive life. Unfortunately, as a record number of women are approaching menopause, a reexamination of those data finds them wanting.

Feminist scientist Anne Fausto-Sterling, who explored menopause research in her book, *The Myths of Gender,* found it riddled with "deep hatred and fear of women" and tainted by the assumption that women are "by nature abnormal and inherently diseased" because their reproductive systems stray so far from the male norm. "One begins to wonder," she writes, "how it can be that within so vast a quantity of material so little quality exists."

One reason for the dearth of good data may be that much of the fundamental research on menopause was done by outsiders, male doctors whose experience with menopause—and, thus, their data—came from the most convenient source: their women patients. Of course, patients are, by their very nature, sick people, so doctors tended to see the pathological side of menopause: the hot flashes, depression, osteoporosis, or sexual problems. More often than not, the patients in these early studies were not experiencing natural menopause at all but had had both ovaries removed, which causes a sudden rather than a gradual drop in estrogen production typical in natural menopause. Subsequent studies have shown that women going through surgical menopause have more severe symptoms. This focus on a special population has allowed the image of menopause as "an estrogen deficiency disease," as a time of "living decay," to hold sway in the medical community and among women.

Though scientists are usually alert to eliminating confounding factors from their work, the entire body of menopause research is rife with them, tucked among the data, unnoticed. Patricia Kauvert spent weeks combing through 108 studies cited in a widely quoted review of menopause literature, looking, she says, "for the questions that had not been asked." What she found dismayed her. "The information provided on who these women were was very limited and even things we know are related to risk, such as their weight, whether or not they smoked, things epidemiologists say are relevant, are simply not there at all. The women were in a way invisible."

The anonymity of the test subjects was fed by and further feeds the myth that when a woman's reproductive life is over she becomes a nonentity; when her ovaries shrivel, so does she. In fact, the myths of menopause may be simply a corollary to the realities of female aging, when a woman's "service to the species is over," as a 1970 article in *The American Journal of Obstetrics and Gynecology* put it, and her value drops like that of a used car. That view, the prevailing medical view of menopause at various times for centuries, "found a safe and too often undisturbed place in the pervasive sexism that still permeates our society," says Amherst psychologist Bonnie Strickland, Ph.D. It allowed the alleged "symptoms" of menopause, a veritable litany of misery, to go unchallenged. The studies found what the researchers expected to find. After all, if a woman's life was over thirty years before her actual demise, why wouldn't she be miserable?

Yet current studies show that most women's menopause experience may be quite different. More recent research, which looked at healthy women, has found that menopause is far from a tragedy in a woman's life. Most women don't seek medical treatment for menopause because they simply don't suffer from its myriad "symptoms." In the Massachusetts Women's Healthy Study, a survey of 7,500 women, 70 percent reported feeling relieved or neutral about the arrival of menopause. Only about 3 percent reported any negative feelings. Similarly, a study done at the University of Pittsburgh found that menopausal women were psychologically comparable to their menstruating counterparts. They weren't angry, anxious, depressed, or stressed out at any higher rates than other women. In fact, many women report what anthropologist Margaret Mead called "menopausal zest," a joyous feeling of being free of menstrual cycles, pregnancy fears, and childrearing responsibilities at last.

In 1992, the media, responding to the aging of the baby boom generation, turned its attention to menopause. Menopause was a cover story in *Newsweek,* on the front page of the Sunday *New York Times,* the subject of a raft of new books by such literary luminaries as Gail Sheehy and Germaine Greer, and, of course, a hot topic on "Oprah." Unfortunately, while the media touched on the growing revisionist view of menopause, it virtually pounced on any woman who had had a hot flash, growled at her family, went on a crying binge, or lost her sex drive. The books, articles, and TV spots told the old, familiar stories, unwittingly reinforcing the view of menopause as a kind of premenstrual syndrome (PMS) to the third power. Sheehy even appeared on "The Oprah Winfrey Show" with three women who had undergone surgical menopause and who were identified as "Amy, Susan and Sheila: Menopause Ruining Marriage."

But the media did make one truth clear: The nearly 40 million American women who would be experiencing menopause in the next two decades were going in virtually blind. The medical community was not going to be able to answer even the simplest questions, such as, Is what I'm feeling normal? Because of the lack of data on healthy women's experience of menopause, there is no baseline information on the normal experience of menopause. No one even knows how many women experience hot flashes, believed to be the most common symptom of menopause. Yet there is evidence that the hot flash is certainly not universal. The Japanese, who have precise terminology for every bodily function, don't have a word for

it, though one rare cross-cultural study found that a small percentage of Japanese women experience them.

This information gap becomes especially acute when a woman
is faced with the question of how to treat her menopause, which is
far more than hot flashes and dry vaginal tissue. As a woman's ovarian estrogen production declines, she also loses her protection
against heart disease and osteoporosis. Though the precise mechanism by which the hormone protects against these diseases is still
little understood, there is good evidence that estrogen replacement
can prevent them and save lives. By some estimates, HRT may cut
hip fractures by 60 percent and death from heart disease by almost
half.

Yet HRT is still the subject of hot debate. For all its benefits, it
has its dangers—and its unknowns. When weighing her risks and
benefits, a woman is, in essence, asked to pick from a menu of diseases that pose her risk. If she takes the estrogen, she may avoid
heart disease and osteoporosis, but she runs a three- to eightfold increased risk of developing uterine cancer. There is also evidence
that her risk of breast cancer may go up as well, though that itself is
the subject of intense debate. (Just how confused the breast cancer
question has become is illustrated by one issue of *The American
Journal of Epidemiology.* On January 1, 1991, the journal published
three papers on the topic. One found that neither short-term nor
long-term estrogen use increased the risk of breast cancer, the second found that estrogen use for more than fifteen years doubled the
risk, and the third found that estrogen use for at least eight years increased the risk of breast cancer by 25 to 30 percent.)

To avoid uterine cancer, a woman may choose a regimen that
contains progestin, which counters the cancer-causing effect of un-
opposed estrogen on the uterus. In fact, says Massachusetts General
Hospital researcher Isaac Schiff, M.D., "it's almost malpractice to
use estrogen without progestin in a woman who has a uterus." However, there have been no studies done on the risks and benefits of
long-term use of progestin, nor has its efficacy as a therapy for heart
disease and osteoporosis ever been determined. There are some data
that suggest progestin may actually cancel out some of the cardiovascular protection estrogen provides. There is also nothing known
about its role in breast cancer, nor about the safety and effectiveness

of the various forms of combined therapies on the market. In fact, the FDA has never approved progestin for use in treating menopausal symptoms although it is widely prescribed.

To further add to the confusion, the protective effects of HRT in cardiovascular disease have been called into question recently. Leading HRT researcher Elizabeth Barrett-Connor, M.D., of the University of California at San Diego, has charged that many of the studies that suggest a 40 and 50 percent reduction in heart attack risk among women taking estrogen are biased because they are looking at special populations: white, middle-class, educated women who are healthier than average. Indeed, the two major studies that showed dramatic declines in cardiac deaths among estrogen-taking women do focus on women who are more likely to be "healthy, wealthy, and wise." The population of the Nurse's Health Study are female registered nurses; the Leisure World Study includes 8,881 residents of a Southern California retirement community. When Barrett-Connor took a look at a group of estrogen takers at a California retirement community, she found that they were more likely to exercise, eat a healthy diet, see their doctors, have regular cholesterol tests and mammograms, and not smoke than those who weren't taking the drug—all measures that may reduce risk.

"Despite considerable current enthusiasm for estrogen replacement therapy as a panacea," concluded Barrett-Connor, "only a randomized clinical trial can adequately address these biases and resolve this question."

The only study underway that may answer some of those questions soon is the one Barrett-Connor directs, the Postmenopausal Estrogen/Progestin Interventions Trial, which is examining the effects of several different HRT regimens, including estrogen alone and estrogen combined with progestin, on risk factors for cardiovascular disease, osteoporosis, and diabetes. However, it is a small study, limited in duration (three years) and in number (only 840 women). The Women's Health Initiative, which started in 1993, will assess hormone therapy in addition to lifestyle factors, but those results may not be available, except as preliminary data, until the next century.

But there is another HRT trial underway. One public health official has called it "the largest uncontrolled clinical trial in the history of medicine." Despite the uncertainty about the risks and benefits of HRT, many doctors are urging it on their female patients whose only "ill" is that they no longer get their periods. Their rationale is that heart disease poses a far greater threat to a woman than cancer, which is true. But they appear to be as confident as most women are confused. The message about HRT is at best mixed, but that is not the message many primary care physicians are getting. In the June 15, 1990, issue of *Patient Care,* an article counseled physicians: "Do you still worry about giving estrogen replacement therapy to menopausal patients? Don't."

By all evidence, they don't. Studies have shown that 75 to 95 percent of gynecologists say they would prescribe estrogen therapy for most of their patients. Obviously, many have. According to a 1992 report on menopause and HRT by the U.S. Office of Technology Assessment, 1990 surpassed the previous peak year of 1975 for the number of prescriptions of noncontraceptive estrogen dispensed from retail pharmacies. In that year alone, there were more than 30 million prescriptions filled. But there were even more written. Preliminary data from the Massachusetts Women's Health Survey found that among patients receiving HRT for the first time, 20 to 30 percent never filled their prescriptions because, unlike their doctors, they were not convinced of the benefits or the safety. Another study found only a 30 percent compliance rate among women given estrogen alone.

Why such a chasm between doctors and their patients? One of the few studies that asked women how they made their decisions about HRT reveals some interesting answers. For one, many seem unconcerned—or, perhaps, unaware—of the long-term health risks of menopause without HRT. Others complained of the side effects. But many of the women also complained of feeling "disenfranchised." Not only were their doctors unable to give them good information about the risks and benefits of HRT, their doctors didn't even listen to their concerns.

Some women's health groups are urging women to be cautious about HRT. But women, particularly baby boomers, don't seem to need that advice. Medicine's track record on hormone-based medications has not given them any reason to trust—or follow—doctor's orders. Some of these women are or know DES daughters, whose mothers were given the synthetic hormone known as DES (diethylstilbestrol) to prevent miscarriage in the 1950s and 1960s. DES was subsequently found to cause cancer, infertility, and other problems in second- and even third-generation progeny of women who took DES. Many baby boomers are also among the first women to take the early Pill, which most experts now agree contained an overdose of estrogen that caused heart attacks and strokes.

Other perceived "errors," such as the Dalkon Shield and the silicone breast implant, have made many women mistrustful of physicians who they believe are insensitive, even cavalier, about women's lives. That mistrust may play a role in medicine for many years to come. HRT may well be an "elixir of youth," a postmenopausal wonder drug that could save millions of women from premature disability and death. But until all the evidence is in that it is not another experiment in which they are the unwitting guinea pigs, many women are likely to take their chances with nature, not medicine.

7
MIND
GAMES

"Still Crazy
After All
These Years"

It's easier to shut women up by giving them antianxiety pills than by trying to figure out the connection between their symptoms and the social context of their lives.

—*Jean Hamilton, M.D.*

In July 1987, Margaret Jensvold, M.D., began a fellowship with the Menstrually Related Mood Disorder Program at NIMH, a position that was the next in a long line of important steps that would get her to the final appointment she yearned for—that of medical researcher and tenured faculty member at a major university. At the age of thirty, this gifted doctor, who had been labeled by the Association for Academic Psychiatry as one of the six most promising psychiatry residents in the United States, was well on her way. Yet, at age thirty-six, it is clear to her that her lifelong goal has been permanently derailed. She has given up any hope of being offered an academic appointment; of obtaining government research grants to conduct studies on her primary interest, PMS; or of heading her own research lab.

Jensvold's dream started to crumble shortly after she began her fellowship at the NIMH. She couldn't help but notice that as the only female researcher she was repeatedly excluded from important work-related activities. "When I started at NIMH, I assumed that I would be treated comparably to the male physicians who were my peers," the soft-spoken Jensvold says. "But, instead, I was excluded from virtually all professionally meaningful opportunities in stark contrast to how the male fellows were treated."

When she asked to be allowed to participate in the same work as her colleagues, she says that her supervisor, Dr. David Rubinow, accused her of being narcissistic, demanding, and impossible to get along with. According to Jensvold, he asked her to undergo psychotherapy as a condition of employment with a male psychiatrist of *his* choosing. She felt she had to go along with his demand or she would be jeopardizing her position at NIMH. Not that it would have mattered if she had declined. Jensvold was denied the third year of her fellowship anyway. The doctor, a psychiatrist whom she found out later was not only employed by NIMH itself but worked out of the same office as her superior, diagnosed her as crazy.

Today, *crazy* carries many new labels. A half century ago, she might have been called hysterical. But in the 1990s, Jensvold was tagged with the new name for crazy: self-defeating personality disorder (SDPD) with paranoid traits. "This is the ultimate blame-the-victim diagnosis," she says. "When they say I am paranoid, they are saying that I am imagining it. When they say I am self-defeating, they are saying that I caused it. When they say it is my personality, they are saying that the problem is intrinsic to me, not anything in my environment or anything being done to me."

In fact, it was *all* being done *to* her. She had dared to step outside the standard acceptable role for women—passive, submissive, and compliant—and had asked to be given responsibilities comparable to the male fellows. In the macho world of medical research, strong women are not readily accepted by the men in charge. As products of a medical education that stresses a biological or internal cause for all illnesses, her male superiors sought a medical diagnosis that could explain Jensvold's outbursts and accusations. They were not trained to look at her environment, one where sexual discrimination of women is dished out routinely. Instead, their hired-gun psychiatrist declared Jensvold to have a serious mental disorder. It was their reality against her reality. Theirs won.

Unfortunately, Jensvold's nightmare at NIMH parallels many women's experiences when they enter psychiatrists' or psychologists' offices. Believing they will receive the benefit of the latest in medical and psychosocial advances, they instead find themselves players in some Freudian drama, where their life experiences are written off as fantasy and their responses to these "make-believe" traumas are viewed as a form of mental illness. "They are not listened to and either underdiagnosed and not taken seriously or over-diagnosed and stigmatized," says Jensvold.

It's not that the doctors who determine what's normal and what's not are insincere men; it's just that their training does not make them sensitive to the reality of women's lives. There is a bio-medical bias in American medicine that tends to see the illness *in* the patient. The notion that sociocultural factors could influence illness has been ignored or scoffed at as nonscientific. How long has it taken for the medical establishment to notice that if people change their diet and behavior, they become healthier? Or that if people are happier, their immune systems function better? Or if they are able to tame the stress in their lives, they're likely to live longer? The fact is that many biological–medical illnesses are linked to external phenomena.

Medicine, with a kind of "mindless arrogance," as one therapist put it, has historically disregarded women's experiences, failing to see them as unique and different from men's and linked in countless ways to their physical and mental states. Even today, says feminist psychologist Laura Brown, Ph.D., of Seattle, "many psychologists and psychiatrists are treating women without a fundamental knowledge base regarding female socialization and the impact of gender inequality on every aspect of women's lives."

The consequences of such disregard are staggering. Instead of seeing women's actions as a natural response to living in a society that devalues them, many male psychiatrists, who are enforcers of the status quo, look for a medical or internal explanation, a "craziness" to explain these women's "aberrant" behaviors. They ignore or trivialize the great emotional stresses that confront women daily and how that influences their behavior and mental state. They fail to see, for example, how the extraordinary amount of sexual abuse, violence, and discrimination against women can contribute to or exacerbate symptoms of depression. Or how the smoldering rage that comes with constantly being dismissed as inferior might inflame the emotional symptoms of PMS. Or how what appears at first to be self-defeating tactics might instead be a means of self-protection (as in the deferential manner of an abused wife to her husband) or a demonstration of exceptional bravery (as in taking a personal stand against sex discrimination, as Jensvold did).

Mental health professionals are as much a product of the culture as everyone else, and that is reflected in the psychological care they give their patients. Studies have shown that many male therapists still view healthy women's innate nature as dependent, childlike, selfless, and undemanding. Those who buy into those stereotypes are more likely to find women maladjusted or worse, mentally disordered, when they step outside their preordained roles or suffer despair when confined to them. These experts sit in judgment over women whose lives are invisible to them and whose experiences they don't seek to understand or acknowledge while they toss out labels and diagnoses that do nothing to help uncover some of the real roots of women's emotional distress.

When the patient is female and the therapist a traditional male, the conflicts between the biomedical and the sociocultural views of illness and between the dominant (male) social order and the subordinate (female) one swirl together to produce a pernicious brew. Meanwhile, the specialized needs of women in various states of mental health or mental disorder often go unrecognized.

NEW LABELS, OLD STORIES

Nowhere is this pernicious effect more evident than in the dangerously misogynist diagnosis of SDPD. This highly controversial diagnosis labels as mentally ill women who behave in traditional, socialized, feminine ways, meaning women who are self-sacrificing, who put other people's needs ahead of their own, or who willingly settle for less when they could have more. Comments Canadian psychologist Paula Caplan, Ph.D., "It sounds more like a description of the good-wife-and-mother pattern than a psychiatric disorder."

Indeed it is. Developmental psychology textbooks have always preached that behaving in selfless ways and being able to delay their own wants and needs are signs of women's emotional maturity. But in the mid-1980s a group of psychiatrists decided that those feminine behaviors once considered ideal were, instead, self-defeating and the hallmarks of serious psychopathology. Shortly thereafter, the new diagnosis of SDPD was born and then given legitimacy when it was included in the appendix of the 1987 volume of *The Diagnostic and Statistical Manual of Mental Disorders* (*DSM*), considered the bible of mental health professionals.

This took on special significance because the *DSM,* which is produced by the American Psychiatric Association, a group whose membership is 86 percent male, is the primary source of diagnostic criteria used by therapists to make crucial decisions about who is normal and who is not. To many therapists, feminist and otherwise, it seemed that the American Psychiatric Association was bent on institutionalizing a category of mental disorder aimed primarily at women but that entirely neglected the specific social factors and oppression with which women in this society must contend. Yet there was no corresponding category that described an extreme form of men's socialization, such as macho personality disorder, even though, as Paula Caplan pointed out, everyone knows men who might fit that diagnosis.

Psychiatrists and psychologists of both genders, alarmed by the new SDPD category, deluged the American Psychiatric Association with letters and petitions representing more than 6 million Americans and Canadians who strongly objected to the inclusion of what was clearly a gender-specific disorder. It was obvious to them that the criteria for SDPD were, in actuality, tactics that women had been trained to adopt in order to win approval and acceptance, to get what they wanted and needed. They were in effect the survival strategies of any subordinate group (such as women or people of color) who must get along with those who dominate them (such as men or whites).

The pros and cons of this diagnosis were hotly debated, often (though not entirely) split along gender lines. As long as the American Psychiatric Association insisted on keeping SDPD on the books, women kept up the battle of words and found, to their surprise, that it was working. Ironically, the Jensvold case proved to be one of the most potent arguments against the diagnosis: Suddenly, it was being used against one of their own. Fearing defeat, a subgroup of psychiatrists who believed in the integrity of the diagnosis mounted a last-ditch letter-writing campaign to keep SDPD on the books. Their efforts failed. Even the psychiatrist who had first proposed the diagnosis in 1975, Duke's Allan Francis, who chaired the *DSM-IV* task force, admitted that *he* had changed his mind. In explaining his turnaround, Francis echoed the feminist opposition: "Much self-defeating behavior occurs for reasons other than the specific masochistic unconscious motivations that are meant to be at the heart of the self-defeating personality disorder," he wrote. "It is usually impossible within the context of a general psychiatric evaluation to determine whether the individual pattern of self-defeating behavior is an expression of unconscious motivation that would play out over and over again regardless of the environment in which the individual exists, or whether the self-defeating pattern of behavior is an understandable and perhaps adaptable result of the need to survive in a harsh and punishing environment." In June 1993, the personality disorders subcommittee of the American Psychiatric Association finally agreed to drop SDPD from the next volume of the *DSM*.

Although this at first appeared to be a resounding victory for feminist therapists and others who opposed SDPD, it's not that simple. Even though SDPD isn't an official diagnosis, many therapists fear that it still will have a lingering impact in a male-dominated society where this pathological description of women finds many true believers. Women will still be at the mercy of mental health professionals for whom the diagnosis resonates with truth and who will counsel their patients accordingly. In fact, it's happened before. Homosexuality was listed in the *DSM* for years as a mental disorder, and psychiatrists spent many client-hours trying to undo whatever vague or supposed psychological damage had caused the "condition." Even though it was later declassified as a mental disorder by psychiatrists, there are still many who have never changed their opinion that homosexuality is not a sexual preference but an illness that can be treated. Consequently, the experts who fear continued fallout from the diagnosis of SDPD have not relaxed their vigilance.

Indeed, it's the potential for misuse that kept the debate on SDPD on a front burner during the past decade, and for good reason. By definition alone, a personality disorder is notoriously difficult to treat or cure because it is believed that the character flaw is intrinsic, at the very core of the person, and not likely to be influenced by outside interventions. By diagnosing a patient with a personality disorder, the therapist then pursues a line of treatment that focuses on why the patient inherently wants to be unhappy, rather than on what in the patient's life is making her unhappy as though in these patients unhappiness is a kind of birth defect for which little treatment will be effective. Add the term *self-defeating* to this diagnosis, and the opportunities for blaming women for bringing on their own suffering are boundless. If a therapist subscribes to victim-blaming notions, a woman patient might be considered self-defeating if she stays in a bad relationship where her role in the household and her decisions or opinions are devalued by her partner even though she has been socialized to believe that subjugating herself to her partner is "normal" behavior and it is perhaps her only *economic* choice. Without the SDPD label, her behavior might be viewed as clever and adaptive—the *opposite* of self-defeating behavior—because she knows that she could be rejected, even homeless, if she acted otherwise. In reality, what appears to be self-defeating behavior might, in fact, be a woman's best means of surviving in what is for her a harsh and punishing environment.

The label of SDPD can also be misused to attack women who step outside their traditional sex-role stereotypes. Margaret Jensvold was considered self-defeating when all she was doing was seeking to correct what she perceived as the blatant sexual discrimination that hampered her work and professional progress at NIMH. Taken one step further, this diagnosis could be maliciously applied to any person who sets out to change what he or she believes to be a social injustice. Any reformer, any dissident, any person who objects to or criticizes the status quo or prevailing majority view, who attempts what seems to be the impossible, is in danger of being similarly branded. Martin Luther King, for example, whose beliefs and behaviors landed him in jail and ultimately accounted for his untimely death, could surely have been tarred with the same diagnostic brush.

Perhaps the most egregious misuse of the diagnosis, however, is among women who have been the victims of sexual, emotional, or physical abuse. Battered women characteristically experience a dangerous plummeting in their self-esteem as a direct result of the violence they experience from their partners, often on a daily basis. To protect herself, a woman may try to become the "better person" her partner demands that she be—more giving and subservient and self-denying. Among therapists who work exclusively with battered women, those behaviors are easily identified as survival skills, ones these women employ simply to stay alive in what can be called the invisible war zone. But they are easy to misdiagnose as well, especially if a therapist has little or no understanding of the dynamics of the abusive relationship, which is often the rule. Then, says Paula Caplan, "applying the label of SDPD to these women is nothing short of a pernicious form of victim blaming."

Interestingly, the authors of the *DSM* recognized that potential for misuse, too. The manual cautioned therapists against using SDPD in cases of abuse—a directive, as it turns out, that was "ignored wholesale," as one expert flatly put it. The reason? Many mental health professionals don't know their patients have been abused. Studies have shown that patients are often reluctant to talk about physical and sexual abuse, and despite statistics showing that as many as half of all women have been abused, their therapists don't ask about it. Even when therapists don't officially diagnose patients who have been victimized with SDPD, it's something not far from their minds. A study from Duke University found that among therapists dealing with rape victims, most were likely to use victim-blaming treatments, such as focusing on aspects of the woman's behavior that might have led to her attack.

The findings of the Duke study support what mental health professionals have feared all along: that even excluded from the diagnostic manual, SDPD can and will be used to negatively label women and blame them for their own victimization. Indeed, psychiatrists and psychologists have heard numerous patients complain about previous therapists who told them regularly that they had brought all their problems on themselves. "This has left the patients feeling more powerless than before to change their behavior," says Caplan, "since they feel, If I bring it on myself, I might as well give up and stop trying." If they are told that it is unconsciously motivated, it's even more frightening because it means that they can never be sure why they are doing anything or making any choice.

In cases of wife battering, the diagnosis is particularly devastating. A therapist who takes the approach that the abused woman enjoys her misery and has an unconscious need to suffer not only does her no good, but actively makes her worse. Women are unjustifiably given the message that there is no point in their trying to get out of an abusive or otherwise distressing relationship or situation, because their sick, unconscious motives will inevitably lead them straight into more trouble.

Yet experts who have worked with battered women have found

that that's not the case at all. Los Angeles psychiatrist Marjorie Braude, M.D., says that women who are able to leave an abusive husband usually go on to have infinitely better relationships. If their so-called self-defeating behavior had been an intrinsic flaw, as they had been told, they would have proved it by repeating their own mistakes.

SDPD has also been used against women in the courtroom, particularly in child custody proceedings and cases of sexual harassment. Seattle psychologist Laura Brown, who has testified against the use of SDPD, says that in child custody hearings, the court looks at how well an individual can parent a child. "If you label a woman as having a severe personality disorder in which she sabotages herself, it could be argued (and has been) that this person won't be able to understand the needs of her child," she says.

In charges of sexual harassment or discrimination, the person accused simply needs to wield SDPD against his accuser to convince a judge or jury that the woman brought about her own problems, like the rape victim whose short skirt is waved before the jury as proof that she "deserved it." It is Jensvold's belief that the NIMH psychiatrist who labeled her with SDPD was building a case for his colleague, Jensvold's boss. With that diagnosis, Jensvold's harasser could claim that she either imagined the discrimination or that she brought her situation on herself. Says Jensvold, "The messages conveyed by the harasser's words and behavior are: I am the boss; you are the employee. I give the orders; you follow them. Or I am the man; you are the woman. You do what I say. And if you don't like it, then you have a serious problem. You obviously have problems getting along with people. You're not a team player. You're a trouble-maker. There's something wrong with your personality/history/point of view." The effect of this line of reasoning is to take the focus and blame off the abuser and place it squarely on the shoulders of the victim. It's the perfect defense for harassers, just as it has been in the past for rapists.

In Jensvold's opinion, her actions on her own behalf have not been self-defeating, but self-*empowering*. If nothing else, her dispute with NIMH politicized her. She joined the chorus of voices opposing the diagnosis that stopped her career dead and helped eliminate it from the therapists' bible, if not, perhaps, from therapists' minds.

PREMENSTRUAL TENSION OR MENTAL DERANGEMENT

Unlike SDPD, premenstrual dysphoric disorder (PMDD), a fancy term for PMS, *is* still on the books, despite strong opposition from respected mental health professionals. With this new and controversial diagnosis, psychiatrists have made the pronouncement that women's biology, in the form of premenstrual hormonal fluctuations, tends to make them mentally deranged.

This presents a particularly sticky situation for women. In the past, women who complained about symptoms having to do with the menstrual cycle were labeled neurotic. Consequently, women considered it a step forward when the diagnosis of PMS became a reality, giving biological credibility to what they knew to be true all along, that their symptoms were not "all in their heads." Now the new category of PMDD comes along and, like the old "raging hormone" theory of the past, says that women are unreliable, unpredictable, incapable of holding an important job, in fact, mentally ill, if they suffer from mood and behavior disturbances associated with their monthly cycles.

Few people doubt that women experience a variety of symptoms from behavior swings and swollen breasts to food cravings and lack of energy at certain times in their menstrual cycles. Indeed, according to surveys, about 40 percent of menstruating women complain of mild to moderate effects. But the experts caution against labeling those symptoms as a mental disorder, in other words, pathologizing what is perhaps biologically normal for them. The fear is, once stamped with that brand, a woman will have an increasingly difficult time convincing her family, friends, and employers that she is psychologically sound. Says Paula Caplan, "In a sexist society, anything that *can* be used to argue that women are deficient or 'sick' tends to be used to do so."

Those who support the diagnosis of PMDD don't view it as inherently discriminatory. Jensvold, a menstrual cycle researcher who has experienced the effects of discrimination first hand, says many psychological disorders have a biological base; for example, schizophrenia, eating disorders, and bipolar disorder. "Some women have severe psychological symptoms varying over the menstrual cycle, and they deserve to have their problem acknowledged and dealt with both in treatment and research." She admits, however, she fears that the psychiatric label will be overgeneralized to all women when, in fact, the vast majority of women are minimally affected or not affected at all by their cycles.

There is also some concern among feminist therapists in particular that the biological explanation of PMDD will discourage any discourse about the impact of women's environment on their symptoms. Traditional medicine has always tended to look for hormonal explanations for women's mental illness, says psychiatrist and PMS researcher Michelle Harrison, M.D., of Pittsburgh. Interestingly, she adds, "We don't find the same focus on male hormones even though there is scientific evidence linking aggressiveness to testosterone that far outweighs anything we've ever seen in women."

Those who believe in this so-called biological primacy tend to underestimate the role of life situations in a person's behavior patterns and overestimate the importance of biological functions. The fact is that although most medical people seem to believe that premenstrual mood swings are related to hormone fluctuations, it's not borne out by research. In one study that compared women with severe PMS to those without symptoms, researchers found no hormonal differences between the groups. However, they did find that women who had the worst PMS problems were also the ones most likely to be married and caring for small children all day. Doctors who are not tied to the narrow biological primacy doctrine recognize that the social context of a woman's life can indeed be at the root of PMS symptoms.

Harrison saw firsthand how PMS often mirrors a woman's life. One of her patients who was suffering with severe PMS for nearly a year revealed that during that year she was being harassed by her boss, who also happened to be her husband's boss. "She was afraid that if she complained they would both lose their jobs or her husband would beat up the boss," says Harrison. A psychiatric label would not have improved her patient's symptoms, says Harrison, since her work situation had as much to do with her PMS as anything biological.

Clearly, most women who say they have PMS don't have a mental disorder. What they have is premenstrual tension, which is a gynecological, not psychiatric, condition. A woman who experiences bloating, some breast tenderness, food cravings, and irritability is not mentally ill, says Jensvold. Doctors need to be made aware of the distinction, however, since it determines how their patients are viewed by those around them and what the course of treatment should be. Indeed, various therapies that have proven helpful for many women with uncomfortable monthly symptoms may not even be suggested if the women are given a psychiatric label. Treatments involving nutrition, vitamins, and exercise are not widely recommended (perhaps not even known) by the psychiatric community, and calling premenstrual tension a psychiatric problem makes it even less likely that a woman will be learn about a treatment that might really help her.

A psychiatric diagnosis for PMS might also give women the false impression that they can blame their angry outbursts or irritability on their cycles, relieving them of responsibility for behavior that otherwise would be unacceptable. The danger is that by not taking responsibility for her actions, a woman may unwittingly reinforce her view of herself—and society's view of her—as a victim with the sense of powerlessness that that engenders. Consequently, any opportunity she might have had to grow and gain control through psychotherapy may be lost. With a sensitive counselor, a woman can diminish her symptoms and learn to live with the rest. A psychiatric label will just make her "crazy."

DEPRESSING THOUGHTS

A woman given the diagnosis of clinical depression, on the other hand, increases her chances of receiving the correct therapy. Yet, even though women are particularly vulnerable to this often disabling and quite common mental condition (one in seven will have a major depression in their lifetimes), they are frequently misdiagnosed and consequently mistreated. Part of the problem is that many women do not recognize their symptoms as depression and neither do their family physicians, the doctors they are most likely to consult first. Women will show up with vague complaints such as headaches, dizziness, fatigue, or stomach ills, not connecting them to the deeper problems they may be masking. Their doctors, trained to look for the biomedical explanation for illness, are inclined to evaluate their symptoms from that perspective. They'll concentrate their efforts at determining whether those chronic headaches, for example, are due to a brain tumor or whether the fatigue is related to anemia but neglect to find out if there could be an emotional component contributing to their patients' symptoms. Even if a woman does reveal some troublesome life events, her story will often be discounted or trivialized, and her physical symptoms and her emotional upheaval attributed to a kind of generic stress.

So locked into the biomedical model are they that many traditionally trained physicians, including psychiatrists, still dismiss the concept that a traumatic experience in a woman's life might precipitate depression. A male colleague of Jean Hamilton, M.D., of Duke University, a man she describes as "generally quite sensitive to women's issues," told her that rape, although a terrible social problem, couldn't cause depression because depression is a medical illness. He believed, says Hamilton, that rape could lead women to be demoralized, but that because biology is at the root of a medical illness, depression could not be caused by a "social problem." That narrow view prompted San Francisco psychiatrist Karen Johnson to recommend, only half in jest, a "one-day experiential opportunity"—getting raped—for those having a hard time imagining that being raped might cause depression. "If psychiatrists can't understand something like this, who can?" she said.

The fact is that women suffer from depression twice as often as men do and, probably in large part, for reasons that are directly related to the culture in which they were raised and live. Women's traditional roles are held in low esteem, they are far more likely to live in poverty, be single heads of households, have less education, or be unemployed or underemployed. But perhaps the single most important societal contributor toward women's increased vulnerability to depression is the disproportionate amount of sexual abuse that women in our culture experience. One study found that 64 percent of women who were depressed had experienced sexual abuse before the age of seventeen. Other studies have found that when the numbers of women who have suffered physical or sexual abuse are teased out of the statistics, the rate of depression among men and women is equal.

Interestingly, there is a notable exception to that two-to-one, female-to-male ratio, which occurs in a culture within a culture: the Amish. Studies show that Amish men and women suffer from depression in equal numbers. Some believe that the reason for this parity is because men's and women's roles are equally valued in that insular community.

There are no studies that show unequivocally what is at the root of women's increased vulnerability to depression. Some believe that because boys and girls suffer from depression at equal rates until adolescence, that it's hormonal changes and not socialization factors that account for women's higher rates. But those who take issue with that theory stress that it's during those same turbulent years that the cultural assault on women is most strongly felt, and self-esteem, which is closely linked to depression vulnerability, takes its steepest plummet.

Unlike boys, who are proud of their developing physiques, young women often feel betrayed and ashamed by theirs. They think of themselves as fat and ugly in a society obsessed with anorectic thinness. They may, as one study showed, find that their budding breasts and curving hips have made them "prey" in the jungle called junior high where they are subjected to sexual harassment by their classmates. And unlike boys, girls face a conflict over whether to suppress their competence and assertiveness—needed to curry favor with boys—or to display those positive traits and be socially rejected. Year after year, girls are fed a steady diet of textbooks that ignore women's achievement and advertising that stresses sex over substance. They learn in subtle and not so subtle ways just what their ultimate value is and what parts of their anatomy matter most.

The decline in self-esteem that becomes apparent during the teen years does not disappear as women mature. On the contrary, that women are second-class citizens in this society is reinforced on a daily basis in paychecks that are a fraction of men's, in glass ceilings that keep women from achieving high status positions as frequently as men, in the devalued status of wife and mother roles, in the sexual violence and discrimination disproportionately affecting women, and in the powerlessness that permeates many women's lives. As one therapist commented wryly, "I don't know why *more* women aren't depressed."

Not only does the mental health community fail to understand what makes women prone to depression, it is equally in the dark about how to treat depression in women. Though they have a smorgasbord of antidepressant drugs from which to choose, little is known about how those drugs act in women. Not only have women been excluded from many of the major clinical trials of these medications, but even when they have been included, the data were never analyzed to detect gender differences. Says NIMH depression researcher Susan Blumenthal, M.D., "This is all the more disturbing because 70 percent of all psychotropic medication in this country is prescribed to women." In fact, it was discovered only later, after women began taking these medications as part of treatment, that they were far more likely to experience adverse side effects and twice as likely to die from fatal drug reactions as men taking the same drugs.

Finding a therapist who incorporates gender sensitivity into his or her practice is not a given either, although it's probably more likely with women counselors. Psychiatry and psychology programs simply don't address those concerns in their educational programs, and so they turn out practitioners often ill-equipped to treat women. Even though the organizations representing the mental health professions have recognized the importance of gender sensitivity in training, there is still a lack of integration of gender issues into the core curriculum of graduate programs. When classes are offered, they are designated as electives, and introducing them and maintaining them is usually seen as the special province of women, not the central concern of the training program. Those who recognize the inadequacies of their education are left to patch together the training they need from readings, continuing education courses, and consultations with other like-minded professionals. It's not the best solution, though, because there is no standardization of the skills and knowledge that these therapists bring to their female patients.

Research has not helped to eliminate gender discrimination within its sphere either. According to the American Psychological Association, sex bias in research has had and continues to have far-reaching implications, including what topics are chosen to be studied, what people are selected for those studies, the generalization of findings from men to women, and the formulation of concepts and theories. Because studies have not been adequately designed to take gender differences into account, inappropriate conclusions about mental health and disorder continue to be drawn. Findings about men, for instance, are assumed to be true of women. For example, the identification of the type A personality as a risk factor for heart attacks prompted experts to warn that as women entered the workforce and became ambitious workaholics, they, like men, would be felled in their prime. But the study of type A personality was done in 4,000 men, and the study results just didn't apply to women. Single working women still had the lowest rate of heart disease of any sub-group. Being ambitious and hardworking doesn't kill women. As another study proved, it's being unappreciated and having little control that is most detrimental to women's health. By focusing on stress in the workplace—a man's place—researchers missed the fact that it's housewives who are more likely to be stressed to death.

Though many experts in the mental health field recognize the need to fund research that would advance knowledge about women's lives, about their social and sexual development, their work and family roles—the so-called sociocultural or psychosocial components—that's exactly the area that is least likely to receive money. These women's health concerns are still considered fringe issues and of little importance to those who make funding decisions. Indeed, biomedically oriented research proposals have a much greater chance of making it through the public health service review process than do psychosocial proposals. And in typical vicious-cycle fashion, when fewer psychosocial proposals receive funding, mental health researchers are discouraged from applying, creating an even greater decrease in that area of mental health research.

There is at least a recognition in some quarters of the mental health community of the importance of addressing issues of sex bias in research and a modest institutional commitment to make changes. To that end, scientific societies, such as the American and Canadian Psychological Associations and the American Sociological Association, have established research guidelines and appropriate educational materials to help eliminate sex bias not only from research but from the language used in professional journals and publications.

Mental health professionals tend to take the long view concerning their expectations for the future. Laura Brown says, "I have seen the struggle for women's rights, and there have been many twists and turns in the road. Twenty years ago women couldn't get credit in their own name, and now they can. Twenty years ago, women didn't get athletic scholarships, and now they do. Twenty years ago, women didn't constitute more than 50 percent of the Ph.D.'s awarded in psychology, and now they do." Perhaps by virtue of the numbers alone, she says, it is not unreasonable to expect change.

Margaret Jensvold is optimistic, too, but she tempers it with a caution born of bitter experience. Now a psychiatrist in private practice and director of the Institute for Research on Women's Health in Washington, D.C., Jensvold believes institutional changes come slow and hard. After all, she points out, the fight over the diagnosis that derailed her career took seven years. That kind of battle—when the enemy is the comfortable status quo—requires personal sacrifice. But the changes come. And that's what keeps her fighting.

It's a lesson she learned early in stories her parents told her about her great-grandfather, John Ridlon, M.D., considered to be the father of American orthopedic surgery. As a young physician, Ridlon propounded the then controversial concept of setting fractured bones. He was fired from his post at Columbia University when he refused his chairman's order to take a cast off a broken hip before six weeks. Ridlon went on to Northwestern University, where he practiced and gradually won acceptance for his unorthodox technique, which saved thousands from needless pain and debilitation.

"I guess whatever personality I have runs in my family," says Jensvold. "They taught me if you believe in something that is good for society, stand up for what you believe in. You may be fired, you may be criticized or blamed. But eventually people will appreciate what you did. Hopefully," she adds, "within your lifetime."

8

VIOLENCE

The
Invisible
Wound

For most women, violence is a daily concern. Even the woman who isn't dodging drug dealers' bullets in her neighborhood has curtailed her life out of fear. She doesn't go out at night alone. She slings her purse straps across her chest like an ammo belt. She glances into the back seat of her car before unlocking the door. A blind date raises a question far more frightening than Will he like me? Today, a woman asks herself, Will he rape me?

One study found that being a woman means having a high fear of crime, particularly of rape. Men, it turns out, have different fears. When novelist Margaret Atwood asked a male friend why men feel threatened by women, he told her, "They're afraid women will laugh at them." When she asked a group of women why they felt threatened by men, they responded, "We're afraid of being killed."

That fear is not unfounded. Violent crimes against women—committed mainly by men—have risen dramatically in the last two decades. In 1990, according to a U.S. Senate report, more women were raped than in any year in U.S. history. Perhaps the most frightening statistics are those that represent a woman's lifetime risk of being victimized: One in four women is physically battered. One in five women is raped. One in three is a victim of childhood sexual assault. And most of those crimes against women are committed by people they know, often by the men—husbands, boyfriends, fathers—they love. Though violence is a crime that leaves no segment of society untouched, women are disproportionately its targets, suggesting to some researchers that gender-based victimization is one of the most destructive consequences of sexual inequality and, perhaps, the ultimate backlash against feminism.

As might be expected, the health care burden victimized women represent is staggering. Some 1.5 million women receive medical treatment for abuse each year. As many as a third of all women seen by doctors have some history of physical or sexual abuse. Women who were abused or molested as children or adults see their doctors far more often than other women—50 percent more often, in some cases. Studies have found that nearly three-quarters of all female psychiatric inpatients have been physically or sexually abused, as have two-thirds of women in outpatient therapy. Domestic violence is the most common cause of injuries among women, accounting for more than car accidents, muggings, and rapes combined. In many emergency rooms, the battered woman is a more common sight than a patient with appendicitis.

For many women, the violence they experience is translated into a constellation of physical and emotional symptoms, including post-traumatic stress disorder (PTSD), the shell shock experienced by soldiers returning from Vietnam. Today, the largest single group of PTSD sufferers is not combat veterans but rape victims. A woman who has been victimized may also suffer from seemingly unrelated illnesses—chronic pain, headaches, irritable bowel syndrome, eating disorders—as well as from alcohol and drug dependency and sexual and psychiatric problems. She is more likely to commit suicide or to be murdered. Violence, in fact, is one of the leading risk factors for illness, injury, and death among women. Yet, in the medical setting, violence is unnoticed and untreated.

For physicians and therapists, identifying a woman who has been victimized isn't always easy. Rape, incest, and partner abuse are among the least reported crimes, making what statistics that do exist merely clues to a social problem that may be massive in its dimensions. Even when victimized women visit physicians or therapists, their real trauma may be masked by aches, pains, depression, or vague complaints. In one study, about half of all women who had been sexually assaulted did not tell their therapists that this was the real reason for their seeking psychological help. Their reticence is explicable. Abuse victims are often afraid; rape victims, ashamed; and incest victims suffer from what psychiatrist Anne Bernstein, M.D., calls "the unknowable trauma": a horror against which they are so defenseless that some develop amnesia to escape it, keeping the secret even from themselves.

But many experts believe that many physicians deliberately do not probe beneath the bruises, the headaches, and the anxiety. Although victimized women may not reveal the source of their pain, neither does anyone ask. "It's striking that physicians almost never ask their patients about violence," says Mark Rosenberg, M.D., director of the office of injury control at the CDC in Atlanta.

This conspiracy of silence has serious ramifications. Because no one asks, speaking about the violence becomes a taboo. The victimized woman remains silent because she believes that the lack of interest her physician shows in what is at the root of her physical or emotional illness means it is something she's not allowed to discuss in the medical setting.

Although her real problem goes undiagnosed, the victimized woman does get treatment for her secondary ills—her headaches, insomnia, depression, or dependence on drugs and alcohol. Suddenly, instead of having a problem, she *is* the problem. Often, write abuse experts Evan Stark, Anne Flitcraft, and William Frazier, physicians "draw from their arsenal of cultural labels those which permit them to treat the victim of abuse as a stereotypic female." She is a drug user, an alcoholic, a hypochondriac. She is "masochistic" and "self-defeating."

A label gives the physician a way to pigeonhole baffling and seemingly unrelated symptoms into something he or she can understand, diagnose, and fix. One reason a physician doesn't ask about violence, some experts suggest, is because there's nothing in the doctor's black bag that will "fix" it. If a doctor uncovers something that can't be cured, he or she risks feeling incompetent. So a doctor does what doctors can do: refers the victim to a psychiatrist or writes out a prescription to help her sleep or to lift her depression. Obviously, affixing a label to such a difficult case may put a physician at ease but is likely to harm the patient. In one study, one in four battered women was given tranquilizers or pain medications, a dangerous therapy for a woman who statistics show is at high risk for suicide. A victim who is given tranquilizers or referred to a psychiatrist also begins to assume what her physician obviously assumes: that this is "her problem," that what has happened is her fault. Medicine, writes Stark and his colleagues, "disposes of battering by characterizing it as a psychiatric problem for the victim." The battered woman then becomes victimized again, this time, as one researcher put it, by "bad medical care."

Predictably, many women thus misdiagnosed return again and again to their doctors. The battered woman may reappear dozens of times with injuries of increasing severity, which earns her not attention, but blame. Why, everyone asks, does she stay? But what sends most victims back to the medical setting is their untreated wounds. Experts say that a battered woman whose abuse isn't addressed when she seeks treatment often feels more isolated and discouraged from escaping. Helpless, she also becomes hopeless. A number of studies have found that victims of violence and sexual abuse whose underlying problem is undiagnosed are at high risk of developing more serious psychiatric illness. When their pain is unacknowledged or not treated seriously, it simply gets worse. "No surprise, I say," writes Canadian psychologist Paula J. Caplan, Ph.D., "because if I have a broken leg and the doctor puts a cast on my arm instead, my leg will certainly get worse."

BEYOND THE MEDICAL GAZE

The reasons violence so often is misdiagnosed—or goes undiagnosed—are myriad. Part of the problem is that physicians are not trained to view violence the way they do bacteria and viruses, as disease etiology. For example, despite its vast medical consequences, domestic abuse is included in only 53 percent of all U.S. medical school curricula and most of those devote no more than ninety minutes to the topic. Until recently, the major medical journals ignored it. A study of how emergency room (ER) personnel dehumanize battering victims was reported in *The Journal of the American Medical Association* in 1990 only after it was published in an obscure journal called *Gender and Society.* Early, theory-building studies on domestic abuse were prejudiced by the researchers' inability to study batterers, who refused to talk to them. They then turned their attention to "the wife-beater's wife," as one early study called her. She *would* talk to them, so they went about the task of finding out what was wrong with *her.* Undeterred by having only one side of the story, and the victim's side at that, the researchers found that she had brought on her own suffering because she was masochistic, frigid, manipulative, and controlling. Someone had to be at fault, and she was there. More recent research takes a more sympathetic view of the abused woman, but as one researcher put it, "the attitude lingers on."

Some hospitals have nothing more than ad hoc protocols for dealing with victims of violence. When treating battered women, ER physicians may lose their only chance for early intervention in a condition that "may begin with a slap and end in homicide" because they have no guidelines for identifying and dealing with abuse victims, nor is it considered their medical obligation. Rape victims, unless they are bruised or bleeding, may fare no better. For example, in one hospital in Virginia, rape victims may wait four and five hours in a crowded, noisy ER before they are seen by the on-call resident.

Studies have found that this is not an isolated case. What may be worse, in many hospitals that do have established procedures for dealing with abuse victims, the medical staff simply does not follow them. In one study done at a Chicago hospital, nurses who were supposed to refer abuse victims for psychiatric or social work consultations did so less than 10 percent of the time. The invisible wound was also the invisible crime: Though many of their patients were seriously hurt by their attackers, the nurses filed police reports in less than half the cases.

The reluctance of physicians to see and treat intimate violence is partly explained by tradition. Physical and sexual abuse of women has been regarded as something "beyond the medical gaze," a private matter, or one better left to the law or the psychiatrists. Many physicians feel it's not part of their job to treat a "social problem," even one with such profound medical repercussions.

"When doctors come out of medical school, they want to deal with blood and guts, MRIs [magnetic resonance images], and X rays, not what's happening at home," says Susan Hadley, M.P.H, di-

rector of WomanKind, a training program to help medical personnel identify and treat victims of domestic violence at Fairview
Southdale Hospital in Edina, Minnesota. "Even though what's happening at home will determine how a patient heals from any kind of
medical problem, they see it as a touchy-feely kind of thing. It isn't
their job. They know how to stop a woman from bleeding to death
when her aorta is cut, but they don't have any training for dealing
with a woman who has been beaten by her husband."

Not only are physicians not trained to see violence, for various
reasons many simply do not want to. One researcher calls it "physician blindness." In a now landmark study of a New Haven, Connecticut, ER, a team of researchers combing medical records easily
identified 340 abuse cases ER personnel had missed. Though physicians identified one in thirty-five women they saw as a victim of intimate violence, the researchers found the reality was closer to one
in four. Even at Susan Hadley's hospital, where training is ongoing
and resources exist for battered women, some physicians choose to
remain blind. Hadley recalls one doctor who discharged a woman
who, he noted on her chart, had clearly discernable finger marks on
her arm. "Now, how you can miss that is inconceivable to me," says
Hadley. "He saw the finger marks, but he didn't make the connection, so she wasn't referred to us for help. What was he thinking? I
don't know. Maybe he didn't consider it a big issue. If you don't have
a broken jaw or a skull fracture, it's not a big issue."

Even when they see it, some physicians find ways to avoid dealing with it. A survey of thirty-one Florida ERs found that ER personnel varied from responsive to hostile in their treatment of rape
victims. In one hospital, residents would hide until shift change so
they would not have to perform rape exams because of their fear
they might have to testify in court. One nurse told the researchers
that a physician in her ER "will see a child with a cold before he will
see a rape survivor" because he "doesn't want to get involved." Many
physicians said they felt conducting a forensic rape exam was a waste
of their time and expertise.

In 1990, researcher Nancy Kathleen Sugg, M.D., of the University of Washington in Seattle, asked thirty-eight family care
physicians in a large health maintenance organization serving
mainly white-middle class women why they didn't intervene in cases
of domestic violence. Eighteen percent explained their reluctance to

probe into the troubled lives of their patients by referring to the story from Greek mythology of Pandora's box about a young girl who opens a mysterious box releasing a torrent of calamities into the world. Many told Sugg they were afraid of offending their patients if they broached the subject; others said they so closely identified with them they didn't suspect abuse, which they expected to see among poorer, less educated women. Most had never had any training in dealing with domestic violence, and half said they felt frustrated and inadequate by their lack of tools to help. But the largest majority—71 percent—told Sugg they were simply too busy. Their greatest fear was that domestic violence would eat up too much of their scarce time.

The extent to which physicians try to distance themselves from victims of violence is clearly and elegantly detailed in a 1989 study done by Carole Warshaw, M.D., at Cook County Hospital in Chicago. Warshaw approached her research with the hypothesis that the notations physicians and nurses made on ER charts would reveal the way they thought about their patients. So Warshaw, behavioral sciences instructor in Cook County's primary care residency program, read all of the charts for women trauma patients during a two-week period, identifying those who specifically mentioned being deliberately harmed by someone else. What she found was dismaying. Though medical personnel dutifully recorded the extent of the women's injuries, in only one case was abuse mentioned as a cause. In the rest of the cases, says Warshaw, it was "specifically avoided." In some cases, when the violence was noted by the triage nurse, the doctors' later notations obscured it. Doctors never determined a woman's relationship to her assailant in three out of four cases, although 85 percent of the injuries they treated were moderately severe or severe, nearly 10 percent were life-threatening, and all of them were crimes.

Many doctors used what Warshaw calls "disembodied language" to detail a trauma. Injuries were described eerily in a passive voice as "blow to head by stick with nail in it" and "hit on left wrist with jackhammer" as though the victims had been dismembered before the attack. One woman's assault was described as "beaten to face and head with fist."

"What they recorded was the mechanism of injury, how the blow impacted on the body, not on the person," Warshaw wrote.

"The entire battering was reduced to an interaction between a fist and an eye. . . . It removes the fist from the person attached to it."

By reducing a woman to her injured body part—the proverbial gallbladder in room 3—the physician is able to focus on "what he can fix," says Warshaw. But failing to see her within the context of her life, he effectively sends her home untreated—and with a life-threatening condition. "That laceration on her face isn't what's dangerous to her at that moment," says Warshaw. "It's what she goes home to that's dangerous."

That kind of narrow vision of the patient seriously handicaps a physician's clinical abilities. Warshaw believes the "medical model," the way physicians are trained to think, contributes to what appears to be callous disregard for the victim. Doctors are taught to remain detached. They learn to objectify, to see a body unrelated to life events, which creates a blind spot into which violence simply disappears. Medical school, with its thirty-six-hour days and oppressive hierarchy, tends to dehumanize doctors, who then dehumanize their patients, says Warshaw. "Doctors get out of their human being mode. Medical training does not support physicians dealing with their own feelings. It wrings out that capacity. It is abusive. You have to suppress your own needs and your own feelings in order to take care of other people. I think it then becomes hard to empathize with other people when no one's doing that for you."

In one case study Warshaw reported, a sensitive intern was able to bring a woman's severe high blood pressure under control in part by allowing her, for the first time in twenty-five years, to talk about the years of physical abuse she suffered at the hands of her husband. If the physician had followed the strict biomedical model, he never would have raised the question, says Warshaw, and never would have uncovered the emotional trigger of the woman's physical illness. Significantly, when the intern moved on, the woman was treated by a new doctor who, though he knew of her history of abuse, never brought it up again. "She says it's all in the past and she's 'okay now.' Her doctor notes, however, that her blood pressure is no longer 'okay,' " says Warshaw.

Detachment and objectivity, while appearing scientifically grounded, are actually motivated by psychological need, Warshaw says. It is not a way for doctors to be better doctors, but a way for them to protect themselves from painful experiences. Physicians may have personal reasons for maintaining a psychological distance from the victim, not the least of which is not becoming emotionally enmeshed in someone else's problems. Many resort to victim blaming, looking for reasons the victim brought on her own trouble, as a form of self-preservation. "If you can discount the victim, you can preserve your belief in your own invulnerability," says psychiatrist Judith Herman, M.D., a leading expert on incest. "You can think, It won't happen to me because I didn't do those bad things that the victim did. Doctors aren't the only ones who do this. The tendency to blame victims for what happened to them is pretty universal."

Others may want to avoid those uncomfortable feelings of inadequacy the physicians in Nancy Sugg's survey felt when confronted by a problem they never learned to treat. To the untrained clinician, the psychological aftermath of violence can be confusing. For example, repeated victimization, the so-called sitting duck syndrome, is associated with childhood sexual abuse and domestic violence. Studies have shown that incest and domestic abuse victims are likely to be harmed again, either by others or themselves. Research by psychologist Diana Russell found that the risk of rape, sexual harassment, and battering is double for incest victims. But this is frequently misunderstood by physicians and therapists, who are likely to see it as a "character flaw," a propensity for choosing abusive relationships, rather than the result of victims being rendered helpless by repeated traumatization, says Herman.

Domestic violence is a particularly frustrating issue confronting doctors. Abused women often leave and return to their abuser four or five times before they make their final escape. Even shelter workers admit they become angry with the women who refuse to press charges or who go home to more abuse. Without any understanding of the dynamics of the abusive situation, a physician may feel no sympathy for a woman who comes in bloody and bruised from a beating and then leaves with the man who beat her. "I've heard physicians say, 'Why doesn't she just leave?' " says Susan Hadley. "They don't understand that domestic abuse is a form of mind control. It's a kind of one-to-one cult."

A battered woman is a prisoner of an intimate war, subjected to both physical and mental abuse, which strips her of her self-confidence and forces her to live in unrelenting terror. She knows that leaving may put her in more danger. The beating she receives at home is merely a taste of what is promised her if she tries to run away. In fact, most women who are killed by their abusers have already left them. Says Hadley, "When I hear someone in the ER asking, 'Why do they put up with it, why do they stay?' I answer, 'No one asked the POWs [prisoners of war] in Vietnam why *they* stayed.' "

What can't be overlooked is that physicians are also products of a social milieu in which women are devalued and violence against them is not only tolerated but is a form of entertainment. "Anti-woman bias in clinicians is about as pervasive as it is in the general society," says Herman. Some physicians may want to distance themselves from the victim because her plight strikes too close to home. Some may have come from abusive families or experienced violence in a relationship. Others may be afraid of identifying too closely with the abusers. Recent studies of male college students found that as many as 30 percent admit they have committed rape and up to 70 percent, posed with a hypothetical situation, could envision themselves striking a spouse.

Also, the medical profession historically has been largely white, male, and ruling class and has displayed little interest and concern for women's problems. Women have always been on the periphery, as nurses and social workers, but not part of the research or theory-building class. "They were allowed to care for victims but not ask the questions, pose the hypotheses, or do the research," says Judith Herman. It has taken twenty years of chiding and cajoling by women's groups to produce even a flicker of medical attention to violence as a public health problem. "There has been a change, but it has not come from within the profession," says Herman. "From initial denial we've come to recognize that yes, rape occurs, yes battering occurs, but there's still a tendency to see it as unusual and deviant and to not recognize how endemic it is and how pervasive its effects are. That deeper awareness has not occurred outside of feminist circles."

VICTIMIZED AGAIN

Victims may find no more help and understanding in the mental health setting. Psychiatrists and other therapists are hampered by the selective inattention given to violence and sexual abuse as a cause of psychiatric illness. Most widely used measurements of stress don't ask about sexual abuse or violence. Therapists are rarely taught to take sexual histories that might uncover hidden trauma. "You're taught in a general psychiatric work-up to ask questions about hallucination and delusions, which aren't that common, but not to ask questions about violence in the home or about sexual abuse, which is very common," says Herman.

Therapists are also trained to look for the source of a patient's problems in the patient herself, a strategy that is helpful in many psychological disorders but dangerous when the patient's problems stem from sexual assault or battering, which leave her vulnerable to self-blame. In fact, a therapist's training may work against the victim in many ways. For one, it may be a rich source of outdated stereotypic notions of women as prone to rape and incest fantasies and of deriving sexual pleasure from masochism. Many therapists, Freudian or not, may be influenced by Freud's early theories of female neurosis, which were based on the stories his female patients told him of being sexually molested by their fathers and other male adults. Freud originally believed that the stories were true, but under pressure from his colleagues and because of his own discomfort with the implications of his findings, he renounced them. Instead, he blamed his female patients' deep psychological pain on their frustrated sexual desires for their fathers.

Many of those early theories have been discounted and replaced by new theories and therapies. The application of the PTSD diagnosis to the jumble of symptoms that follow sexual and physical assault has given clinicians a way of comprehending the profound impact violence has on a woman's life and new, more effective ways to treat her. But the news apparently travels slowly if at all. Indeed, several studies have found that most practicing clinical psychologists don't read or base their work on psychotherapy research.

In fact, one study, published in *Psychology of Women Quarterly* in 1990, found that many therapists working with victims of sexual assault are likely to tailor treatments around their own prejudices. Even when they are aware of new concepts, they tend to fall back on outdated therapies that focus on victim blaming. Ellen Dye and Susan Roth, of Duke University, surveyed 257 practicing psychologists, psychiatrists, and social workers in the cities of Durham,

Raleigh, and Chapel Hill, North Carolina, to determine their attitudes toward sexual assault victims and how those attitudes predicted how they would treat them in therapy. They found that therapists in general didn't believe the kind of rape myths that would blame the woman for provoking the attack, but of those who did, psychiatrists were more likely than other mental health professionals to hold such negative attitudes. Nevertheless, a relatively large percentage of survey respondents admitted to using treatment approaches that focused on the woman's behavior and role in her victimization. Sixty-four percent said they would work with a victim on developing more appropriate, less seductive behavior with men, and 56 percent said they would discuss with her ways in which she may have unconsciously desired or enjoyed the assault.

Why, when the tools for effective treatment are there, do therapists return to old familiar ways? One might argue that this is human nature. But studies of ER personnel may offer some more revealing clues. In the late 1980s, physician Susan V. McLeer, M.D., and her colleagues at the Medical College of Pennsylvania looked at the rates of victim identification in the medical school's ER before and after a system was set up to detect injuries resulting from battering. A number of studies have found that in hospitals that have victim identification guidelines, detection of battering cases jumps 180 to 500 percent and more women are referred to supportive services.

McLeer and her colleagues found that prior to a protocol introduced in 1977, ER personnel identified 5.6 percent of all female trauma patients as victims of domestic abuse. Within a year of setting up a system, ER personnel identified 30 percent of all the women they treated for injuries as abuse victims. But when the research team went back for an eight-year follow-up, much had changed.

The medical faculty and students who had been behind the protocol were gone and so was the protocol. It had been a mere flash-in-the-pan, the faddish interest of a few people who had moved on, and no one else seemed to think it was necessary. There was no monitoring system to ensure that the protocol was followed, nor was domestic violence included in the medical school curriculum. In 1985, it also appeared that domestic violence had all but disappeared too. By the time the follow-up was done, ER personnel were identifying only 7.7 percent of the injured women they saw as victims of violence. But a check with community agencies serving the area provided a far different picture. They reported an increase in the number of battered women seeking services.

What happened? In the absence of strong institutional support and incorporation of the issue of domestic violence in medical training, it became just another interesting experiment no one really saw as crucial. In the parlance of psychologists, its importance had never been "internalized." Susan Hadley, who did a similar study, says she has found that the only reason her program in Minnesota is so successful is that it has the full support of the hospital and "I never go away."

As of 1991, hospitals across the country learned they could not ignore the victims of intimate violence. That year, the Joint Commission on Accreditation of Health Care Organizations announced it was requiring all hospital emergency and ambulatory care departments to train staff to identify and treat female victims of domestic abuse or face loss of accreditation status. Hospitals must have an identification process, maintain a list of community support organizations, document abuse in medical records, and provide education on domestic abuse to the appropriate staff.

A year later, calling domestic violence "a cancer that gnaws at the body and soul of the American family," then Surgeon General Antonia Novella helped the nation's largest doctors' organization, the AMA, launch its campaign to encourage doctors to diagnose and treat family violence, which it called America's deadly secret. In April 1992, the AMA began making available to physicians guidelines for detecting and treating victims of intimate abuse. (Though a step in the right direction, the guidelines betray the long-held bias against identifying and treating the perpetrators of domestic violence. Doctors are not encouraged to ask a woman's abuser about how he handles his rage, so attention is again focused on "the wife-beater's wife.") The AMA had no choice but to act. It had done its own survey that found that more than 60 million Americans were either victims or knew someone who had been a victim of violence in the previous year. It also found that nine out of ten felt that doctors should get involved when they suspect family violence.

But will they? The AMA guidelines may make it easier for physicians to recognize a patient who has been victimized, but unless doctors receive the training, the tools, and the resources to cope with violence as a medical issue, they may resist recognizing it as a "crisis of epidemic proportion, every bit as virulent and destructive as the AIDS epidemic," as it was described by Robert McAfee, M.D., then vice chairman of the AMA board of trustees.

A diagnostic tool is also unlikely to overcome societal tolerance of violence against women or the psychological resistance to opening the Pandora's box it represents. Rape, battering, and incest are emotion-fraught issues, unresponsive to standard medical care. Unless that standard is changed, unless violence is recognized as a disease risk factor every bit as deadly as smoking, unless doctors begin to see it as their medical obligation, they will never learn that they do have something to give their patients to help heal the invisible wound. It has been there all along. Pandora found it, so the myth goes, huddled alone at the bottom of a box she was not supposed to open. It was hope.

9

"FALLEN WOMEN"

Alcoholics

and

Drug Abusers

Women substance abusers are not identified as frequently as men, nor do they receive treatment as frequently as men. And because men's experiences have constituted the norm or standard, women have traditionally—and incorrectly—been viewed as sicker and more difficult to treat than their male counterparts.

—*Tonda Hughes, Ph.D., R.N.*

These days, the biggest challenge facing Julianne Harris (not her real name) is getting her four-month-old twins to settle down for a nap. She relishes that hour or so of peace and tranquility, a rare treat in a day jam-packed with diapers, feedings, and bathings. But for Julianne, a twenty-nine-year-old former bookkeeper and Joan Lunden look-alike, it's a challenge she embraces with joy and optimism. Indeed, she sails through her days with confidence and energy, the picture of young motherhood, a baby perched on each jean-clad hip.

But up until a few years ago, Julianne faced a different kind of daily existence, one she endured alone and in an alcoholic haze. Her days were spent sprawled on the sofa with a glass in one hand and the TV remote control in the other. She didn't even bother to eat. "At my worst, the only thing I managed to do was walk to the liquor store to replenish my supply," she says, "and I would think I had accomplished a lot." Over a period of seven years she saw her life spiral out of control, fueled by the 2 gallons of vodka that she downed each week.

Although her family suspected that she probably drank too much, they didn't know the extent of it. Like so many women alcoholics, Julianne remained hidden to them, her friends, her co-workers, even her doctor. She became one of the millions of closet drinkers, overwhelmed by guilt and shame, shunned by society and ignored by medicine and research.

Although 40 percent of those who abuse alcohol or drugs are women, it's easy for them to remain virtually unnoticed, like so much dirt swept under a carpet. In fact, they feel like dirt much of the time. Like Julianne Harris, most chemically dependent women must contend with the disgust and repulsion of family and friends. In fact, those reactions often reinforce an addicted woman's reluctance to admit to a problem or to seek help for it. "I would make excuses so I didn't have to be around other people," says Julianne. "I didn't want to see their looks of disapproval. I knew I had a problem, but I didn't want anyone else to know. It was too humiliating."

The scientific community has hardly been more open-minded. Traditionally, substance abuse has been regarded almost entirely as a male affliction, an unfortunate assumption that has compounded the invisibility problem for addicted women. Researchers, who have had little interest in studying those who didn't fit the "norm," simply excluded women from their studies or just averaged their data in with the men's. Indeed, of the more than 110,000 substance abusers studied by various researchers over a period of thirty years, only about 7 percent (8,000) were women. Even when looking for possible hereditary predisposition, researchers have more often chosen to study the biological connections between sons and their alcoholic parents, disregarding whether the findings would be applicable to daughters of alcoholics. And because recovery programs have been studied using only addicted men, they have remained insensitive to the special needs of addicted women.

What little is known about substance abuse in women has only served to underscore the desperate need for more research. Women alcoholics, for example, develop severe liver disease after a shorter period of time than men drinkers do and after consuming far less alcohol, although no one has bothered to find out why. The disease progresses faster, too. More women than men die from cirrhosis of the liver, the most common health complication of alcoholism. According to the National Institute of Alcohol Abuse and

Alcoholism, women alcoholics have death rates 50 to 100 percent higher than those of male alcoholics. A greater percentage of female alcoholics die from suicides, alcohol-related accidents, and circulatory disorders.

Women are also at an increased risk of developing multiple addictions, far more so than men. Women are prescribed two-thirds of all psychoactive drugs, such as Valium and Librium, and are more likely to be prescribed excessive dosages. Indeed, 25 percent of women in treatment for alcoholism have serious prescription drug problems as well.

Apparently the interest of the scientific community has yet to be stirred to any significant degree. In 1990, for example, the National Institute of Alcohol Abuse and Alcoholism spent under $7 million on research related to women out of a total budget of $132 million, while pleas from those who study and treat women with chemical dependencies are largely ignored. When research money is spent, most goes to studies of the role of drugs and alcohol on women's reproductive functions or on the influence of substance abuse on women's positions as wives and mothers. The research community, as it does in other arenas, fails to recognize that "women are more than just baby carriers and care givers," says substance abuse researcher Tonda Hughes, Ph.D., R.N., of the University of Illinois. The effect of alcohol and drugs on women themselves, on their psychological and physical health, remains unmapped ground as do the social and economic pressures that influence their addictive behaviors. As long as both interest and money remain in short supply, chemical dependencies in women will continue to be ignored, underreported, underdiagnosed, and most definitely undertreated. Consequently, it will be decades or longer before knowledge of the causes, risk factors, long-term effects, and treatment of addictions in women approaches that of men's.

THE STIGMA OF THE FEMALE ADDICT

In society's eyes, women are still held to a higher code of conduct than men. They are seen as the gatekeepers of social standards and morality. Excessive drinking is simply incompatible with that narrow view. No one likes a drunk, but when the drunk is a woman, she is despised. In ancient Roman times, women who were caught drinking were put to death by stoning or starvation. Although the penalty for drinking isn't death anymore, it's still torture for most women. Indeed, drunken women are labeled as fallen women, dangerously promiscuous, and generally out of control. Snubbed by society and riddled with guilt, they are driven into hiding, becoming closet drinkers, like Julianne Harris, or secret pill poppers or both.

Not so for men, however. In typical double-standard fashion, a drunken man is not only tolerated, but is either viewed as "macho" by his buddies or excused with a wink and a boys-will-be-boys attitude. Julianne, who used to play in a coed softball league, says that she eagerly guzzled beer with the guys until she noticed the dirty looks shot her way. "They made it clear that drinking the way *they* did wasn't ladylike."

But by far the most damaging stigma that women who drink or use drugs must contend with is that of sexual promiscuity. The prevailing attitude is that women who drink excessively become far more sexually aggressive. Yet the research simply does not support that notion, no matter how popular it remains. One study showed, for example, that only 8 percent of 1,000 women surveyed said they became less particular about their choice of sexual partner when they had been drinking. And the proportion hardly varied whether the women were light or heavy drinkers. Instead, the majority of the women reported that they were the targets of sexual aggression by men who had been drinking.

This stereotype of promiscuity among women who drink is not only inaccurate, says psychiatry professor Sheila B. Blume, M.D., of the State University of New York at Stony Brook, it results in promoting the sexual victimization of drinking women. In other words, if she drinks, "well, she's just asking for it." Studies have shown that she gets it, too. In one survey that compared alcohol-dependent women with nondrinking women, 16 percent of the alcoholic women reported being raped, whereas none of the nonalcoholic women had been.

Women who drink in bars are particularly vulnerable to victimization even if they are not themselves heavy or problem drinkers. Julianne Harris says that men often became more brazen when she was out drinking. "They became less afraid to make the first move. Once when I was drunk, a man took advantage of me. It wasn't rape, but I still felt so dirty afterward. It made me want to drink more just to hide the pain," she says, her voice growing soft with embarrassment.

Sadly, women who abuse alcohol or drugs are likely to believe the low opinion that many have of them. "Since the chemically dependent woman grows up in the same society as the rest of us, she applies these stereotypes to herself," says Blume, who also treats alcoholics at South Oaks Hospital in Amityville, New York. When she fails to meet society's standards, she is acutely aware of her own failures, reacting with extreme guilt and shame. Harris says that people called her a slut when she was drunk even though there was no reason for that. Or they'd say "I was just a drunk. It was bad enough to be called a drunk, but '*just* a drunk' made me feel even more diminished and worthless."

The effect of these social stigmas is to drive addicted women into hiding, into invisibility. Indeed, alcoholic women are much more likely to drink alone, at home, early in the mornings or on weekends, and to go to great lengths to hide their problems from themselves and others. Julianne Harris used to make some excuse to go to her room or to the basement or wherever she had stashed a bottle of vodka, and there, alone and hidden away from disapproving stares, she would drink. "Sometimes I'd pour vodka into a glass and put it behind the microwave oven," she recalls. "Since I was always alone in the kitchen when I cooked, I could sip from my secret source without fear of discovery. But when the house was empty, I would drink all day."

SLIPPING THROUGH THE CRACKS

The fact is that it's far too easy for women addicted to alcohol or drugs to remain in hiding. It's as if no one cares enough to even look for them, and in a sense that's true. The existing systems that expose men with addictions and get them into treatment programs don't necessarily work for women. That's because they were all designed with the male substance abuser in mind. It's *his* behavior when he drinks or uses drugs that has been used as the model for detection. Women simply don't follow the same behavior patterns that men do when they're addicted.

When men have chemical dependency problems, they are more likely to have trouble on the job or trouble with the law. Women, because they are more likely to drink alone and at home are, consequently, far less likely to be caught driving under the influence, drunk at work, or making a public scene. Not surprisingly, employee assistance programs, drunk driver rehabilitation programs, and public intoxication programs are all heavily male dominated. Indeed, the male-to-female ratio among the latter two programs is nine to one. Adds Blume, "Employee assistance programs, which use impaired job performance as a problem indicator and job jeopardy as a motivator, have also been more successful with men."

Families, too, whether intentional or not, often undermine any efforts the addicted member makes to seek treatment. Julianne Harris's family tried to get her committed to a mental hospital, a choice *they* felt was more respectable for their upper-class daughter than the drug rehab program she preferred, which they equated with street junkies. Sadly, studies have shown that about 25 percent of women's families are actually opposed to their seeking treatment of any kind, contributing to these women's invisibility and prolonging their addictions. Aware of and sensitive to the social stigmas associated with female substance abuse, these families fear exposure of their shameful secret. Or more selfishly, they may not want to lose the services of the person who also happens to be the primary family caretaker.

Drug-dependent women are also far more likely to be divorced or separated, so the only people who might be aware of their problem are their own children, and the kids are not about to turn in the people who care for them. Besides, women fear losing custody of their children if they acknowledge that they need help for an addiction—with good reason. In some states, a woman who is addicted to drugs or alcohol is legally labeled as a child abuser or child neglecter. Paradoxically, a woman who continues her dependency without seeking help does not have to face this charge. By remaining invisible, she gets to keep her children, although it comes at the expense of her own recovery efforts. Only the state of New York has recognized what a disincentive this rule is for women who want to kick their habits. There, a woman who is participating in a treatment program is not automatically assumed to be an abusive or neglectful parent, at least not without additional evidence.

When women do decide to seek help, it's usually because of trouble with their health or trouble with their families. But unlike the drunk driver and public intoxication programs that favor the needs of men addicts, there are no public assistance programs for the marriage or health problems that are more consistent with women's addictions. The best these women can hope for is that the people they most often turn to—their doctors, health clinics, or even family and social service agencies—will somehow detect their drug or alcohol problems. In fact, divorce lawyers could be good at detecting chemical dependencies in their women clients if they would allow themselves to do so, claims Blume.

What *about* doctors? Who could be better equipped to uncover the hidden alcoholic than a doctor talking face to face with his or her patient? Although this sounds perfectly logical, it simply doesn't happen—not nearly as often as it should, considering that diagnosing ills is what doctors are trained to do. Yet physicians are often reluctant to diagnose *this* particular problem, especially in their women patients, because they're as aware of the negative stereotypes as everyone else is. In surveys, doctors admit that they often shy away from alcoholic patients because evaluating them, confronting them with their suspicions, and then managing their cases all take large blocks of time, the same excuse many use for not diagnosing patients who are victims of domestic violence.

Doctors are at a disadvantage. Like battered women, women with chemical dependencies are more likely to visit their doctors with vague symptoms such as headaches, anxiety, or insomnia. And, like victims of domestic violence, they leave with a prescription for Valium or some other sedative rather than what they really need—a referral to a drug treatment program. It's the vigilant and concerned doctor who can see through the facade. Julianne Harris's doctor was fooled every time. No matter what illness drove her to the doctor, she'd always mention something about being under a great deal of stress, which, she says, was a complete lie. "I would say that for the past two weeks I've really been drinking a lot. I'd never tell him that I'd been drinking heavily for the past five years. The doctor always took my word for it and never probed further." Instead, Julianne would occasionally receive a prescription for Valium for her so-called stress problem.

Granted, doctors don't have a great deal to go on in their quest to identify a substance abuser. Alcohol screening tests, for example, sound like a good idea. But even if these screening devices were used all the time (which they're not), they're still bound to miss a proportion of women with addictions, because the tests were developed for and tested on men. The Michigan Alcoholism Screening Test, for example, was tested on men at first, and then repeated with another group of people, only 5.5 percent of whom were women, says chemical dependency researcher Tonda Hughes, Ph.D. A shorter version of the same scale (called the Short Michigan Alcoholism Screening Test) was also originally tested on only male subjects. Although some questions have been changed to incorporate women's life experiences, they are still more geared to uncovering men with addictions than women. Questions about getting into fights or arguments, for example, or drinking-related arrests, trouble at work, or being hospitalized due to alcohol problems are not nearly as relevant for women as they are for men, she says.

Neither are the questions that ask the patient if they ever drink first thing in the morning or before noon. Though women whose addiction is limited to alcohol might be detected with that line of questioning, those are still the patterns more typical of men alcoholics. The fact is, alcoholic women are twice as likely to combine their alcoholism with a dependence on sedative drugs, so they may be more inclined to start their days with Valium or other tranquilizers. Indeed, women who have multiple addictions may not touch a drop of alcohol until the evening hours.

A clinician who asks his women patients how much alcohol they drink each day may also be missing the ones with problems. Studies show that women who drink excessively consume only about *half* what their male counterparts do, although both have the same level of impairment. Until recently, doctors blamed body water content for the difference. According to that theory, because women have less body water than men do, alcohol becomes more concentrated in their systems. But there's more to it than that. When researchers finally got around to studying alcohol metabolism in both men *and* women, they uncovered the most important difference. They found that women have far less of the stomach enzyme that breaks down alcohol, gastric alcohol dehydrogenase, than men do. This enzyme decreases the availability of alcohol to the whole body, so that the less of this enzyme there is, the more intoxicated the person becomes. Because women have less of the enzyme, more alcohol enters their systems. Alcoholic women, the researchers found, have virtually none of this alcohol-metabolizing enzyme.

In spite of this new knowledge, the charts and tables that are used to calculate blood alcohol levels have yet to be revised. Those tables are designed to determine when it's safe to drive by taking into account the number of drinks a person has had, body weight, and the time elapsed since the last alcoholic beverage. But those tables still apply to men only, so regardless of what they say, women would be well advised to consume half the amount of alcohol recommended as safe on the charts before attempting to get behind the wheel.

TREATMENT INSENSITIVITY

When women manage to emerge from the shadows of alcohol or drug addictions and attempt treatment programs, they are likely to find the road to recovery a particularly difficult and lonely one. Detection systems have failed women so completely that there are from four to ten times as many men as women being treated for their addictions, even though addicted men outnumber addicted women only two to one. Vast numbers of women with dependencies still go untreated, whereas those who do get help are forced to participate in programs that have been designed with the male addict in mind.

As in other areas of medical research, women have been systematically neglected, particularly by those who study treatments for alcoholism and other drug dependencies. Researchers have relied almost entirely on male volunteers, and the results are simply generalized to both men and women, a process that does nothing to advance the knowledge of women's addictions or how best to treat them. "It's like operating in a vacuum," says addictions therapist Marsha Vannicelli, Ph.D., of Harvard University Medical School. "Maybe the study results based on men do apply, and then again, maybe they don't."

Because men have been the ones most often studied, they have also become the standard or norm against which women are measured whether women fit that particular picture of "normal" or not. Most often, of course, they don't. Instead, women are relegated to what's called a special population group, a designation that allows those who design treatment programs to exclude their needs in favor of the needs of those all-purpose standard setters—white males. In that way researchers, policy makers, and doctors can leave existing programs as they are whether they work for all their patients or not.

For women, they are often quite problematic. Male-based treatment programs commonly fail to recognize the importance of the excessive guilt and shame that women suffer, to understand the impact of women's life experiences on their addictions, and to treat them as grown-up individuals who want and need to take responsibility for their lives. Julianne Harris, for example, went through three different rehab programs over a period of one and a half years and fell off the wagon each time before finding a therapist who was sensitive to her style of coping.

As with many women alcoholics, Harris found the therapy strategies used by her counselors to be confrontational rather than supportive, a method that has proven to suit men's behavior patterns much more than women's, says Hughes. Women are already so shamed and demoralized by their addictions that a confrontational approach is counterproductive for them, diminishing their already low self-esteem even further. Typically, says Julianne, the therapist would "scream at the group and tell us that we were idiots. They wanted us to get angry and yell right back to get it out of our systems," she says. In all the groups she participated in, nearly every man did just that. In fact, they got so worked up that she expected to see fist fights break out. "But the men really seemed to get something out of it; you could see that they felt better afterward, relieved," she says. "The women, though, would completely shut down. They'd start to cry and simply freeze and not be able to speak at all. I always felt worse about myself after those sessions and would dread each and every one."

Male-based treatments also tend to discount or trivialize the impact of women's social and economic experiences on the development of their chemical dependencies. Women are not just rationalizing when they relate the onset of their addiction problems to life events such as divorce, sexual abuse, joblessness, or childbirth, says Blume, and those events need to be addressed for treatment to be successful. Julianne's drinking, for example, began as an antidote to the humiliation of discovering her first husband in bed with their next-door neighbor. But it progressed rapidly to needing alcohol to boost her confidence for everyday situations, too, even something as routine as picking up the phone to call about a potential job. Yet, the programs she participated in didn't seem interested in her personal story. "The impression I got was that they had heard it all before many, many times, and so they didn't have to listen to what I thought or felt. Instead, they just wanted to tell me what the problem was and then give me the standard treatment."

Just as detrimental to successful treatment outcomes are the stereotypes and false beliefs that many therapists themselves have of chemically dependent women. The fact is, therapists hold the same negative attitudes as society in general. Women, particularly addicted women, are considered weak and therefore needing extra protection. Julianne found, for example, that the rehab programs tended to treat her as if she were a helpless child who needed constant tending. "It was as if, because I was a woman, I couldn't be trusted on my own to follow the program and do what was expected," she says.

Though therapists may believe that they are being supportive and helpful, the effect is anything but that. Says Vannicelli, "In my experience I have found that many women patients, and alcoholic women in particular, need to learn a different message about themselves, namely, that they are or have the potential to be competent, mature women and that they are not doomed to be helpless little girls forever." Indeed, Julianne says that it felt good to take responsibility for herself. "To say, wait a minute, I can do this. If I really want to stop drinking, then it's up to me. Being successful was the best confidence builder."

Chemically dependent women have also been falsely stereotyped as being sicker and harder to treat than their male counterparts. The fact is, however, that women *appear* sicker or less motivated to recover only if they are compared against the male standard. In actuality, of fifty-one studies that compared the treatment outcomes of both sexes, forty-three showed no difference between men and women, seven showed that women had done better than men, and five showed that men had done better than women.* The notion that women have a poorer response to treatment is simply not supported by the existing research, says Vannicelli, who reviewed thirty years' worth of medical literature. "If anything, the weight of the evidence seems to lean slightly in the opposite direction."

And that's with treatment programs designed specifically for the chemically dependent male. What if there were programs sensitive to women's needs? What if there were programs that provided child care for those who needed it; that took women's social and economic status into consideration; that addressed the greater guilt and shame that women experience; that offered supportive rather than the male-oriented confrontational strategies; that included vocational training to improve women's employment opportunities; that worked on assertiveness training and building up long beaten-down self-esteem; that compared results with what's typical for women, not men? Would the outcomes be even better? The truth is, practically no research has been done to find out. Nobody even knows for sure if women do better in all-female groups rather than the more traditional mixed-sex groups, whether a female therapist is better for women than a male therapist, or whether individual counseling is better than group therapy.

"If treatment is done the right way, women respond well, too," says Julianne Harris, who says a day doesn't go by that she doesn't feel blessed. She had her turnaround, which has given her a new life, filled with hope "and diapers," she laughs. But she lost valuable time—most of her twenties—in her search for the right treatment. "I was lucky that I found someone who listened to me," she says. "But I shouldn't have had to find that someone in the Yellow Pages."

---

*The number of studies adds up to more than fifty-one because some studies reported data on more than one sample.

10
POOR
WOMEN,
POOR
HEALTH

*Poverty should not be an offense
that is punishable by death.*

—*Harold P. Freeman, M.D.*

In 1990, two researchers from Harlem Hospital published a shocking study that made headlines across the country. Colin Mc-Cord, M.D., and Harold P. Freeman, M.D., in a study published in *The New England Journal of Medicine,* revealed that black men in Harlem had shorter life spans than men in Bangladesh, one of the poorest countries in the world. Receiving less publicity was another finding of the Harlem study: If the extraordinarily high death rate among girls under five in Bangladesh were eliminated, black women in Harlem, like the men in their community, were less likely to survive to age sixty-five than their counterparts in Bangladesh.

Harlem was hardly an isolated case. McCord and Freeman identified fifty-four pockets of premature death in New York City alone, and almost all of those were populated largely by minorities. Other studies have identified similar enclaves of abnormally high mortality, most in areas with the highest proportion of racial and ethnic minority groups.

Studies like these sent a handful of researchers scurrying to investigate racial differences in disease incidence and death rates.

Those thinking they would find some genetic basis for the disparities in most cases have been disappointed. Race, as it turns out, is merely a risk factor for poverty, which, as Harold Freeman poignantly told a congressional panel in 1991, has become "an offense which is punishable by death."

Poverty is a leading risk factor for illness and premature death in the United States. The poor are more likely to be sick, to be uninsured, to get poor-quality medical care, and to die at an early age—often five to seven years before more well-off Americans. They are also more likely to be women, often women of color, making poverty both a gender and a racial issue. Over the past three decades, poverty has become feminized. Since 1970, the number of female-headed households has doubled, and they are four times more likely to be poor than other families. Among those poor households, the number headed by African-American or Hispanic women is nearly twice that headed by white women. If the present trend continues, according to the National Advisory Council on Economic Opportunity, by the year 2000, the poor will be made up almost entirely of women and their children for whom good health is simply another commodity they can't buy.

If women's health has been neglected in the United States, the health of poor women has been ignored. There's very little disagreement on the reason for that: The poor don't vote, and women and racial minorities are an easily dismissed constituency. As New York Governor Mario Cuomo noted in a speech attacking "welfare scapegoating," the trend toward blaming programs for the disadvantaged for poor economic conditions: "Who's going to march against you, a fifteen-year-old girl with a baby? She doesn't even get to the polls."

"Everyone is biased against the poor, and if you are also a woman and a woman of color you are powerless three times," says Kayla Jackson, program associate for reproduction and women's health at the National Council of Negro Women.

The results of being powerless are manifest:

• Most low-income women of all races perceive themselves in poor health, with almost three-quarters of poor minority women and two-thirds of poor white women reporting poor health, according to a government report. Rural poor women are more likely to consider themselves to be in poorer health than women who live in cities, another study found.

• Minority women have higher rates of infant mortality than white women; among African-Americans the rate is twice as high.

• Though more white women get breast cancer, more black women die from it. In fact, women who live in poverty, regardless of their race, are 1.5 times more likely to die of breast cancer or have a recurrence of the disease than women of higher socioeconomic status.

• Minority women have higher rates of diabetes, hypertension, and cardiovascular disease.

• Death rates from heart disease are twice as high for black as for white women.

• Nearly three-quarters of the women with AIDS are either African-American or Hispanic.

• Except for cervical cancer, cancer rates among Native Americans are relatively low because they don't live long enough to get cancer.

When experts talk about the health problems of the poor, they generally begin by talking about lack of access, the inability of the poor to get good medical care. Though lack of insurance coverage may be the pivotal issue, even universal health care will not be a panacea. Poor women suffer from lack of access to many things— good education, good jobs, respect, proper nutrition, support, self-esteem—that can affect their health. Poor women also don't have access to the same health information as middle-class women. They are less educated, may speak another language, and simply can't afford the books and magazines middle-class women read to become good health care consumers. They may be in no position to judge whether the medical care they are receiving is appropriate or feel empowered enough to do anything about it if they think it isn't.

Poor nutrition can have a significant impact on the health of pregnant women and their babies, who are more likely to be born with low birthweight, which is associated with the high infant death rate among minorities. Poor nutrition may also affect the high rate of cancer among poor people. A 1991 National Cancer Institute study found that living in poverty can increase the risk of certain cancers by as much as 20 percent. Diet and other lifestyle factors may play a role. For example, the poor generally eat a high-fat diet, which is associated with cancer risk and, because of high cost, don't consume many fruits and vegetables, which, as recent studies have suggested, may prevent cancer. Some poor families also face hunger and malnutrition because the money they receive simply won't stretch to pay for rent and groceries, too.

Lack of educational and career opportunities, which directly affect economic status, have far-reaching effects on poor women's health. Most poor women are engaged in a day-to-day struggle for survival. They may be unemployed, homeless, or single parents whose greatest concern on any given day is putting food on the table, not getting a mammogram or a blood pressure check. It's a life full of stress, which can lead to stress-related illnesses, smoking, and abuse of alcohol or drugs. Studies have shown that smoking is decreasing among all groups except the poor. "There's a big class difference in smoking," says Virginia Ernster, Ph.D., head of the department of epidemiology and biostatistics at the University of California at San Francisco. "The less educated you are, the more likely you are to smoke."

Cassie Parsons (not her real name) is aching for a smoke. Sitting in the pink-walled examining room of her gynecologist, she rattles off the litany of illnesses that forced her to quit her job as a nurse's aide—diabetes, asthma, emphysema, congestive heart failure, hypertension, arthritis, "and stomach problems"—and admits abashedly, "Yeah, I still smoke." She knows she shouldn't. "I did cut down from three packs a day to half a pack. But it's hard," she says. "I'm under a whole lot of stress."

Cassie's life could define stress. Married and a mother at twenty, she was a single mother of two by the time she was twenty-one. She had a third child, now fourteen, by the man who eventually became her second husband and has three grandchildren. Grossly overweight and virtually toothless, Cassie appears to be a woman in her late fifties. She is only forty-five. Her husband was a detail man in a car wash until his diabetes and depression worsened, forcing him to take permanent disability. She remembers coming home from work to find him sitting on the front porch of their house, staring into the night with a gun in his lap. "He's on Prozac, so he's doing better," she says. "It's been real stressful for him, too."

It's clear that for Cassie, whose own depression goes undiagnosed, smoking is simply nonprescription Prozac. Her hand, adorned by a mother's ring with two blue stones and one green, taps on her purse. "I sure wish that doctor would get here," she says, looking jittery. "I could sure use a smoke now."

THE INSURANCE GAP

Without a good education, many women like Cassie are relegated to low-paying and low-status jobs where they are less likely to have employment-based health insurance or to be able to afford private insurance. Lack of insurance—or inadequate coverage—is associated with poor health care and with high mortality rates from some diseases. For instance, one reason African-American women have higher death rates from breast cancer is that by the time they see a doctor, their cancer is incurable. At Harlem Hospital, Freeman found that 49 percent of the patients who were diagnosed with breast cancer were in the late stages of the disease. Unable to pay for a private doctor, an uninsured woman is unlikely to have a mammogram, which could detect her cancer in early stages. She is more likely to seek treatment in a hospital ER only when the painless lump she felt a few months before suddenly begins to hurt. ERs— usually crowded, busy places—are not equipped to diagnose and treat breast cancer.

Likewise, a woman who rarely if ever sees a private doctor may never have her blood pressure checked. Poor minority women are at higher risk for hypertension than other segments of the population. Nor is she likely to have a Pap test for cervical cancer, another cancer that, when caught early, has a 90 to 100 percent five-year survival rate.

In 1991, lack of health coverage became a serious problem for a record 36 million Americans under the age of sixty-five, a rise of nearly 1 million over the previous year. Fifty-five percent of those without private or public insurance were from families making less than $20,000 a year, barely enough money to cover food and shelter, let alone medical expenses. Many of them—roughly 16 percent— are the working poor who are, in the words of Freeman, "too rich for Medicaid but too poor for Blue Shield."

Because women are more likely than men to be in low-paying, temporary, or part-time jobs, they are less likely than men to have private medical insurance and employment-based coverage. Hispanics are 2.5 times and blacks 1.8 times as likely to be uninsured as whites. However, poor women of all races are more likely to have public insurance—Medicaid—because they are poor. But even Medicaid is of limited use. By some estimates, only about 40 percent of the poor are covered by this public health insurance. Most of them are women and children. But the bulk of Medicaid expenditures—roughly two-thirds—go to cover costs for the elderly not reimbursed by Medicare.

The process of applying for Medicaid is a formidable obstacle to many poor women, who, if they work, may have to take time off, risking lost wages. Many don't have transportation to the application site and may have young children and no money to pay a babysitter. Often, it is forty-five days between the time they apply and learn if they qualify for Medicaid benefits. Similarly, in some cases, pregnant women or mothers of young children may have to wait to learn if they are eligible for the Special Supplemental Food Program for Women, Infants, and Children, known as WIC, which supplies food, nutrition screening, and counseling to pregnant women, new mothers, and infants and children under the age of five. WIC has been a very effective program in reducing infant deaths and low birthweight as well as getting more vulnerable women and children into the health care system. Yet 40 percent of those who are eligible don't receive it.

Even those who are covered may not get the care they need. For example, a study by GAO found that 63 percent of uninsured or Medicaid-covered women received incomplete prenatal care. Other studies have found that this is particularly true of women in nonurban areas, who have less access to medical care than women living in cities. Many pregnant women who are uninsured or on Medicaid do not have their first prenatal visit in their first trimester, a factor associated with having a healthier baby. Studies have shown that women who don't see a doctor or midwife some time in the first three months of pregnancy are at higher risk of having a low-birthweight baby. That risk is compounded for poor women who tend to have babies at younger ages, often in their teens, another factor associated with having a small infant. Though teen pregnancy among the poor offends many middle-class sensibilities, it is understandable.

For many poor, uneducated teens, motherhood may seem like their only available career option.

Whereas for many, Medicaid is the only gateway to the health care system, it is virtually worthless if a woman cannot find a physician willing to accept it. Nurse-practitioner Jackie Gaines, who works for Health Care for the Homeless, a program providing medical services for fifty-two homeless shelters in Maryland, refers to the Medicaid card as "a hunting license." Many physicians refuse Medicaid patients because the reimbursement is so scanty and the paperwork so long. One study found that nationwide, 44 percent of physicians providing obstetric services turn away Medicaid patients. The gynecologist Cassie sees works for the Women's Center, a program sponsored by the Memorial Hospital of Burlington County in New Jersey and housed in a refurbished welfare office. The center is the only place in this far-flung rural county near Trenton where indigent women can get gynecological and obstetrical care.

Once a woman finds a physician or clinic who will accept her, the wait for an appointment and then to see a doctor can be lengthy. "If you try to go to the public maternity clinic sponsored by the Chicago Department of Health, it could take three months on the average to get an appointment," says Aida Giachello, Ph.D., assistant professor at the Jane Addams College of Social Work at the University of Illinois at Chicago. "If you try to go to the clinic that is part of the county system, you may have to wait nine months. By that time, you will have delivered."

Once a woman gets an appointment, she may have an all-day wait to see a doctor because many public clinics schedule block appointments, shoehorning as many women as they can into office hours. Poor women testifying at a conference of Maryland health care leaders told stories of arriving at a clinic for an 8:30 A.M. appointment and not leaving the clinic until 3 P.M. For most women, a six-and-a-half-hour wait is an insurmountable obstacle because of the difficulty in getting transportation and child care.

Cassie never got to see her doctor that day. He was delayed by emergency surgery and there was no other doctor scheduled to take his patients. "But it's always like this," she grumbled as she gathered up her things to leave. "It's not easy for me to get here in the first place, now I've got to find some way to get here again." If her daughter-in-law, with her two-week-old son in tow, hadn't driven her, Cassie would have had an hour trip on two buses, a painful journey because of her emphysema and arthritic knees.

POOR TREATMENT

Although Cassie usually sees the same gynecologist each time, many poor women get fragmented care, rarely seeing the same doctor twice. Women with special needs, drug treatment, for instance, may be unable to find a treatment facility that will accept Medicaid.

For the poor who use ERs for primary care, the picture may even be worse. A study done at a California ER found that seriously ill patients who sought care in the ER left after waiting more than six hours to be seen. The researchers found that those who left had the same need for medical care as those who stayed. Ironically, when asked by the researchers why they left, many said they felt "too ill" to stay. Others had to return to work, to care for children, or left because they had transportation problems, all familiar obstacles for the poor seeking medical care.

In some cases, those obstacles can be lethal. At Harlem Hospital, Harold Freeman saw a story that repeated itself over and over again: Women, too concerned about feeding and sheltering their children to be worried about a painless breast lump, are turned away from the ER where they're considered "not sick enough." Sent to public clinics, they may be asked for proof of medical insurance, which they don't have, and face a lengthy and difficult registration process which may seem "more painful than the painless lump."

"In this manner," Freeman writes, "poor people are often triaged negatively back to their communities, returning months later with an incurable cancer."

Even if they do manage to get into a hospital, the care they receive may be substandard. A number of studies have found that some urban public hospitals and those serving minorities and people on public health insurance offer low-quality care. A study of ninety-nine Illinois hospitals, published in 1991 in *The Journal of the American Medical Association,* found that women who were uninsured or poorly insured and went to urban hospitals were more likely to be diagnosed in the late stages of breast cancer. It also found that of those poor women who were diagnosed in the early stages, many did not receive radiation therapy after a partial mastectomy, considered the standard of care for the treatment of breast cancer.

The researchers suggested that it was the economic conditions at the hospital that led to the poor-quality care given to poorly insured women. For many poor women, the struggling urban hospital, which may have trouble attracting high-quality personnel and may be slow in adopting state-of-the-art treatments, is the only source of health care they have. Along with economics, racism may also play a role in the quality of care poor minority women receive. A study of 7,812 patients with breast cancer treated in 107 hospitals across the country found that black patients, most of whom had Medicaid or were uninsured, were less likely than white patients to be tested for hormone receptor status of their tumors, which could affect their prognosis and dictate how aggressive their treatment should be, and to be referred for rehabilitation after a mastectomy.

An earlier study, which looked at the racial differences in the treatment of pneumonia, found that nonwhite pneumonia patients received far fewer hospital services than white patients despite the equal severity of their illness. They received fewer consultations, fewer surgical procedures, and less intensive care than the white patients, and those differences in treatment were found not only between hospitals but within the same hospital.

Poor women may face other biases that may influence their access to health care. "Immediately, you walk in and you are a welfare recipient, receiving Medicaid benefits, so you are lazy, you are not a good mother, you don't take care of yourself, and you probably abuse drugs. That's often the perception caregivers have of poor women," says Kayla Jackson. "When that is the way you think about the person you are caring for, that person, who is unhealthy, is going to stay that way."

Homeless women face even greater barriers. Says Jackie Gaines, "I had one medical director tell me he had just had his waiting room redone and he didn't want *that* element in his waiting room."

The clinic Cassie uses could be a model for how it should be done, from its location in a small strip shopping center accessible to bus routes to its carpeting and walls the colors of a Monet painting to its staff—four doctors, five nurses, a social worker, and a nutritionist—who are encouraged to dispense respect along with medical advice. "We like to say everyone wakes up with an IALAC card—I am loveable and capable," says Helene Fedele, R.N., who runs the Women's Center. "Unfortunately, many of our clients don't know where their card is anymore. We make it a point never to beat on them. They're already beaten up. They don't need that here."

But Cassie still feels that there's a health care hierarchy and she's somewhere at the bottom. "When you're low income, the doctors don't have time to sit and talk to you," she says. "They don't want to know about you. Unless you come in here crying and half broke down, they don't ask how you're doing. They don't care as long as you're in and out."

Sometimes, she says, she thinks if she could pay with cash and not a charity card, she'd get better. "Instead of giving me a bunch of pills that don't help," she says, "they'd give me one pill that works."

Nevertheless, Cassie keeps all her appointments, even the ones that have to be rescheduled. Some women who sense that caregivers are hostile to them simply don't return. Studies of pregnant women found that women who have bad experiences with caregivers, who sense they are unfriendly or who don't feel supported, don't go back for prenatal care. Unfortunately, personal biases aside, the way the public health care system is set up, bad experiences are almost unavoidable. By their very nature, most public clinics tend to be crowded, noisy, and often hostile places with harried staffs who have no choice but to treat patients as if they were on an assembly line.

Increasingly, physicians treating poor populations face both language and cultural barriers many fail to breach. This is a particular problem in Latino communities, although it exists among Asian and Eastern European immigrant populations as well. A survey of health care providers in Chicago, which has a large Hispanic population, found that many held negative stereotypes about their Spanish-speaking patients, which led to many misunderstandings. For example, says Giachello, former president of the Latino Caucus of the American Public Health Association, many Hispanic women don't seek prenatal care until it comes time to make arrangements for delivery because they don't connect pregnancy, a natural state, with a need to see a doctor, whom they perceive as someone who cares for the sick. Many don't comprehend the concept of well-baby visits to the doctor. "In the Hispanic culture, you don't take your baby to the doctor if it is healthy because of the likelihood of a baby who is healthy getting sick as a result of exposure to sick children in the waiting room," she explains.

Though the logic is hard to argue with—indeed, a number of studies have found that children *do* pick up illnesses in pediatricians' waiting rooms—women who miss appointments are met with hostility. "When the women do return to the office, the nurses tend to penalize them, criticizing them for not keeping their well-baby appointments without considering that they might have had a good reason based on their own common sense," says Giachello.

The Chicago survey found that even among those who worked with Latinos, there was little familiarity with the Latino culture. "What was more unfortunate," says Giachello, "not many of them were very interested in learning about Latinos either."

That same insensitivity exists among researchers, says Giachello, who, when they do include minorities in their study populations, tend to view them like Victorian missionaries: judgmentally, through the prism of the dominant culture. "They take certain kinds of behavior and values out of context and analyze them from their own perspective," she says. "Their results then enhance negative stereotypes, like the Latino male being macho."

AIDS, which affects a disproportionate number of minority women, has brought into relief the inadequacies of current research protocols that fail to take into account some of the obstacles poor women face in getting medical care, from transportation costs to child care responsibilities, and that also preclude them from enrolling in clinical studies. Part of the problem is that researchers are usually quite different from the typical person at high risk from AIDS—different in race, different in gender, different in income level and in education. Those marked differences mean that the scientists need to make an extraordinary effort to identify with their potential study subjects in order to find ways to attract them to clinical trials. They may also have to deal with the distrust many minority women and men feel toward the scientific community. Though many explain that distrust as part of the Tuskegee effect, referring to studies done at Tuskegee Institute in which black subjects with syphilis were deliberately left untreated, it is far more likely that the average minority woman has experienced so much racial prejudice and insensitivity that she looks on scientific research as just another form of exploitation at best and as a tool of genocide at worst. Given the poor, fragmented medical care she does receive, she may also be disillusioned and distrustful of any health care provider who claims to want to help her.

Of all the obstacles women face in their struggle for quality health care, poverty is likely to be the most formidable. Though physicians and scientists are beginning to understand the need to become sensitive to society's disadvantaged—both in the clinic and the laboratory—society itself seems to have become less tolerant of the poor. Welfare scapegoating has become a legitimate political tool, a way for politicians to deflect attention away from their inability to inject any real life into a flagging economy. Playing to the prevailing myths of welfare—that it is a disincentive to work or that women have babies simply to increase their welfare payments—dozens of states have cut both general assistance and Aid to Families with Dependent Children (AFDC), eliminating health benefits for thousands of men, women, and children. According to a study by the Washington-based Center on Budget and Policy Priorities, in 1991, benefits in the AFDC program—made up almost entirely of women and children—were reduced more than in any year since 1981, with forty states freezing or cutting benefits. General assistance cuts mainly affect men, though some jobless single and older women also rely on the program.

At a time when unemployment and poverty were on the rise, some states carved deeply into programs that help the disabled poor, keep marginal families from becoming homeless, and even those that provide winter coats to poor children, making few ripples among a generally approving public. Michigan was hardest hit. There, state officials dropped 82,000 people from general assistance, slashed AFDC payments by 13 percent, and eliminated special needs payments for AFDC recipients, including pregnant women.

Other cutbacks may have far-reaching effects on women's health. In New York, for example, Medicaid recipients are restricted to fourteen physician visits a year. New York will now only pay for eighteen lab procedures and sixty prescription items a year. Though most healthy recipients won't be affected, those with chronic illnesses and the elderly poor could have their health grow worse and may end up costing the system even more.

Some cuts have been aimed directly at poor women. Title X, the federal family-planning program serving roughly 4 million poor women, has been slashed repeatedly. Over 1,000 Title X clinics have closed since 1981, depriving women at highest risk of sexually transmitted diseases, unwanted pregnancies, teenage pregnancies, and low-birthweight infants of family-planning information and primary care. Those same women have been denied the right to a legal abortion since 1978, when the Hyde Amendment gave states the right to refuse to provide public funding for poor women's abortions.

Many poor women also do not use birth control for many reasons, including cultural. But the most serious problem they face is that they simply don't have access to it, prompting former Planned Parenthood Federation head Faye Wattleton to suggest in a *Los Angeles Times* article "that poor and young women are effectively coerced to have children."

However, a number of states seriously considered coercing women on welfare *not* to have children by paying them up to $500 to use Norplant, a surgically implanted, slow-release contraceptive that is effective for up to five years. Those measures drew charges of racism, because the majority of women on welfare are black, and horrified many women's health advocates who remembered the sterilization scandal of the 1970s, when women on welfare were forced to have their tubes tied.

Though gender bias is rapidly becoming an intolerable aspect of health research and care, there has been no such public outcry about measures that deprive the poor of what has increasingly come to be seen as a right. In fact, says Olivia Cousins, Ph.D., chairperson of the board of directors for the National Women's Health Network, the unavailability of good-quality health care for the poor "makes a lie out of the philosophy that health care is something that should be a birthright, not something you should have to pay for."

Though Americans may have to pay a high price for universal health care, some Americans now pay a high price for not having it. They're women like Cassie who, at midlife, suffers from a host of old woman's diseases that have robbed her of her health and her income and will likely cut short her life. For Cassie, poverty has been a cruel thief in other ways.

Shifting around in the small plastic chair in the examining room, a mild exertion that makes her draw in a deep gulp of air, she ducks a question about why she waited so long to see a doctor for her ailments, which she has had for many years but were only recently diagnosed. "I know I should've . . . But I've never been one to go running to the doctor unless something was really wrong. I've always been this way," she finally explains. She pauses, as though she knows that this answer is not enough, and then reveals the real reason.

"The truth is," Cassie says, "I really don't *care* if I live or die."

11

MATERNAL VERSUS FETAL RIGHTS

Whose Life Is It Anyway?

A fetus has more rights than a woman does....A cadaver has more rights than a living, breathing woman does when she's pregnant.

—*Vicki Paterno, M.D.*

The question left by a doctor on her answering machine was haunting Ruth Macklin. Macklin, a bioethicist, usually sorts out medical moral dilemmas in the classroom or during case conferences at the Albert Einstein College of Medicine in the Bronx, New York. But occasionally a doctor will call with an ethics emergency. This time, Macklin wasn't there to return the call and she was curious about the outcome.

"He wanted to discuss the case of a woman, twenty-six weeks pregnant, who came into the hospital with some symptoms," she explained. "Her physician recommended that she stay in the hospital, but she wanted to leave. His question was, What is our obligation to this twenty-six-week-old fetus?"

That was the question that disturbed Macklin. "What," she wondered aloud, "about his obligation to the woman?" She paused. "I bring this up," she said, "because it illustrates a trend I've noticed among doctors. What they are increasingly doing is putting the interest of the fetus above the rights and interests of the pregnant woman. What were they going to do to this woman? They could suggest to her, cajole her, seek to persuade or convince her to stay. But if that didn't work, were they going to incarcerate her in the hospital? Were they going to take away her liberty because of their perceived obligations to this twenty-six-week-old fetus?"

Macklin was not indulging in fanciful, *Brave New World* speculation. By 1992, what seemed unthinkable had already occurred. Women had been held against their wills in hospitals, forced by court order to risk their lives by undergoing surgery doctors deemed necessary to save their unborn children. They were jailed for smoking, drinking, taking drugs, even having sex against doctor's orders while they were pregnant because of the potential harm to their fetuses. By the time Macklin listened to her phone message, more than 150 such cases had been documented by the American Civil Liberties Union, cases that established medical and legal precedent for imprisoning women when fetal well-being was presumed to be at stake.

While the antiabortion forces waved photos of bloody fetuses at clinic doors and the other side drafted armies of escorts and bought bullet-proof vests, a central question of the long and rancorous abortion debate had been quietly and unofficially settled. Though the high courts have repeatedly confirmed that the state is constitutionally bound to place the interests of a woman over those of a fetus, a kind of frontier justice has prevailed in the obstetrics wards and ERs across the country. There, medical professionals have allied themselves with law enforcement officials, declaring the fetus a person with full legal rights. But the ruling from this particular tribunal carried with it an unanticipated corollary: When the fetus has rights, a woman does not.

By becoming pregnant, a woman may be forced to give up what had previously been her legal due: her life, her health, her privacy, her bodily integrity, her ability to make decisions for herself and her children. Indeed, pregnancy even robs her of her right to be seen as a competent person or as a person at all. Instead, she is the "maternal environment," a "walking womb," nothing more than an organic incubator. Not coincidentally, it is this view of women as nothing more than fetal containers that has kept them invisible in clinical research on many of the diseases and treatments that critically affect their lives.

As the cases mounted, the stories sounded chillingly similar:

In 1986, nineteen-year-old Ayesha Madyun, in labor for two days with her first child, was admitted to Washington's D.C. General Hospital. When her labor didn't progress after eighteen hours, and her baby risked a fatal infection, her doctors decided a cesarean section was necessary. Madyun, who wanted to have natural childbirth, refused. But hospital officials would not take no for an answer. The hospital sought and won a court order to force Madyun to undergo the surgery, which carried a small but undeniable risk of putting *her* life in danger.

A forced cesarean section may have hastened the death of twenty-six-year-old Angela Carder, who was six months pregnant and dying of cancer when she entered George Washington University Hospital in Washington, D.C., in 1987. Not only was Carder denied chemotherapy because of the danger to her fetus, she was also forced to undergo the surgery, which her doctors had warned would kill her. At 26 weeks, her fetus had a slim chance of surviving, but hospital administrators sought the court order because they were afraid of incurring liability if her baby died. Carder, though heavily sedated, had told doctors at one point she didn't want the surgery. But she was not permitted to decide for herself. Nor were she or her family permitted to "speak" for her baby. Instead, the court appointed a legal guardian who argued that the operation didn't pose a serious risk to Carder because the young woman was going to die anyway. Carder did die two days after the operation. Her baby, a girl, died shortly after birth. A doctor later testified that the surgery had contributed to Carder's death.

In 1985, Pamela Rae Stewart, twenty-six, and eight months pregnant with her third child, was told by a physician at Grossmont Hospital in San Diego that her baby was in a breech position and she was suffering from a pregnancy complication called placenta previa, a condition in which the placenta nourishing her unborn baby was implanted so low it was covering her cervix. Any change in her cervix and Stewart risked hemorrhaging. She was given medication to delay labor and advice to stay off her feet and avoid sexual intercourse, which, in her condition, could induce premature labor. With two small children at home, Stewart was unable to stay in bed, and she admitted she did have sex with her husband the day her son was delivered by cesarean section. Born severely brain damaged, the baby died five weeks later. Doctors ordered drug screening of both

Stewart and her son, which turned up traces of amphetamines and marijuana. They reported Stewart to the local child protection agency, which in turn notified police. Stewart was later arrested and charged with her baby's death.

In 1989, Kimberly Hardy, twenty-three, was a single mother of two and a crack cocaine user when she entered Michigan's Muskegon General Hospital in labor with her third child. Her blood was tested for drugs—a hospital policy—and when her son, Areanis, was born small and sickly, he was held for observation and also screened. The hospital reported the positive results of the blood tests to local authorities, who charged Hardy with child abuse and, in a novel twist on a felony usually used to imprison drug dealers, with delivering drugs to a minor. In Hardy's case, the law was reinterpreted to cover those few minutes after her son's birth before her umbilical cord was clamped when her cocaine-tainted blood still pumped into his tiny body. That same year similar charges had been brought against a Florida woman, Jennifer Johnson, an admitted cocaine user, who gave birth to two healthy babies who tested positive for metabolites of the illegal drug.

In 1989, a South Carolina mother of one, Monica Young, eighteen and unmarried, was seven months pregnant when she checked into the Medical University of South Carolina in Charleston complaining of abdominal pain. Her drug test—again, a hospital policy—revealed evidence of cocaine use. Two days later, two policemen came to Young's hospital room and arrested her. She was led, in handcuffs, to a waiting patrol car. She was taken to a preliminary hearing in leg shackles and held for trial on an $80,000 bond. She spent six weeks of the last trimester of her pregnancy in the Charleston County jail still suffering from abdominal pains.

How did this happen? How did what is perhaps the most intimate relationship a woman has—with her fetus—suddenly become adversarial? In the 1980s, several dramatic and controversial political, social, technological, and legal changes coincided, forcing a new consideration of the fetus as a person with rights that sometimes clashed with the rights of the woman who carried it.

Medicine began to regard the fetus if not as a person, at least as a patient. New technology in the form of prenatal tests—ultrasonography, electronic fetal monitoring, amniocentesis, chorionic villus sampling—allowed physicians to peer into the womb, then enter it to diagnose and even perform surgery on the fetus as a patient separate from its mother. In fact, obstetrics texts now refer to the fetus as the physician's "second patient." (The extent to which medicine now views the fetus as a patient to which it has obligations is illustrated by a new text from a leading medical publisher. The book, from Saunders, is called *The Unborn Patient*.) Doctors who once treated the fetus indirectly by keeping its mother healthy now were expected to directly monitor the health of their second patient, even treat it if necessary, while it was still in the womb. Women who once went to obstetrics departments for their prenatal care and childbirth started noticing a new sign on the door: Maternal–Fetal Medicine.

New technology as well as a growing specialty called neonatology, which focuses on the newborn, gave physicians a new ability to keep preterm infants alive at earlier stages of gestation. This has pushed viability—and with it, the notion of fetal "personhood"—farther and farther back, into the second trimester of pregnancy, when many elective and genetic abortions take place. Though there remains no agreement on when personhood, indeed, when life begins, technology has complicated an issue already thickly tangled. For parents, ultrasound provides them with more than just a grainy prenatal Polaroid for their baby books. Increasingly, couples who learn through amniocentesis that their unborn child has a severe genetic defect must make a decision on whether to abort a fetus whose heart they have actually *seen* beating. Doctors themselves face a thorny moral and intellectual issue. Just how are they to view their second patient—the twenty-six-week-old fetus squirming on the ultrasound screen—who may be, with technology, old enough to survive outside the womb but who, under the law, can also be aborted if its mother's health or life is in danger?

Further complicating the matter, medical research, by identifying potential dangers to the developing embryo, has provided physicians with new ways to help keep this newly accessible fetus healthy and, thus, the obligation to do so. When they seek prenatal care, pregnant women are routinely counseled by their doctors to avoid drinking, smoking, drug use, and exposure to toxic chemicals and may even be handed diets and exercise advice to ensure that they deliver a healthy baby. In fact, during the 1980s, a new concept in obstetrical care was born. Prepregnancy medicine, popularized by the book *Before You Conceive,* written by Connecticut OB-GYN John R. Sussman, M.D., with B. Blake Levitt, stresses the need to prepare the body before it carries and nourishes a fetus and encourages women to see their obstetrician *before* they get pregnant. It also reinforces the woman's tremendous—and apparently sole—responsibility for the outcome of her pregnancy.

At the same time these advances were changing the view of the unborn in medicine, the fetus also appeared to be acquiring legal rights. Courts were allowing children to sue their parents for prenatal behaviors that resulted in harm. In Michigan, for example, a court allowed a suit against a woman because the tetracycline she took while pregnant had discolored her child's teeth. Parents were permitted to name their unborn children as heirs to estates or to file wrongful death or injury suits if a fetus was harmed or killed in an accident or criminal attack. Though most legal experts point out that most of those actions confirm parental, not fetal, rights and that being permitted to sue is not the same as winning a suit, the notion of the fetus as a legal entity began to gain footing.

All of these medical and legal quantum leaps were taking place in a social and political milieu marked by violent divisiveness over issues such as abortion—the ultimate clash of maternal and fetal rights—and, by association, women's rights. During the twelve-year Reagan–Bush era, reproductive freedom, once considered a social achievement, had become a political target. The Republicans had mounted up significant debts to the antiabortion movement and were paying off by pledging allegiance to the pro-life agenda. Many opponents feel that agenda has less to do with saving fetuses than it does with eroding the new economic and social gains of women, which are tied to reproductive freedom. With the debut in the sixties of the oral contraceptive and the 1973 Supreme Court decision in *Roe* v. *Wade,* motherhood became a choice rather than an inevitable consequence of sex. Women were free to explore—and, perhaps, conquer—the worlds that had traditionally been the sole provinces of men. To many opponents, the antiabortion movement and its political parent, the ultraconservative religious right, which blame feminism for everything from the soaring divorce rate to crime in the streets, are nothing more than a backlash against this breaching of male bastions.

Though a new, more woman-friendly administration took over

in 1993, it was clear that women had lost some ground in this turf war. Abortion and anything even remotely connected to it had become a political hot potato. For example, many believe that it was, in part, fear of reprisals from the antiabortion movement that cast a pall on contraceptive research in the United States. During the 1980s, the nation that pioneered modern contraception was virtually out of the business. The father of the Pill, chemist Carl Djerassi, Ph.D., told an audience at Planned Parenthood Conference in 1990 that "only Iran and the U.S. went backward in family planning in the 1980s."

During those dozen years, abortion also became a litmus test for seekers of high office. Supreme Court nominees, candidates for cabinet posts, and those hoping to fill top jobs at NIH were grilled on their views, presumably to assure that institutions and policy as permanently as possible reflected the conservative view that fetal life was more sacrosanct than any other. Bills authorizing fetal tissue research were marked for doom, and the French antiabortion pill RU-486 was placed under an import ban although both the fetal tissue research and the innovative pill had proven effective in treating debilitating and life-threatening illnesses such as Parkinson's disease, late-stage breast cancer, and brain tumors.

By some miracle, abortion stayed legal. But through their clinic door picketing and Washington politicking, the antiabortion forces were successful at limiting women's access to abortion services and, in some cases, contraception. For some women, getting an abortion in the 1990s may be almost as difficult as it was when they were done for cash by spurious doctors in back alleys. Many poor women lost their access to birth control with the closing of more than 1,000 public family-planning centers during the Reagan–Bush years. In thirty-seven states, they couldn't get abortions either because the Hyde Amendment prohibited use of federal funds to pay for them.

Even if she had the money to pay a private physician for an abortion, a pregnant woman might have some difficulty finding one willing—and able—to do it. Threats of violence—and real violence, in the case of the murder of Florida abortion doctor David Gunn—have kept doctors from performing abortions. Consequently some states have only a handful of clinics where abortion services are available. South Dakota has only one. It can be quite daunting—and, perhaps in some cases, prohibitive—for a pregnant woman to travel hundreds of miles to the clinic, then be forced to battle her way inside through a phalanx of protesters praying, waving photos of bloody abortuses, and screaming, "Baby killer!"

The new technology that had given them a second patient coupled with the fetus-first frenzy that was rapidly dominating politics seemed to have swung doctors into a petrified state of ambivalence. Among physicians, abortion is a procedure nearly everyone believes should be available but which few want to do. Despite surveys showing that most OB-GYNs, like most Americans, support a woman's right to an abortion, physicians regard those who perform abortions as "not quite their peer or equal," says Allan Rosenfield, M.D., an OB-GYN who is dean of Columbia University School of Public Health. Many physicians believe that if they do abortions, their practices will be ruined as local pro-life groups throw up permanent pickets, driving other patients away. Perhaps frightened by a similar prospect—only, in this case, of losing public and private funding—medical schools have done their part to make sure that the pool of doctors skilled in performing abortions is small. The procedure is not taught in about 30 percent of the schools and is only optional in most of the others. "To my knowledge," says Rosenfield, "it is the only procedure in which I as a doctor can decide if I will or will not be trained."

DOCTOR KNOWS BEST

Technological advances, legal rulings, and the conservative political climate of the eighties may explain why fetal rights have become such a powerful social and ethical issue. But they aren't sufficient to explain why, in the medical setting, the rights of the fetus have begun to take precedence over the rights of women. Why was Angela Carder's life of secondary concern to doctors than that of her twenty-six-week-old fetus? Why was Kimberly Hardy's drug addiction treated by her doctors as a criminal act committed against her child and not as an illness from which she was suffering? Why did doctors ignore the wishes of Ayesha Madyun, resorting to a court order to allow them to cut into her body without her consent to save her child's life at the possible sacrifice of her own? How did the second patient suddenly become *more* important than the first?

The head of Harvard Medical School's OB-GYN department, Kenneth J. Ryan, M.D., has suggested one answer: that the moral quandary being called maternal–fetal conflict might more accurately be described as physician–patient conflict. It was often not only fetal well-being doctors were championing when they sought court orders for surgery or sent police to their patient's hospital rooms. What they were often championing was their own belief that they knew best, a belief that is more familiarly called paternalism.

"Doctors get used to always making decisions and always having people listen to us," says Vicki Paterno, M.D., a California pediatrician and feminist with an interest in the issue of maternal–fetal rights. "We start believing that we know what's right and what's better. In fact, *not* becoming paternalistic is a very difficult thing to do."

With their ability to invade the womb, it is easy to understand how doctors might believe they know more about a fetus than its mother does. But though technology has given doctors a clear view of the fetus in the womb, it should not have obscured their view of the woman in whom it resides. Technology did not change the right of patients—all patients—to bodily integrity, self-determination, and autonomy.

In fact, the principle of patient autonomy—the patient's right to decide—is an accepted ethical tenet in medicine. It gives the patient who is deemed competent the right to do both the foolish—refuse lifesaving treatments—and the morally reprehensible—refuse to donate organs to save another's life. Medicine has not added a Catch-22 to this principle. Refusing lifesaving treatments does not prove incompetency nor does acting immorally. But exceptions to this principle have always been made for women. As bioethicist Albert R. Jonsen, Ph.D., wrote in 1988, doctors have long "distrusted and disdained" the preferences of their women patients. They were not alone. Respect for preferences of women "has not been a notable virtue of western culture," he pointed out. Nor, might he have added, has been respect for their competence. It was medicine, after all, that invented "that unique female disorder, 'the vagrant uterus,' from which we have the term 'hysteria,' " a handy diagnosis for the woman who dares challenge a doctor's opinion or defy doctor's orders.

When University of Illinois researcher Veronika E. B. Kolder, M.D., and her colleagues looked at twenty-one cases of court-ordered obstetrical intervention, including fifteen for cesarean sections, one of the things they wanted to know was how doctors determined maternal competence. What they found was that none of the women who had refused treatment recommended by their doctors had been found incompetent by a psychiatrist. In fact, only in three of twenty cases was a psychiatrist even called in for consultation. Yet in fifteen cases, doctors decided to override their apparently competent patients' refusal of a surgery whose death rate, though still fairly low, is two to four times higher than natural childbirth. It is likely that not one of those doctors would have sought legal recourse if the procedure their patients turned down had been heart bypass surgery or chemotherapy, even if they believed it would have saved their patients' lives.

What Kolder and her colleagues did find that they believed was significant was that most of these women were from that strata of society likely to face many kinds of discrimination. They were African-American, Asian, or Hispanic women being treated in teaching hospital clinics or who were on public assistance. Almost half were unmarried and about a quarter did not speak English as their primary language. It seemed "reasonable to assume," the researchers said, that had these been private patients in smaller hospitals, doctors would have been "less inclined and less able" to perform court-ordered procedures. Though they stopped just short of accusing the physicians of prejudice, the implication was clear: Being a woman, poor, a member of a minority group, non-English speaking, *and* disagreeing with your doctor is enough proof in some quarters that you are not competent enough to make decisions about yourself and your child.

The physicians and hospital administrators also apparently believed that for some of these women, incompetence was a familial disorder. In the few cases in which the hospital sought to remove fetal custody from the mother, in essence appointing a guardian for the unborn child, the courts never granted custody to next of kin. Instead, the unborn child's interests were given the proxy voice of a doctor, lawyer, or hospital administrator, whose concerns, not the least of which is liability, are likely to be quite different from those of a loved one.

It is also telling that in most of these cases, hospital administrators and lawyers were aware of the situation for a day or less before seeking court intervention, a rather short amount of time to settle an ethical issue that is still being hotly debated. Most of the judges arrived at their decisions with equal haste. In one case, a judge gave his approval over the telephone.

As part of her study, published in *The New England Journal of Medicine,* Kolder also surveyed the heads of maternal–fetal medicine fellowship programs across the country, and found astonishing support for what was going on in these hospitals. Almost half believed that a woman should be compelled by court order to undergo treatment to protect her unborn baby or be held against her will in the hospital so her compliance to her physician's advice could be assured. And more than a quarter believed that Big Brother should play Big Doctor. It was their opinion that the state should keep women who refuse medical treatment "under surveillance" while they are outside the hospital system.

With such widespread support from their peers, could these doctors have been so wrong? Their motives are certainly compelling. In many cases they were dealing with full-term babies, some just a surgical incision away from birth. When weighed against a woman's right to freedom and bodily integrity, don't the scales tip in favor of saving a life? The problem with that argument is that it makes at least two false assumptions: that women are not interested in saving the lives of their unborn children, which would make them morally incompetent, and that doctors are always right, which would make them infallible.

Even the American Academy of Obstetricians and Gynecologists, in a statement opposing compelled treatment, admitted that "medical knowledge and judgment has limitations and fallibility." In fact, Kolder found that in six of the cesarean cases she and her colleagues studied the doctors were absolutely wrong. Some of the women who fled the hospital went on to have normal vaginal deliveries of healthy babies. Only two of the babies had any significant problems and none died.

Unfortunately, the technology that has helped bring about healthier babies has also allowed doctors to play God, although not nearly so omnisciently. Most of the court orders in the Kolder study were sought because a doctor diagnosed fetal distress. This is an often misdiagnosed condition that may have contributed to the nation's high rate of medically unnecessary cesarean sections, according to a 1990 report by the Public Citizen Health Research Group. Between 1980 and 1985 there was a 225 percent increase in the reported incidence of fetal distress, which cannot be explained by any decline in maternal or fetal health. What did change in those years was an increase in the use of electronic fetal monitoring.

Many, if not most, women who deliver their babies in hospitals are strapped to a fetal monitor, which gives constant digital measurements of fetal heart rate. However, studies have shown that fetal monitoring can be grossly inaccurate. In one report, only 4 percent of the women who had abnormal fetal monitor readings actually had a fetus in true distress, as measured by abnormalities in fetal blood samples. Not only is it unreliable, the intervention it leads to most often is cesarean section, a major abdominal surgery.

"One study I looked at figured monitoring saves 1 out of 1,500 infants," says Vicki Paterno. "If C-section mortality is 1 out of 1,000, for every 2,000 babies you save, you sacrifice 240 women."

The question then becomes, Do doctors have the right to force women to potentially sacrifice their lives for their unborn children? "I would do it for my kid in a minute. Most women would," says Paterno. But, she adds, "we as doctors have no right to make other people do what we would do."

Nor, other experts point out, does a physician have the right to presume that a woman's decision to refuse treatment to save the life of her child is unreasonable and evidence of her incompetence. After all, her decision may be quite reasonable to her: She may have other children to care for, her religion or culture may forbid it, she may be afraid to take the risk, or she may think the doctor is wrong. The results of overriding that decision can be devastating, as the Kolder study illustrated. A Nigerian man who supported his wife's refusal of surgery and had been physically ejected from the hospital committed suicide a few months after her court-ordered cesarean section. His was the only death associated with any of the twenty-one cases of compelled treatment.

What becomes clear from all of these cases is that women are viewed as incapable of making competent decisions, apparently by virtue of their being pregnant. What may be worse, as in the case of Angela Carder, their lives are seen as less important than the life they carry within them. Though a woman may have a moral obligation to make sure her fetus is born healthy, "a moral obligation should not be transformed into a legal obligation," says Ruth Macklin. "We have to recognize that a pregnant woman is still an adult woman. The fact that she has a life growing within her should not change her rights to freedom and privacy."

The fact that she has a life growing in her should also not make her subject to standards—moral and legal—not applied to nonpregnant women or men or even to cadavers. The law is clear on that issue. Judges have consistently refused to order other adults to donate kidneys or bone marrow to relatives even when lives would be saved. As one Washington State judge who refused to issue a court order for a cesarean explained, "I would not have the right to require the woman to donate an organ to one of her other children, if that child were dying. . . . I cannot require her to undergo that major surgical procedure for this child."

Even cadaver organs cannot be harvested without the consent of the family. Says Vicki Paterno, "If a woman decides not to have a cesarean section because of the risk to herself, I think you've got a hell of a nerve to force her to do it when you can't even get an organ out of a cadaver. If you go ahead and do it, you're saying that a fetus has more rights than a woman does. You're saying a cadaver has more rights than a living, breathing woman does when she's pregnant."

THE PREGNANCY POLICE

Though the physicians in the Kolder study may have believed they were acting in the best interest of one of their patients—and doing "what was best" for the other—there is strong evidence that the damage such actions do to the doctor–patient relationship may in the long run do more harm than good to both patients. After all, at least six of the women defied the court orders and escaped from the hospital. In some cases, presumably, they went on to deliver *without* medical care.

Getting good prenatal care is perhaps the single most important factor in producing healthy babies and preventing maternal mortality. It is crucial when a pregnancy is compromised either by medical complications or the constellation of problems brought on by poverty, including poor maternal health, inadequate nutrition, smoking, and substance abuse. Yet, say some experts, it is the women most likely to have these kinds of problem pregnancies who are going to be driven away from prenatal care if they begin to regard physicians as "the pregnancy police."

In fact, as an article in *The Journal of the American Medical Association* warned, the relationship between pregnant women and their doctors is indeed becoming one "of adversaries, like police officer and criminal suspect." Doctor–patient privilege has been routinely disregarded for pregnant women if it was suspected their prenatal behaviors—using drugs or, as in the case of Pamela Stewart, not following doctor's orders—had harmed or could harm their unborn children. For example, instead of getting her help, the obstetrician and nurse to whom Florida's Jennifer Johnson confided her drug addiction called authorities.

Medical personnel certainly could not be faulted for their concern. They were seeing the results of a growing social tragedy: as many as 750,000 babies born every year exposed to illegal drugs in the womb, facing early death, personality disorders, learning disabilities, and other problems. Two in one thousand babies born to alcoholic mothers suffer from fetal alcohol syndrome, which is one of the top three causes of birth defects and mental retardation.

Sometimes, their frustration bordered on desperation. "Something must be done to protect these babies," said one doctor, whose hospital treats 120 drug-addicted infants per year. He unknowingly echoed the words of the South Carolina prosecutor who, working with the local university hospital, cast the dragnet that sent Monica Young, pregnant and in pain, to jail for her last trimester. "Someone's got to do something about protecting the babies," Charleston city solicitor Charles Condon told a *New York Times* reporter.

But the kinds of punitive measures doctors, in consort with local law enforcement officials, are using against women suggest that "protecting the babies" may be a smokescreen obscuring their real agenda. The truth is, like the women who were forced to undergo cesareans or who were tied to their hospital beds in the name of fetal rights, these women were being punished, as one attorney asserted, "for being bad mommies."

Clearly, sending a pregnant woman to prison is not acting in the best interest of her unborn child. Prison was not the best place for Monica Young to spend the last weeks of her pregnancy, nor is jail time good therapy for a drug habit. "Prisons aren't exactly drug-free environments," points out Sara Mandelbaum, an attorney with the Women's Rights Project of the American Civil Liberties Union. If the health of her baby was the primary concern, wouldn't her doctors have sought help for Kimberly Hardy, not turned her over to police?

The assumption on the part of the medical personnel and their legal allies seems to be that these women are intentionally causing their children harm, like the "morally incompetent" women who refused doctor-ordered bed rest and surgery in the Kolder study. "Yet I have yet to hear of a case where a woman chose to start using cocaine during her pregnancy," says Alison Marshall, a Washington, D.C., attorney who helped represent Kimberly Hardy and serves as general counsel for the National Association for Perinatal Addiction Research and Education. "These women were addicts before they became pregnant, so there is not the intent or volition to cause harm to that unborn child. I think people are rushing to judgment when they don't understand how difficult it is to break an addiction."

Sending a woman through the court system to get her drug treatment also suggests that help has to be thrust upon her because she's not responsible enough to seek it herself, something that is often not true. Many opponents of prenatal prosecutions point out that very little drug treatment for pregnant women exists. Jennifer Johnson and Kimberley Hardy had both previously attempted to get into drug treatment programs and were turned away. How can a woman be punished for not seeking help when there isn't any help? "A study done about a year ago found that on any one day in this country, there about 250,000 pregnant women who need drug treatment but there are only about 10,000 treatment slots for them," says Ira Chasnoff, M.D., a pediatrician and founder of the Chicago-based National Association for Perinatal Addiction Research and Education.

Many drug treatment programs refuse to treat pregnant women, largely because of liability fears. A study done by researcher Wendy Chavkin for the Rockefeller Foundation found that more than half of the seventy-eight New York City drug treatment centers surveyed refused to accept pregnant addicts and almost all refused pregnant crack addicts on Medicaid.

Chasnoff says drug treatment centers might be more willing to treat pregnant addicts if they hired obstetricians to take medical responsibility for the women. "However, the most common thing we hear from treatment programs is, 'We can't find an OB who's willing to provide care for our patients,' " he says. Doctors have the same liability fears as the treatment programs, and many still don't know how to identify a woman on drugs nor how to talk to her about her drug use, Chasnoff says.

But that may be only a partial solution. There's no guarantee that if a woman manages to find a treatment program that will take her, she'll come out drug-free. Research on how well drug treatment works has been done almost exclusively on men and most programs are tailored to male substance abusers, who rarely have child care responsibilities. A man also may not face the same kinds of economic barriers as a woman, who may get accepted into a program only to find she doesn't have the bus fare to get there.

There is increasing evidence that prenatal prosecutions aren't protecting the babies at all. Pregnant women are indeed staying away from their doctors' offices despite claims from prosecutors that their dwindling arrests mean the threat of jail terms has curtailed drug use among pregnant women. "Women don't get off drugs that quickly," says Alison Marshall. "When I see an overnight turnaround like that, it leads me to believe the women must be going somewhere else."

That thought alarms Ira Chasnoff. He cites studies that show that even if a woman continues to use heroin during her pregnancy but receives good prenatal care, she has a better chance of having a healthy baby. "It's not great," says Chasnoff, "but it will improve the outcome." But if pregnant addicts are suddenly disappearing from the medical system, as he believes they are, Chasnoff warns: "You now have children in double jeopardy—their mothers are using drugs *and* getting no prenatal care."

Chasnoff believes that doctors do need to intervene when there's a risk a baby will be born addicted. But, he says, that intervention should not entail a phone call to the local police. "It has been shown that if you can identify the drug-using woman during pregnancy, get her off drugs, get her into an adequate treatment program, you can prevent most of the complications these babies face at the time of delivery."

The problem is, says Chasnoff, physicians seem to be unable to identify women drug users without the aid of mandatory drug testing or, worse, their own stereotypes. In fact, in a study Chasnoff and his colleagues conducted, they found the only women doctors report are like those in the Kolder study—poor minority women— raising again the specter of discrimination. The 1990 study of pregnant women in Pinellas County, Florida, found that despite similar rates of substance abuse among pregnant white and African-American women, a black woman was ten times more likely to be reported to authorities than a white woman. One reason for that, says Chasnoff, is that drug use is far more visible among the poor and minorities because those are the populations that have been studied. "There is a population of white middle-class women who have the money to get good care for themselves and their children but who are using drugs during pregnancy. We don't know what happens to those children because those women have *never* been studied."

And one only has to look at what else has never been studied to complete the pattern of gender discrimination that underlies the entire issue. No one has examined the role men play in pregnancy outcomes, nor have any fathers been arrested in the nationwide crackdown on prenatal child abuse. Although the charges against Pamela Stewart were based in part on the fact that she disobeyed her doctor's dictum that she refrain from having sex, her husband, with whom she had sex, wasn't arrested.

In 1990, a pregnant Wyoming woman named Dianne Pfannensteil went to her local hospital for treatment after being beaten by her husband. However, it was Pfannensteil who was arrested and held on child abuse charges after hospital personnel told the local district attorney's office that she had been drinking. (Those charges were later dropped.) The hospital did not report Pfannensteil's husband, nor did law enforcement officials pursue him on child abuse charges though physical abuse has recently begun to be recognized as a serious threat to the lives and health of pregnant women and their fetuses. A group of Harvard researchers, writing in *The Journal of the American Medical Association* in 1992, pointed out that abuse of pregnant women is not rare, occurring in as many as 11 percent of all pregnancies seen in obstetric clinics. But the studies of the risks to mother and child are quite rare. The researchers were able to find only one small study that looked at the harm done to the fetus when its mother was physically or sexually abused.

Likewise, very little human research exists on the impact to the fetus of drugs taken by the male. There are a few that show that drugs can be measured in a man's sperm. In fact, a study done in 1991 at Washington University in St. Louis found that cocaine binds to sperm and could potentially be carried to an egg at fertilization, though the effects it could have on a fetus are unknown because the theory hasn't been tested in humans. There is also some evidence that alcohol abuse by a father may affect the birthweight of a new-born even if the mother is drug free. But those studies are few and far between.

"Not many agencies have wanted to address the issue of male drug use," says Chasnoff. "It's very difficult to find funding for those kinds of studies." The reason? "Everyone assumes it's the woman who is at fault. The responsibility for the child's outcome is a mater-nal issue. And," he adds, "it's because the people who make the laws and develop policy and do the research are mostly white middle-class males."

THE SLIPPERY SLOPE

Though most of the major medical organizations have taken a strong stand against both court-ordered obstetrical interventions and criminalization of prenatal behavior, the "pregnancy police" are still on patrol. As of 1993, there were still a handful of cases pend-ing—a case of court-ordered hospital detention in New York, pre-natal drug abuse cases in South Carolina, Pennsylvania, and Kentucky—despite a trend by the higher courts to rule in favor of the women. All of the drug convictions—including Jennifer John-son's—have been overturned. Oftentimes, the charges against the women were dropped, as they were in the cases of Pamela Stewart and Kimberley Hardy, because the child abuse or drug-dealing statutes under which they were arrested were never meant to apply to unborn children. The courts even gave some postmortem satis-faction to Angela Carder's family: In 1990, an appeals court ruled that even a pregnant woman who is terminally ill whose fetus may be viable cannot be forced to undergo a cesarean to save the fetus.

Sara Mandelbaum, who has represented three women in drug cases, says that in light of the outcomes, she is sometimes baffled why doctors and prosecutors continue to pursue them. Though there's popular support for them and there's always political hay to be made from antidrug and motherhood issues of any kind, they're a losing battle, both in the courtroom and the delivery room. In an effort to protect these babies, no one is really helped.

Maybe, she suggests, it's a case of mommy bashing, like the postfeminist headlines that told women they were "bad mommies" for going back to work too soon, leaving their babies with strangers, choosing careers over motherhood. "Women are always being told they're not good enough mothers," says Mandelbaum, "that they're not providing the ideal environment for babies. Women are being held responsible for more and more things that are not in their control."

What frightens many people, like Sara Mandelbaum, are the so-called slippery slope arguments: that once women are held legally responsible for what happens to their unborn children, once doctor's orders take the force of law, pregnant women may find themselves subject to prosecution for anything from smoking to lingering in a room where there are smokers. Might the day come when a woman is required by law to quit her job because her obstetrician insists on it to save the life of her unborn child or to face jail because the drink she took before she knew she was pregnant may have led to a birth defect?

There was a time, before the Pamela Stewart case, when Laurie Zelon would have considered such notions far-fetched. But the California attorney, whose practice is confined to business litigation, has since changed her mind. Once she began reading about the Stewart case, she said, she became angry and called her friend, pediatrician Vicki Paterno. The two women began compiling a file of medical studies and legal rulings on court-ordered obstetrical interventions and prenatal prosecutions. "I had seen some trends that alarmed me as a woman," said Zelon, "and I just wanted to keep track of things."

But as the cases began to multiply and her file expanded, she began combing newspapers and journals with another goal in mind: to keep track of what *might* happen. "My feeling is that first you have an idea—that the fetus has rights and by the act of becoming pregnant a woman gives up her rights and is entitled to be treated as a vessel—and then you find the justification so you can implement the idea. That's why I clipped this article." She rustled through the file on her desk. "It was in *The New York Times* on January 31, 1992, a front page article headlined, 'Studies Find a Family Link to Criminality.' What struck me was this quote." She read: " 'A criminal is made when the mother drinks and smokes or uses drugs and causes her baby to grow up with a learning disorder.' I read that and said, 'I have to keep this.' That's scary to me," said Zelon. "That's really scary to me."

12
SEX IN
THE OFFICE
The Unhealthy Touch

We show a videotape to medical boards of a dentist trying to copulate in a woman's mouth. It helps them get over their denial that doctors really can do awful things to patients.

—*Gary Schoener*

Beth Morgan (not her real name), a high school teacher from New England, was still reeling from a brief physically abusive relationship when her fiancé suggested that she see a psychiatrist to help her deal with the emotional toll the experience had taken. He highly recommended a close friend of his, a psychiatrist whom he had been seeing professionally as well. Beth saw the doctor every week and continued therapy after her marriage. At the end of a particularly emotional session, where she had spent most of the hour crying, her doctor began to hug her. What seemed at first to be innocent comforting soon became something else entirely. Beth's doctor proceeded to have sexual intercourse with her. "I left that day stunned and ashamed," she recalls. "I didn't know what to do, where to go with it. I was in the first year of my marriage, and I had just had sex with this doctor, the person who also happened to be my husband's friend and someone we both trusted completely."

Beth continued going back for her weekly sessions, thinking that surely it wouldn't happen again, but it did. She felt guilty and torn but powerless to say no. "It would have been like saying no to my father or my God," she explains. Finally, after a few more months, she got up the courage to terminate treatment, much to her doctor's disapproval. "He said I was copping out on therapy, that I wouldn't benefit from the whole experience if I didn't finish," says Beth. "But I refused to go back." She kept the secret buried inside, never telling anyone, not even her husband or her mother. Meanwhile, she and her husband continued their social relationship with the psychiatrist and his wife. The strain was unbearable, and Beth turned to alcohol for relief. After eight years of silence and bouts of alcohol abuse, she finally told her story to a fellow Alcoholics Anonymous member whom she trusted. Her road to recovery had begun.

Sadly, Beth Morgan's experience is not an isolated one. Indeed, these violations of trust and expectation happen far more often than most people imagine. Studies of psychiatrists, OB-GYNs, surgeons, internists, and family physicians conducted in the United States and Canada indicate that sexual or erotic contact of doctors with patients occurs with about 5 to 13 percent of practitioners, regardless of specialty. But even that number may seriously underestimate the actual incidence of sexual abuse of patients by doctors because surveys typically depend on the self-reporting of doctors, who may be unlikely to acknowledge unethical behavior, even anonymously. Besides, these henhouse-reports-from-the-foxes are rarely augmented by word from the chickens because the victims seldom come forward—only one in ten women do, by some estimates.

Sexual misconduct by doctors is yet another form of gender-based victimization: The physicians are almost always men, the abused patients almost always women. And not just young and pretty women, as popular wisdom has dictated. Says Gary Schoener, director of the Walk-In Counseling Center in Minneapolis, which treats both victims of physician abuse and their abusers, "We've seen more victims than anyone—thousands—and there is absolutely no pattern whatsoever. We have seen sexually abused patients that range in age from three to seventy-eight. They come in all body sizes, all shapes and all races."

What makes this kind of sexual abuse even more disturbing is that the perpetrators, often respected doctors in the community, usually go unpunished and unstopped because many abusers don't think what they're doing is wrong—or wrong enough—and too few disciplinary boards give more than short suspensions from practice for these ethical and often criminal violations. More often than not, they are protected by their colleagues and their professional institutions because they are part of a conspiratorial old boys' network, which still describes much of the profession.

Victims who decide to press charges against their physicians find they are often discredited by these peer review boards and their stories rejected, almost out of hand. Part of the problem is that many physicians hold the same misperceptions about sexual abuse as the general public. Doctors will proclaim with conviction that the abuse was probably the victim's fault rather than understanding that the power differential in the doctor–patient relationship leaves them with the responsibility to halt any contact. Or that women and children lie about sexual abuse instead of recognizing that abuse is vastly underreported and that false reports are extremely rare. Or that if the patient consented, then it's not considered sexual abuse. Or that it probably wasn't harmful anyway because physical force and violence weren't used. Or that the so-called sexual abuse was in actuality a misunderstanding by the patient about the nature of a procedure being done.

With false beliefs rampant, the impact on the victims' mental and physical health is likely to be trivialized by those who render medical and ethical justice. Though there are governing bodies that profess to enforce the ethics of the doctor–patient relationship, the fact is that most traditional systems such as medical societies and disciplinary boards are stacked in favor of the abusers, while the victims are left with their emotional lives in ruin.

Though the medical community would like to downplay the extent of the damage to the victims of this sexual misconduct, that has become increasingly difficult as more researchers have undertaken the task of documenting this unethical behavior and its aftermath. The College of Physicians and Surgeons of Ontario, Canada, for example, commissioned an independent task force to examine the problem in depth. Its groundbreaking report made headlines throughout Canada and caught the attention of the U.S. medical community as well. What the task force uncovered was staggering in its magnitude, not just in the pain and suffering that the sexual violation had caused the victims, but also in the victims' subsequent lack of trust for doctors, in particular, and the medical system as a whole.

The sentiments from women who had the courage to reach out to the task force echoed common themes. Like Beth Morgan, all felt ashamed, betrayed, and afraid. They suffered from nightmares, guilt, humiliation, and fear or distrust of men. They had feelings of rage and anger. They felt "dirty." Some had thoughts of suicide; a few actually attempted it. Many experienced physical symptoms as well—headaches, blurred vision, stomach problems, vaginal and anal pain, nausea, and vomiting. Perhaps most disturbing was the fact that like Morgan, many of the victims said that they had never told anyone about the abuse before because they were convinced that their accounts would not be believed or that they would be blamed for allowing it to happen. Those fears were particularly strong for people who had a history of psychiatric illness, and for good reason. When they had made previous attempts to come forward, their past medical histories were indeed used against them and their complaints dismissed.

ETHICS ASIDE

Make no mistake: Sexual contact between doctor and patient is always wrong. The AMA states explicitly that sexual contact or sexual relations between physicians and patients is unethical. It's even incorporated into the Hippocratic oath: ". . . I will come for the benefit of the sick, remaining free of all intentional injustice, of all mischief and in particular of sexual relations with both female and male persons. . . ."

And the Canadian task force members used even stronger language to express their view on this subject. They stated emphatically that "there are NO circumstances—NONE—in which sexual activity between a physician and a patient is acceptable. Sexual activity between a patient and a doctor ALWAYS represents sexual abuse, regardless of what rationalization or belief system the doctor chooses to use to excuse it. Doctors always need to recognize that they have the power and status, and that there may be times when a patient will test the boundaries between them. It is ALWAYS the doctor's responsibility to know what is appropriate and never to cross the line into sexual activity."

Beth Morgan says that neither she nor her husband were aware of these so-called boundary issues at the time she started treatment. So the fact that her husband was seeing his psychiatrist-friend on a professional level never raised any red flags for either of them. "It wasn't until much later that I learned that there should be no friendships outside the therapy hour," she says.

Oaths and strong language aside, doctors do step across that line. When they do, it can take any number of forms from what's known as sneaky touch—the doctor's erect penis bumps into a patient's thigh during an examination, for example—to outright rape and everything in between. And they almost always get away with it because unsuspecting women, who place so much trust in their doctors, rarely say no to even peculiar requests. An optometrist, for example, had all his women patients strip to the waist even though they were there for an eye exam. He simply told them that he needed to check for scoliosis (curvature of the spine) because bad posture can sometimes be at the root of vision problems. Not one of them refused. They didn't want to believe that their doctor could betray and exploit them for his own sexual gratification.

Inappropriate behavior can also range from a putative romance—a woman may actually feel attracted to her doctor and be flattered by the sexual advances at first—to sex represented fraudulently as treatment, as it was in Morgan's case. An offending doctor who represents sex as therapeutic may tell his patient that it's going to enhance her self-esteem, provide a beneficial emotional experience, or shorten the grief she's experiencing following a significant loss, says patient abuse expert Nanette Gartrell, M.D., of the University of California, San Francisco, School of Medicine. Beth Morgan's doctor told her that he loved her, that what they were doing was beautiful, and that it would help her grow. Apparently, he was also helping several other women patients "grow" at the same time, she discovered years later.

Another woman told the Canadian task force about a psychiatrist she and her husband had seen together because of sexual difficulties. When he indicated that he wanted to see each of them for individual therapy, she had no reason to be suspicious. Yet at her first session he had sexual intercourse with her, saying that it would be good for her. She said it felt like making love to her father and is still shattered by the experience.

A doctor's office is also no place for seduction or the appearance of it. It's just as out of line for doctors to flirt, make sexual comments or sexual jokes, or stare at a patient's breasts or genitals as it is for them to touch a patient in a sexual manner. Lap sitting, kissing, and sexualized hugs don't belong in the doctor's office, either.

The doctors who engage in repeated sexual malpractice are not like other doctors any more than rapists or wife batterers are like normal men. Those who inflict the most damage are often sociopaths masquerading as concerned physicians with their patients' best interests at heart. These sex abusers go after whatever they want, exploit their victims shamelessly, lie glibly about it or rationalize it, and suffer no guilt feelings whatsoever from their actions.

"That is exactly what a rapist does," says psychiatrist John Fleming, M.D., an expert on sexual abuse. "They go for their own gratification. They act out their own hostility or their own need for feeling a certain physical pleasure regardless of what the other person wants. It's a very scheming, manipulative, dangerous thing to do to another person."

Abusive doctors refuse to see it that way. Studies show that they believe their actions could be beneficial to the patient, although most acknowledge that the contact is for their own sexual pleasure or emotional gratification. These violators never bother to consider the potential harm to their patient-victims nor the unethical nature of their actions. They think that their patients feel good about the sexual contact even though that's completely contrary to what patients report when they are asked. One study, for example, found that nine out of ten patient-victims suffer negative reactions, including depression, sexual dysfunction, panic attacks, even PTSD. Beth Morgan says that she found it almost impossible to have sex with her husband after having a relationship with her psychiatrist. She suffered from depression and stress that was so intense that patches of her hair fell out.

Offenders show a callous disregard for their patients and think that there is an exaggerated concern for their welfare. More often, these doctors worry about the dangers that they have exposed themselves to—professionally and personally—than any injury they may have inflicted upon their victims. Morgan's psychiatrist, for example, begged her not to tell anyone of their past sexual encounters, and she didn't for many years. It didn't seem to concern him that his patient's physical and emotional health was steadily deteriorating before his eyes.

Another doctor who had sex with a patient during his residency says that he finds it hard to believe that he did what he did. But he fretted about the cost to his marriage and the threat to his career, not about the effect of the sexual relationship on his patient, a frequently and severely abused incest victim. "Her life was terribly chaotic to begin with, with multiple moves, suicide attempts, substance abuse, etc.," he says. Did he believe that one more trauma couldn't make it any worse?

DOCUMENTING THE FORBIDDEN

Uncovering the extent of patient abuse has been a mission fraught with stumbling blocks tossed out by those who have something to hide and those who want to protect their own. Indeed, until a decade ago, virtually no studies or surveys had even been conducted on the subject. It's not that doctors aren't aware that the problem exists among their colleagues. It's just that they'd rather keep these skeletons locked in their professional closets even at the expense of the patients who are bound to be future victims. How vehemently they opposed letting the skeletons out became evident when a group of Harvard University researchers, headed by Nannette Gartrell, decided that it was time to get the issue of sexual abuse of patients out in the open to examine it, to prevent it, to eliminate it, to educate colleagues and consumers about it, and to protect patients from it.

They chose to survey psychiatrists, because sexual misconduct by these specialists is believed to be particularly devastating to their vulnerable victims. Trust is paramount; after all, the patient reveals her most private thoughts to this person and spends more hours on a one-to-one basis with him or her than perhaps with any other kind of doctor. By surveying thousands of psychiatrists, they intended to document the prevalence of these doctor–patient sexual violations and the attitudes of those who engaged in it despite its unethical (and, in some states, criminal) nature. The researchers hoped the survey would be used to develop ethics curricula for residency training and continuing education programs. And perhaps more importantly, they expected the data to be utilized to establish more effective guidelines for managing reported cases of sexual abuse.

Perhaps they were naive, but Gartrell's group, all women, had no inkling when they first proposed the survey idea to the American Psychiatric Association (APA), that the original plan would be subjected to unreasonable scrutiny and petty objections. Nor did they suspect that some four years would elapse before they saw any of the survey results in print. At first, various committees within the APA acknowledged openly that sexual misconduct was a severe problem and that the survey was indeed a timely and worthwhile project. But those encouraging statements were, as it turned out, nothing more than lip service. The Ethics Committee, for example, declined to sponsor the survey and the Council on National Affairs declared there were insufficient funds to support it, although it had been suggested at first that funding would not be a problem.

Despite this financial setback, a questionnaire was developed anyway at the authors' own expense. Criticism of the survey by the APA followed. Revisions ensued. Finally, the true nature of the APA's concerns started to surface: that the survey would damage the public image of psychiatry. Privately, it was another matter entirely. "There were a substantial number of powerful, prominent male psychiatrists who were sexually involved with their patients, and that created an internal, unspoken standard that it was acceptable behavior in some circles," says Gartrell. "The APA viewed me as the person who was trying to bring a bad name to the profession rather than recognizing that it was the perpetrators of this unethical conduct who were responsible for that," says Gartrell, who is the former chairperson of the APA's committee on women. "It was a case of blaming the messenger."

The APA continued to raise more questions about the survey. How would the data be used? Shouldn't the extent of sexual misconduct among other specialties be emphasized as well? Couldn't the information on prevalence be given a positive spin? (Meaning, why not point out the percentage of psychiatrists who have never participated in this unethical conduct instead of the percentage who do?) The APA also indicated that in exchange for sponsoring the project it might want exclusive possession of the data. In other words, for giving the researchers their stamp of approval, the APA could literally take the analyzed information, stuff it in a drawer, and forget about it forever.

Rather than submit to the APA's unreasonable demands, Gartrell and her colleagues began a national fund-raising campaign and in six months collected enough money from individual psychiatrists—mostly women—to carry out the survey regardless of APA approval, which, it turned out, they never did get. Even though the APA decided that the questionnaire was indeed scientifically sound, it voted not to use it because "it was not considered a cost-effective means of educating the membership about psychiatrist–patient sexual abuse." The APA never did see how useful the questionnaire could be as an educational device, says Gartrell. About three years after their quest began, the researchers proceeded to carry out the project independently, surveying a representative sample of APA members. They subsequently made the data available to the APA and any other professionals who wanted to use it to devise educational programs.

PROTECTING THEIR OWN

The APA's foot-dragging tactics and its ultimate refusal to support the survey of sexual abuse of patients by psychiatrists can only be viewed as tacit approval of this unethical conduct whether that's what the organization intended or not. It's hard to deny its intent, in fact, when that same protectionism filters down to individual psychiatrists as well, who will rarely, if ever, expose their unethical colleagues, no matter what potential harm may befall their future patients. Indeed, when asked in one survey if they would report a known offender to a professional association or legal authority, not one psychiatrist who admitted to being a repeat offender himself said he would turn in a colleague. And only *8 percent* of those who had never violated a patient said they would turn in another colleague. It's not that these questions were asked in the abstract. More than half the psychiatrists surveyed knew of a colleague who had sexually violated patients.

But perhaps the real tragedy uncovered by this survey is that a woman who is looking for counseling following abuse by a previous doctor is very likely to find herself on the couch of a doctor who has been and may still be engaged in the same sexual violation that she is trying to escape. Researchers found that every single doctor who admitted to being a repeat offender had treated patients who were sexually involved with previous therapists. What's happening, it seems, is that offending doctors are actually referring patients they have abused to colleagues whom they know to be sympathetic to this unethical behavior.

In spite of their dismal record of turning in known violators, however, the majority of psychiatrists who never abuse patients favor mandatory reporting of doctors who do. Not so the repeat offenders. Surveys show that only 15 percent of them are in favor of it. One sixty-one-year-old male APA member who favored mandatory reporting was outraged. "Sexual contact with a patient is tantamount to rape," he said, "and I hope the APA will view it as criminal behavior that belongs in the courts for their jurisdiction."

The fact is, among this professional group, there isn't enough outrage to get the job done. When questioned, doctors don't really believe that offenders will be effectively disciplined even if reported to ethics committees and licensing boards. They have good reason to be skeptical. Between 1972 and 1983, for example, only 23 percent of the 382 psychiatrists charged with ethical violations were found guilty by APA ethics committees. The Canadian task force also found evidence of a weak disciplinary system. Penalties imposed by the discipline committee were meager and reflected a profound underappreciation of the harm done to victims. Decisions to reinstate doctors who had been found guilty of sexual abuse were based, in every case, on insufficient evidence that their future patients would be safe from sexual violations. But they weren't. Indeed, many women came forward to report abuses from doctors who had been deemed rehabilitated and then promptly proceeded to abuse again as soon as they were reinstated.

The view that physicians "look after their own" has not been lost on these victims. They feel powerless against ethics committees made up of medical colleagues (predominantly male) who find it far easier to identify with the accused than with the victim. Indeed, fear and skepticism have caused many more to hold their tongues than to speak out.

When women do decide to brave this hostile environment and file a complaint, it is often the last they hear about it, reinforcing their suspicions of lopsided justice. In one study, for example, 55 percent of patients who filed complaints reported that nothing happened. Some experts suspect a sinister reason for the ease with which offenders avoid discipline and punishment. They think it's conceivable that psychiatrists who are offenders themselves, and therefore sympathetic to their accused colleagues, may be serving on ethics committees.

Women who actually appear before an ethics committee face a daunting experience, one reminiscent of rape trials from a decade or two ago, where the victim was as much on trial as her attacker. Those who complained to the College of Physicians and Surgeons of Ontario, for example, described the process as demeaning, traumatizing, and abusive—more abusive than the original sexual abuse. The victims found that the college didn't believe their stories, trivialized the impact of the abuse, or suggested that the victims were somehow responsible. Weeks or months would elapse without word of progress in the case. The abused women were not always permitted to attend the hearings nor hear the doctors' testimonies. But they had to endure the humiliation of hearing the intimate details of their abuse and their sexual and psychiatric histories revealed and then listen to that information used to discredit them.

Shabby treatment of these patient-victims appears to be standard operating procedure no matter who they are. Even when the accusations come from a fellow psychiatrist, a woman is not spared the wrath of the governing bodies. Gartrell says that one thirty-four-year-old woman, an APA member, wrote to tell of her personal experiences when she complained that her own psychiatrist had sexually abused her. The woman said that it took almost four years for the matter to be resolved. During that time, she was pressured by her residency training director to drop her complaint even after the ethics committee found her former therapist guilty. "I would never refer a patient of mine to the ethics committee," she said, "because the process was so traumatic to me and because ultimately I was not believed or the abuse was seen as insignificant, worthy only of a one-year suspension. I just keep wondering who the ethics committee believes if not a fellow psychiatrist in good standing at a good residency."

An abused patient who decides to bring suit against her physician-abuser will also run up against a system that is designed to protect its own. Psychiatrists who are members of the APA, for example, are covered for personal liability by an insurance company in which the organization owns a 25 percent share. Clearly, it is in the APA's best interest to discourage large payouts to victim survivors who bring suits against sexually abusive psychiatrists. In one highly publicized case, which was featured on PBS's "Frontline," the APA defended an abuser, a psychiatrist who freely acknowledged his own guilt. Yet this known offender received all the resources of the APA, who used defense tactics that involved attacking and libeling the psychiatrist who subsequently treated the victim, says Gartrell, one psychiatrist who spoke out against and subsequently resigned from the APA in protest over the case.

"It was unconscionable," Gartrell says. The whole institutional structure was concerned that if that claim got paid, there would be many more made along the same lines. "I think it was an attempt to frighten us (the women psychiatrists who treat these previously abused women) from helping our victim survivors," she says. "And it effectively did just that."

THE MYTH OF REHABILITATION

Can a physician who has committed sexual offenses against patients be rehabilitated enough to return to practice and pose no danger to other patients? Realistically, not in most cases, say the experts who treat these men. Indeed, those who have been treated for cancer have a higher cure rate than those who have been treated for sex offenses. They may be considered at low risk after effectively completing a rehab program, but they can never be labeled as cured. It's not even possible to know for sure who the best candidates for successful treatment are, because there is no literature that specifically looks at the effectiveness of rehabilitation programs, a situation that leaves future patients highly vulnerable to attacks from supposedly rehabilitated doctors.

Experience at the Walk-In Counseling Center in Minneapolis, however, has shed some light on this murky situation. They have been able to identify certain one-time offenders who have a good probability of successful rehabilitation. A doctor, for example, may be guilty of nothing more than using poor judgment, perhaps because of some personal tragedy that has befallen him—his wife left him or died. He knows what he's done is inappropriate; in fact, he may have even requested treatment on his own, having immediate regrets about his transgression. It's purely situational, and there's no pattern to it.

"Of course, there's always the danger that you've caught a potential sociopath or compulsive sex offender on his first violation," says Gary Schoener, who evaluates offenders for state licensing boards. The track record for treating these highly pathological conditions is very poor. People who can't control their sexual impulses will typically deny everything and lie about it until they are caught, sometimes red-handed. Then they'll suddenly admit their offenses while still trying to minimize what they've done. Sociopaths have a serious personality disorder and feel no guilt at all for their transgressions. They're the hardest to nail down because they're so good at lying. "I've never spotted one immediately," admits Schoener. "They've had to slip up in some way—pleading guilty to the wrong case, for example. Once they're caught, they'll playact 'healthy-professional-who-had-a-lapse-in-judgment.' Their goal is to manipulate out of responsibility, and they often succeed. If they can't convince the authorities of their innocence, however, then they go on the attack, using every nuance of the law and every type of defense to get off."

Though these kinds of offenders are the fewest in number, they account for the greatest number of victims. "We've had doctors who eventually admitted sexually violating thirty or forty women," says Schoener. Beth Morgan's psychiatrist had sexually abused other women patients before, during, and after his violations of her, she learned later at his hearing.

The Canadian task force also looked closely at the potential for successful rehabilitation, and they are just as pessimistic. After reviewing all the files where a doctor had been allowed to practice again, the task force realized that in every case, the decision to reinstate was based on insufficient evidence that these guilty doctors wouldn't abuse again. In fact, the likelihood is high that they will. What little evidence there is indicates that as many as 60 percent of treated abusers relapse. And, indeed, the task force met with many victims who had been abused by doctors who had previously been found guilty and subsequently reinstated.

If the experts have a hard time figuring out who is guilty in the first place and who is most likely to relapse even if treated, it's virtually impossible for an individual woman seeking a therapist, or any doctor for that matter, to know that the one she chooses hasn't violated patients in the past. In fact, she hasn't much more to go on than faith or luck, because this is one area of a doctor's background that has remained off limits to inquiring patients. For women who have been the victims of abusive doctors, it often means that they forgo medical care until and if their trust in the system can be restored. "Every woman absolutely has the right to know if the physician she has decided to see has ever been treated for sexually abusing his patients," says Gartrell. "But I don't know how she'll get that information. Right now there is no way to find that out."

Patients can find out, however, if a doctor has had his license revoked and, in some cases, if he's been subject to board discipline. But there are strict limitations to that information, too. The board, for example, cannot reveal if complaints have been made, only of adjudicated findings. If many accusations have been filed, it can take years before a verdict is handed down. Meanwhile, the accused doctor can continue to practice, and there's no way for his unsuspecting patients to know that he's under investigation. Though the board can tell women if a doctor has been disciplined and then reinstated—that's public record—women may not be able to find this out until *after* the discipline has been meted out, not before or during the hearings. Nor can women find out what infraction the doctor has committed. And there's also no way of knowing what criteria were used to determine whether a doctor should be reinstated.

Once a doctor's license has been revoked, he cannot practice medicine. So, for example, family physicians, or OB-GYNs, or surgeons are literally out of business until and if they are reinstated by their state licensing boards. But for psychiatrists, there's a serious glitch that leaves potential patients unprotected. The sad fact is that though a guilty psychiatrist can be prohibited from ever practicing medicine again as a psychiatrist, this same doctor can still hang out his shingle *anywhere he wants* as long as he calls himself something else, like a psychotherapist, and doesn't prescribe drugs.

The APA has taken an important step to curtail such activity, however, by requiring that the names of psychiatrists expelled for ethics violations be published in *Psychiatric News*, the trade paper of their organization. That lets colleagues know the score but still does little to protect patients. And, in fact, some known sexual violators are out there repeating their offenses under the guise of psychotherapists. Beth Morgan's psychiatrist is one of them. Although his license was revoked thanks to testimony by her and a number of other women he had abused, this doctor is still seeing both male and female patients. He simply relocated hundreds of miles away and now identifies himself as a psychotherapist.

In another attempt to help protect patients, several states have made sexual contact with a patient a criminal rather than just an ethical offense. "New Hampshire, Michigan, Colorado, and Wyoming have statutes about sex within a medical exam," says Schoener. "And there are nine states that have statutes about sex during a psychotherapist meeting—Wisconsin, Minnesota, North Dakota, Colorado, California, Maine, Florida, Iowa, and Georgia. That includes anyone who counsels you, by the way, even if it's your general practitioner or a cancer surgeon."

Unfortunately, all the laws in the world are not going to protect patients from male doctors whose socialization has somehow allowed the violation of women to become an acceptable practice. By addressing this issue in medical schools, however, some experts are hoping to reach at least a few of these future doctors with their message. "Apparently, by the time they're seniors in medical school, it's already too late to instill sensitivity to this issue," claims Gartrell, who teaches an ethics course to future doctors. "Male medical students are men after all. They grow up in this culture that socializes them to be predators. By the time I get to teach them, they've heard much subtle and not so subtle banter implying that it's okay to go after their patients, that it's routine. Their older teachers and residents make comments like, 'Well, wouldn't you like to go out with her.' Or, 'Hey, I bet you're signing her up to take that breast lump out because you really want to feel her breasts.' How can you overcome such ingrained sexism?"

When it is explained to them that sexual contact with patients is unethical and against AMA policy, these students complain that their access to sexual contact is being restricted and then proceed to find the loopholes in that policy. "By this time the women students are so enraged that they can hardly speak," says Gartrell. "They seem to easily grasp the principles involved, probably because they've been on the receiving end of sexual harassment more than once during their training."

Teaching ethics courses to first- or second-year medical students, however, seems to have a much more powerful impact on them. "Maybe I've just caught them before they've had a chance to be invaded by the insensitivity that medical education often breeds," says Gartrell. "But these young men seem better able to understand that their socialization as doctors over the next few years does not include the option to sexually violate their patients."

Part Three

Small Victories

13
THE
VISIBLE
WOMAN

"June 18, 1990, is a big day to remember," said Florence Hasel-tine, pouring a glass of orange juice over her Grape Nuts in the quiet dining room of Washington D.C.'s exclusive—and once men-only—Cosmos Club.

For women's health advocates like Haseltine, June 18, 1990, is a date of great historical significance. It marks the day that women became visible, when an issue that had previously been the province of feminist "troublemakers," one that everyone felt safe turning a blind eye to, suddenly became a national scandal.

Within two weeks of that date, nearly every major newspaper and news magazine in the country had written about the all-male aspirin study, the all-male aging study, the all-male uterine cancer study, and the all-male laboratory rats. Soon, everyone was reading about the studies revealing that women were discriminated against in the treatment of heart disease and about the lack of funding for breast cancer, the disease that kills more women each year than the better-funded AIDS. Perhaps most important, those stories were getting headlines in the journals doctors read. The coverage in the weekly *Journal of the American Medical Association* and in *Science* was even more extensive and hard-hitting than in the lay press, which often went for sound bite over substance. "Within two weeks," said Florence Haseltine, a smile playing at her lips, "we took women's health from a luxury item to an entitlement."

Haseltine regards this as a personal triumph. The director of NIH's Center for Population Studies, Haseltine, one of the few women physicians in a command role at the health agency, stopped just short of whistle-blowing to bring women's health research into the public spotlight. Though not the first woman physician to attempt this, she has been the most successful.

Through her medical career, which took her to Harvard and Yale, Haseltine claims she's gotten used to being "the only one of something." But she was never really happy about being only one of three gynecologists on the NIH payroll—and outnumbered by the veterinarians. But she saw the lack of an OB-GYN program at the agency as symptomatic of a more serious and fundamental ill: the relegation of women's health to second-class status, where it got little attention and money. She turned to some of her high-placed friends for advice. Out of those meetings—held often at the Cosmos Club because she took perverse glee in the symbolism—Haseltine founded the Society for the Advancement of Women's Health Research (SAWHR), patterning its title and logo after the American Association for the Advancement of Science "because it is recognized by all scientists as solid and mature." She knew SAWHR was going to have to command respect from scientists; it was about to peel back the veneer of scientific objectivity to reveal instead "science corrupted" by strong and unacknowledged biases. "But I had to get somebody to help me," she said. "It was clear I could not lobby on the Hill in the job I have." So she placed SAWHR in the hands of one of the leading women's health lobbying firms inside the Beltway, Bass and Howes, run by two women, Marie Bass and Joanne Howes, with strong liberal political connections. "I had to call everybody I knew and pull in all my chips to raise the money to pay them," Haseltine admitted. "But I was willing to spend every cent of my mother's inheritance on this thing."

SAWHR has a working board that includes several other women scientists from NIH, the associate director for government relations for the American College of Obstetricians and Gynecologists, the former publisher of *Scientific American,* doctors, nurses, and philanthropist Nancy S. Vreeland. In 1991, SAWHR tapped into the resources—financial and otherwise—of the pharmaceutical industry, creating a Corporate Advisory Council, which most of the major drug companies joined. A number of major medical associations, including all the OB-GYN groups, and several private foundations have all signed on to provide financial and moral support. "I hit up every rich male I knew who had a daughter who was a gynecologist," confessed Haseltine with a grin. "But many of these societies—we didn't even ask them for money. They just sent it."

Walking the tenuous line between diplomat and nose thumber, Haseltine, as a government employee, had to take personal leave to carry the issue to the Hill, including "taking my little slide projector" to the bipartisan Congressional Caucus on Women's Issues "to show them how NIH worked." She knew that women's health needed to become a political issue. It needed friends in high places, national headlines, and more money. It got all three.

It was through the political machinations of the caucus, cochaired by Patricia Schroeder and Olympia Snowe, that the GAO investigation was launched. The results of that were immediate. By September 1990, director William Raub announced that the NIH was establishing an Office for Research on Women's Health (ORWH) with "authority and responsibility" to act on behalf of the NIH director to monitor and coordinate all activities of NIH institutes, specifically to encourage research on women's health and to ensure that research funded by NIH includes women and addresses their needs, in other words, to enforce that long-standing and long-forgotten policy. So it could do so, Congress gave the fledgling office $1.5 million in its first year which rose to $10.3 million by fiscal year 1992.

Its temporary head, Ruth Kirchstein, M.D., of the Institute of Medicine, was replaced about a year later by a permanent director, Vivian Pinn, M.D., then chief of pathology at Howard University College of Medicine. Within two years, the office had held several conferences, including one attended by over 300 scientists and others to establish a research agenda for women's health and another to determine what barriers exist to attracting women to biomedical careers and to keeping them in the field. The ORWH is also tackling some of the more tangled issues, such as the medical, legal, and ethical questions about the inclusion of women of childbearing years in research studies.

On the political side, the caucus drew up an impressive collection of legislation, known as the Women's Health Equity Act, which, among other things, permanently establishes the ORWH, codifies the NIH policy on the inclusion of women and minorities in research and authorizes nearly $500 million to be spent on women's health issues, including breast cancer research. Much of the legislation, which was introduced twice, was folded into the 1993 NIH Reauthorization Act, which is also the agency's budget.

Across the country, other organizations joined the fray. In November 1990, representatives of medical and consumer organizations were invited by the New York-based American Medical Women's Association to a meeting to discuss the possibility of developing an advanced curriculum in women's health, a continuing education program that would help practicing physicians better understand and treat their women patients. That group developed a twenty-page list of skills and knowledge primary care physicians would need and over three years, with the help of representatives from seventeen medical specialties, turned that list into a course of study built around the life phases of women, from childhood to maturity. Unlike other medical school curricula, this one focusing on women takes in the broad scope of their lives, including the effects of everything from socioeconomics to sexuality to the male-dominated culture in which they live.

At the University of Illinois at Chicago, noted menstrual cycle researcher Alice Dan, Ph.D., helped found the Center for Research on Women and Gender, whose purpose is to promote collaborative research on gender issues, particularly relating to health, work, and culture. In December 1991, the center held its first conference, with SAWHR, on what are clearly emerging as the major goals of the new women's health movement: increasing research on women's health issues, making science an attractive career opportunity for women, and promoting mutual understanding between researchers and the people they study.

In June 1993, SAWHR, *The Journal of Women's Health,* and the American Medical Women's Association cosponsored the First Annual Congress on Women's Health, held in Washington, D.C. It drew double the number of attendees conference planners expected.

More than 400 people, most of them women doctors, filled the sessions on abuse and violence, sexually transmitted diseases, gynecological cancers, reproductive issues, autoimmune diseases, and a dozen or so other topics that are routinely neglected from research lab to clinician's office.

Some organizations whose main focus had been reproduction began to broaden their agendas. In December 1991, the National Women's Health Network, one of the oldest and largest of the women's health advocacy groups, drafted its own "agenda for equity" in women's health research, adding its voice to the growing clamor for quick action by the government on closing the research gap.

The Washington-based Institute for Research on Women's Health, once the only voice, found itself now part of a chorus. Started in 1984 by four women scientists, including longtime NIH critics Jean Hamilton and Margaret Jensvold, the institute had sponsored a series of meetings on the lack of research on women's health issues in the spring of 1988. The Institute for Research on Women's Health developed a research agenda on women's health that primed the pump for SAWHR, founded two years later. The institute's agenda was adopted by Haseltine's group and provided much of the foundation for the Women's Health Equity Act.

In November 1990, two San Francisco physicians, Karen Johnson and Laurel Dawson, stirred up their fellow physicians by proposing that women's health become a multidisciplinary specialty, much like pediatrics and geriatrics. Writing in *The Journal of the American Medical Women's Association,* Johnson and Dawson suggested that women's health specialists be trained to provide comprehensive care for women, who now may bounce from specialist to specialist for treatment of one problem that may have more than one symptom, such as endometriosis or premenstrual syndrome. The new board-certified specialty would incorporate two important points of the newly created women's health agenda: attention to women's psychosocial needs and to women as savvy health care consumers.

Some doctors—women included—fear that a specialty in women's health will build another "pink-collar ghetto" where women's health will again be trivialized, as opponent Michelle Harrison, M.D., warns. Harrison, a Pittsburgh psychiatrist and feminist, says she would much prefer to see a women's health discipline, taught at the master's level, open to all physicians who work with women, from internists to family practitioners to cardiologists. That way, she says, "all specialties . . . become user-friendly to women."

Advocates on the other hand believe that having physicians who specialize in women's health will create a demand for more and better research on women's unique health concerns. "The women of America, women of every class, every color, every sexual preference, should no longer have a legitimate health care concern ignored or minimized by the medical establishment," Johnson told a group of physicians during her spirited—but genteel—debate with Harrison at the First Annual Congress on Women's Health. Only a specialty can assure that, she said, because "physicians do not take a field of study seriously unless we have a specialty."

But what may be the most important event in this sequence was a serendipitous one. In April 1991, cardiologist Bernadine Healy, M.D., became the first woman to head the NIH. Not the administration's first choice, Healy got the job only after a number of men had turned it down. The ultimate in oxymorons—an Irish Catholic Republican feminist—Healy took office and immediately embraced the women's health issue as her own. Within a week of her confirmation, Healy unveiled, by all accounts, the most ambitious research project ever undertaken by NIH. Her effort to redress years of neglect of women's health issues is the fifteen-year, $625 million, multi-institute Women's Health Initiative (WHI). The three-part study, among other things, will examine the effectiveness of HRT and a variety of lifestyle factors, including diet, on heart disease, cancer, and osteoporosis in postmenopausal women, incorporating Maureen Henderson's ill-fated Women's Health Trial on dietary fat and breast cancer risk.

On the face of it, this is all good news. But critics warn that what this new women's health movement lacks is permanence. The Women's Health Equity Act was designed to give it that, by making the ORWH an NIH fixture and the inclusion of women and minorities in research a law. Caucus members—seasoned politicians all—have been concerned that many scientists and conservative lawmakers are simply waiting for the brouhaha to blow over so everyone can return to business as usual. "When we first started talking about this, everybody was treating it like, 'If we just wait this out, it will go away,' " said Patricia Schroeder. Indeed, although four women now serve on the appropriations subcommittee that approves medical research funding, they share that duty with other lawmakers who haven't wavered in their opposition to disease-specific—and, in this case, female disease-specific—allocations. Likewise, Cornell researcher Lila Wallis, M.D., who spearheaded the development of a women's health curriculum, said she has gotten the impression from "some medical institutions and powerful physicians" that the launching of the Women's Health Initiative and the permanent establishment of the ORWH have "solved the problem, and they would like to get on with their usual agenda."

Schroeder admitted she is sometimes pessimistic about the political longevity of women's health in a Congress where, as of 1993, there were only 54 women among its 535 representatives and senators. The Senate Judiciary Committee's grilling of Anita Hill in the Clarence Thomas hearings simply brought home to the viewing public what Schroeder and her female colleagues have been aware of for years: What women know from their experience has to be explained—often interminably—to men who still "don't get it."

She worries that with the loss of Healy—a political appointment of the Bush administration who resigned under Clinton—the institutional focus on women's health will evaporate like dew on a hot day. Even before Healy's departure, said Schroeder, "the good old boys" were "already lining up and attacking her. That Women's Health Initiative must have just pissed them off."

Other critics, such as Jean Hamilton, say it's important to look past the words to the bottom line. The money spent on an issue often speaks volumes about its perceived importance. After all, when the U.S. Public Health Service brought the issue of gender inequities in health research to light in 1985, the NIH set up an advisory committee made up of one representative from each institute and gave them no budget and little time or staff support. It was that powerless committee that put together the policy that NIH felt it could ignore until the GAO report was read to a congressional panel on June 18, 1990. Likewise, as Hamilton pointed out in a speech given at the Second Annual Syntex Women's Health Roundtable in Washington, D.C., in February 1992, the amount being spent on the ORWH is roughly equivalent to the initial funding of NIH's Institute on Aging. However, the institute was established in 1975, when

$10 to $15 million bought more. "If any of us were offered $15 million, we'd take it in 1975 dollars if it were possible," Hamilton said. "So it appears that gender comes up short compared to early funding for aging."

Though the women's health issue has had a public forum, there's no evidence that it has yet seeped into the public consciousness, so there is not yet any substantial grass roots constituency that could wield influence in either the political or medical arenas. The self-care movement of the 1960s and 1970s is credited with inventing the concept of "health care consumer." By demystifying reproduction and encouraging women to become participants in their own care, the early women's health movement created consumer demands—for less paternalistic care, natural childbirth, better and safer contraception—that medicine, industry, and, in some cases, the government had no choice but to meet. Though women have taken to the street for abortion, contraception, and AIDS and lately for breast cancer, no one has marched on Washington to demand something better than estrogen replacement for menopause or that women with angina undergo cardiac catheterization as often as men. Although those are needs every bit as great as warm speculums and low-mortality birth control, they have not yet been recognized by women, whose exposure to the research gender gap may be limited to a newspaper article they read sometime during the week of June 18, 1990, or a television news report on the latest women-are-neglected-as-heart-disease-victims study.

With few notable exceptions, most women's groups have not given more than a nod to the issue. Most have been slow to acknowledge that women's health extends beyond reproduction, feeding into the prevailing notion that all of women's health concerns are below the waist. Many of them have been so caught up in the protracted abortion rights battle that breast cancer, heart disease, and violence seem peripheral issues despite their direct and dangerous impact on millions of women. The press simply magnifies that disproportionate concern by paying more attention to the latest abortion clinic skirmish than to how few women are enrolled in clinical or drug trials. In part, that is because abortion rights has taken on the drama of a war—indeed, by 1993, with the shooting death of Florida abortion doctor David Gunn, it was clear it had become an armed conflict—while health is a tamer, more specialized beat. But it is also because so few of the lay press really understand the signifi-cance of scientific research. In fact, it has been the science journal reporters who have tracked and probed and questioned the real progress of the "gender gap" issue.

For example, while the lay press docilely reported on the "good news"—the groundbreaking WHI—*The Journal of the American Medical Association* and *Science* detailed the strong and widespread criticism of the study, which some suspect is more politically than scientifically correct. Many scientists, including many women scien-tists, have pointed out that the study is large, unwieldy, and, possibly, ultimately undoable. In the WHI, thousands of women will be ex-pected to take daily hormone replacement and vitamins and modify their diets—reducing fat intake to a difficult-to-maintain 20 percent of total calories—all at the same time. Breast cancer researchers, too, are concerned that the trial might come to an abrupt halt once there's enough evidence that the various regimens under scrutiny protect against heart disease. For the breast cancer segment to work, the study must run at least a decade.

There has also been criticism that WHI will be regarded as solving the gender gap problem when it simply is filling in some glaring omissions in medical knowledge about postmenopausal women. There are no studies of that magnitude planned for condi-tions affecting women of childbearing years, who have been most neglected by science, particularly in drug research, because of fears of fetal harm and legal liability. Though many critics have pointed out that not every woman of childbearing years is at equal risk of pregnancy—lesbians, for example, and women who have had tubal ligation—many scientists prefer to steer clear of that group.

However, in 1993, the FDA, after receiving a blistering report from the GAO on the lack of gender-specific information on drugs it approves, told drug companies they must include sufficient num-bers of women and provide evidence of drug safety and effectiveness in both men and women. Also, several universities have approved drug studies of women of childbearing age, and the scientific com-munity is carefully watching how issues of informed consent and fe-tal protection are handled.

The WHI has its ardent supporters, too, including the often cynical Pat Schroeder. "When people complain that the Women's Health Initiative is 'too much too soon,' I have to ask, isn't it better than too little too late? The reason it's so big is because women have been left out of so much for so long," she said.

Some scientists and women's health advocates also have expressed doubts that official words will be translated into official action, particularly in tight economic times. "Too often we have seen cutbacks in overall research funding just when that funding would benefit a particular group that has been ignored," the president of Chicago's Cook County Hospital, Ruth M. Rothstein, testified at one of three roundtable meetings of women's health advocates and consumers sponsored by SAWHR in 1991.

Other scientists say that the crucible is when a grant enters that number-crunching funding machine at NIH. For example, though there is general agreement that research studies need to provide social services to attract women and minorities, some researchers have found there's no guarantee they'll be funded for it. "There is a kind of assent that this might be important, but the bottom line is that NIH funding is for research and not for social services," Wayne Greaves, M.D., chief of infectious diseases at Howard University, told *The Journal of the American Medical Association* in January 1992. Greaves told *The Journal of the American Medical Association* that while his university was funded by NIH to target minorities left out of AIDS research, they've received no real help in getting into a protocol. "It's as if this was an attempt to appease the critics more than a way to truly provide us with the necessary tools, or with direction in getting integrated into the system," he said. "We're on the periphery, taking a peek inside."

Economics may have prompted the early and vociferous opposition to the women's health specialty proposed by Johnson and Dawson. The leaders of several major medical associations, including the American College of Obstetricians and Gynecologists and the American Academy of Family Physicians, have questioned the need for a new specialty that would no doubt draw away their best-paying customers. Women not only make health decisions for themselves but for their families as well. The women's health market is a lucrative one, and many hospitals, angling for a greater share, have established women's health centers, combining a variety of specialists, from gynecologists to psychiatrists, to provide woman-friendly care under one well-decorated roof. There are about 200 such centers across the United States, most of them successful, strongly suggesting that there is a need for a women's health speciality. It may indeed, as the medical organizations fear, draw women away from their other practitioners.

Despite the chorus of criticism and doubt, there is at least one optimistic voice. Florence Haseltine said she's beginning to see a change where it counts: a slow and subtle metamorphosis of the medical profession. Some of the change can be chalked up to fate. Medicine is becoming feminized. The number of women physicians has quadrupled in the last twenty years, and women are about to dominate at least one speciality, OB-GYN, although a 1991 report from the Feminist Majority Foundation and the American Medical Women's Association pointed out that women are still underpaid and underrepresented in positions of power. There is also no guarantee, as many feminists hope, that large numbers of women physicians will humanize medicine by rejecting its largely male-oriented views. Medical education is steeped in those views, and institutional changes, which are needed, often come slowly. Nevertheless, sheer numbers—both of women doctors and women patients—may be enough to bring some needed changes both in medical school curricula and in physicians' offices, where ignoring women's needs could be a costly mistake.

Some change has already occurred. For example, most medical schools now require students to attend a special program on communicating with female patients, which, for some physicians, is roughly equivalent to learning a foreign language. Even the AMA has taken up causes once the lonely province of feminists, from family violence to women's health. The AMA established a contingency fund for women's health research and education programs as part of its Education Research Foundation and launched the Women's Health Campaign, which has produced educational materials and television programming spotlighting women's health concerns.

Though the public may come across an occasional newspaper article or television special, physicians are virtually bombarded by medical journal articles on research inequities and women's health. Not only did a new journal debut in 1992—*The Journal of Women's Health,* edited by Haseltine and another SAWHR board member, Ann Colson Wentz, M.D.—journals as staid as *The Journal of the American Medical Association* and *The New England Journal of Medicine* have hammered fearlessly away at the controversy. In

1992, *The Journal of the American Medical Association* devoted an entire issue to women's health but before that covered topics as wide-ranging as sexual harassment at NIH and the lack of attention to family violence in the medical setting. Bernadine Healy used *The New England Journal of Medicine* as a forum to call for a general awakening to the fact that women have unique health problems that deserve the same attention and care as the health problems of men. In *The Journal of the American Medical Association,* she scattered the blame for women's health research inequities in every corner where it belongs, including "within each of us." Though the general public has been barely aroused, doctors have been forced to sit bolt upright and take notice. "That's what June 18, 1990, did for us," said Haseltine. "It changed the way we think. And that is far more powerful for us than any law."

But for women, it is not enough. As critics charge, to survive beyond mere fad the new women's health movement needs a strong and broad constituency that will make it *politically* impossible to underfund women's health issues or to focus more attention on the health concerns of middle-class white men. The makers of law and policy need to catch themselves up short with the vision of angry women milling on the Mall or pulling down the lever of a political opponent more sympathetic to the cause each time they find themselves making knee-jerk decisions on health that recognize their own experiences and no other.

The women who fought for and won the right to have babies the way they wanted—or not to have babies at all—need to create a similar consumer demand for more and better research on breast cancer, menopause, osteoporosis, and heart disease and for a new treatment paradigm that doesn't dismiss their complaints or fail to view them within the context of their lives. And once women begin to make their demands, they need to maintain the pressure until the paper promises become permanent and applied policy, until lawmakers and policy makers recognize that lip-service-with-a-smile isn't going to work any more. "Women have never learned that when it comes to lobbying," says Pat Schroeder. "If somebody tells them, 'Well, I'm totally against breast cancer,' they think they've won. They need to ask, 'How are you going to vote? Where does this fit in your priorities?' Because if it's priority number 852, it's never going to see the light of day."

And, she points out, packing Congress with women not only isn't realistic, it may not even be necessary. AIDS funding ballooned over the eighties "not because everyone who voted for it is gay," but because the issue had "outside political support," a cohesive grass roots movement that used every tool at its disposal—from pressuring top CDC researchers to holding die-ins at their front door—to get what it wanted, to get what it deserved. Even those who are repulsed by the outrageousness of ACT UP can understand its motivation. Its slogan can strike a chord in all of us: Silence equals death.

When women do learn how to manipulate politics and policy, they find it works. By holding letter-writing campaigns and lobbying influential lawmakers, the Breast Cancer Coalition saw breast cancer funding have its greatest increase ever in 1992. And the experience of a California orthopedic surgeon named Vicki Ratner is another case for grass roots lobbying.

Ratner was a latecomer to medicine. A dental hygienist for ten years, she entered medical school in 1981 at the age of thirty. While there, she developed a little understood and rarely studied condition called interstitial cystitis, a urological disorder resembling chronic urinary tract infection. Because the dozen physicians she saw didn't recognize the disease and, in fact, told her it was all in her head, Ratner diagnosed herself one afternoon in a medical library. But learning she had a disease that urology textbooks filed under psychosomatic diseases of menopause—with no known cause and no known cure—left Ratner in devastating isolation.

So she turned to the media. An article in a local newspaper drew dozens of responses from women suffering the same symptoms. Broader media coverage, including, eventually, a spot on ABC's "Good Morning America," drew thousands of responses from women who had been suffering for years with a disease that didn't exist in their doctors' training or experience. Those thousands of women became the nucleus of the Interstitial Cystitis Association, which, like the Breast Cancer Coalition, discovered that the pen was mightier than almost anything. A letter-writing campaign along with pounding the halls of Congress and testifying before any subcommittee that would hear them got them the attention of a number of sympathetic lawmakers who convinced their colleagues in 1993 to appropriate $4 million for research into interstitial cystitis.

"There is real irony in the Interstitial Cystitis Association experience," says Ratner. "Through life people are taught that if you're sick, you go to the doctor for treatment. The reality, however, for women's health issues, is that it takes a political act, literally an act of Congress, to get the medical community to sit up and listen."

But it can—and must—be done.

Women need to recognize their unacknowledged power—as nearly 52 percent of the population; as nearly half of all workers; as the family comptrollers, who spend more than three-quarters of the consumer dollars; and as the Dr. Moms, who choose the doctor their families see and the over-the-counter drugs they take—and use it the way AIDS activists have used theirs, part rational persuasion, part cudgel.

Women need to, as one women's health advocate put it, "organize the outrage." But first, women need to be outraged. Except for a few dramatic marches, the women's movement has limped along the road to equality. We have, as Flora Davis wrote in *Moving the Mountain,* a history of the women's movement since 1960, fought "just half a revolution." The majority of women, by their silence, have tolerated women's relegation to low-status, low-paying jobs, the overrepresentation of women in the lowest socioeconomic brackets and underrepresentation in positions of power and the reign of political administrations that claim to enshrine family values but are blind to family needs. The term *gender gap* when applied to salaries and position in the workplace may stir in women a simmering anger, but in thirty years that anger has not been strong enough to *close* the gap. Women still earn only three-quarters of what men do. On June 18, 1990, it became clear that what was once a matter of livelihood had become a matter of life and death. The term *gender gap* now applied to women's health; the second-class citizen had become second-class patient. Perhaps now, when inequality can be fatal, women will rise up in rage, step out of the blind spot and *stay* visible, demanding, until it is given, their right to health, their right to life.

KEY SOURCES

1: WANTED

Baltimore, David. "The Funding Crisis Runs Deeper Than Money." *Journal of NIH Research* 2(1990):27–29.

Borins, Elaine. Assistant professor of psychiatry, the University of Toronto. Personal interview, January 20, 1992.

Congressional Caucus for Women's Issues. "Caucus Fact Sheet." Washington, D.C., June 1991.

Congressional Caucus for Women's Issues. "The Women's Health Equity Act of 1991." Washington, D.C., February 1991.

Congressional Caucus for Women's Issues. "Women's Health Equity Act Update." Washington, D.C., December 1991.

Cotton, Paul. "Examples Abound of Gaps in Medical Knowledge Because of Groups Excluded From Scientific Study." *Journal of the American Medical Association* 263 (1990):1051, 1055.

Cotton, Paul. "Is There Still Too Much Extrapolation From Data on Middle-aged White Men?" *Journal of the American Medical Association* 263 (1990): 1049–1050.

Dan, Alice. Center for Research on Women and Gender, the University of Illinois, Chicago. Personal interview, February 18, 1992.

Dresser, Rebecca. "Wanted: Single, White Male for Medical Research." *Hastings Center Report* (January–February 1992):24–29.

Fried, Linda. Johns Hopkins University, Baltimore. Personal interview, March 30, 1992.

Greenberg, Daniel S. "What Ails NIH?" *Journal of NIH Research* 2(1990):29–30.

Hamilton, Jean A. "Biases in Women's Health Research." Based on the paper presented at Gender Science and Medicine Conference, sponsored by the University of Toronto Faculty of Medicine and the Women's Clinic, the Toronto Western Hospital, Toronto, Ontario, Canada, November 5, 1988.

233

Hamilton, Jean A. "Medical Research: The Forgotten 51%." In *Encyclopedia Britannica: Medical and Health Annual.* Chicago: Encyclopedia Britannica, 1992.

Hamilton, Jean A. Professor of social and health sciences and women's studies at Duke University, Durham, N.C. Personal interview, February 24, 1992.

Hamilton, Jean A. "Women's Health Research: Public Policy Issues." Paper presented at the Second Annual Syntex Women's Health Roundtable, Washington, D.C., February 7–9, 1992.

Haseltine, Florence. Director, Society for the Advancement of Women's Health Research, and director, Center for Population Research, the National Institutes of Health, Washington, D.C., Personal interview, May 12, 1992.

Hilts, Philip J. "F.D.A. Lifts Ban on Using Women in Drug Tests." *New York Times* (March 24, 1993).

Johnson, Tracy Lee. Society for the Advancement of Women's Health Research, Washington, D.C. Personal interview, May 11, 1992.

Jordan, Craig. Testimony. Breast Cancer in America: The Status and Promise of Current Research. Hearings convened by the Research Task Force of the Breast Cancer Coalition, Washington, D.C., February 5, 1992.

Kirschstein, Ruth L. "Research on Women's Health." *American Journal of Public Health* (March 1991):291–293.

Mervis, Jeffrey. "Anatomy of the NIH Grant System, or How to Play the Game." *Journal of NIH Research* 2(1990):59–68.

The National Council for Research on Women. "Why Fund Women and Girls?" Press release, 1991.

The National Women's Health Network. "Research to Improve Women's Health: An Agenda for Equity." Washington, D.C., December 1991.

The National Women's Health Resource Center. Forging a Women's Health Research Agenda. Washington, D.C., December 5–6, 1990, February 28, 1991.

Rutter, William. "Cut Review Fat, Boost Cooperation." *Journal of NIH Research* 2 (1990):34–35.

Schroeder, Patricia. U.S. Congresswoman and cochair of the Congressional Caucus for Women's Issues, Washington, D.C. Personal interview, May 11, 1992.

Schroeder, Patricia. "Women's Health: A Focus for the 1990s" (editorial). *Jacobs Institute of Women's Health* (Spring 1992):1–2.

Silberner, Joanne, et al. "Health: Another Gender Gap." *U.S. News & World Report* (September 24, 1990):54–55.

Society for the Advancement of Women's Health Research. "Toward a Women's Health Research Agenda: Findings of the Scientific Advisory Meeting." Washington, D.C., 1991.

Society for the Advancement of Women's Health Research. "Women's Health Research: Prescription for Change," annual report. Washington, D.C., January 1991.

U.S. Congress. NIH Reauthorization and Protection of Health Facilities. *Hearings before the Subcommittee on Health and the Environment of the Committee on Energy and Commerce House of Representatives.* 101st Cong., 2d sess., serial 101–191. Washington, D.C.: U.S. Government Printing Office, 1991.

U.S. Department of Health and Human Services. "Women's Health: Report of the

Public Health Service Task Force on Women's Health Issues," Vol. II.
DHHS Publication No. (PHS) 85-50206, May 1985.

U.S. General Accounting Office. Report to Congressional Requesters. *Women's Health: FDA Needs to Ensure More Study of Gender Differences in Prescription Drug Testing*. GAO/HRD-93-17, B-243898. Washington, D.C., October 1992.

U.S. General Accounting Office. Statement of Mark V. Nadel, "National Institutes of Health: Problems in Implementing Policy on Women in Study Populations." Washington, D.C., June 18, 1990.

2: MEDICAL EDUCATION

American College of Physicians. "Promotion and Tenure of Women and Minorities on Medical School Faculties." *Annals of Internal Medicine* 114(1) (1991):63–68.

American Medical Women's Association. "AMWA Position Statement on Gender Discrimination and Sexual Harassment." Alexandria, Va.: November 1990.

Angell, Marcia. "Women in Medicine: Beyond Prejudice" (editorial). *New England Journal of Medicine* 304 (1981):1161–1163.

Association of American Medical Colleges. "Survey of Specialty Societies." *Women in Medicine Update* 6(1) (1992):2.

Baldwin, DeWitt C., et al. "Student Perceptions of Mistreatment and Harassment During Medical School: A Survey of Ten United States Schools." *Western Journal of Medicine* 155 (1991):140–145.

Bernstein, Anne E. "Gender Equity" (editorial). *Journal of the American Medical Women's Association* 44(3) (1989):84–85.

Bickel, Janet. Director of Women's Programs, the Association of American Medical Colleges, Washington, D.C. Personal interview, February 18, 1992.

Bickel, Janet. "Women in Medical Education: A Status Report." *New England Journal of Medicine* 319 (1988):1579–1584.

Bickel, Janet. "Women in Medicine Statistics." Washington, D.C.: Association of American Medical Colleges, June 1991.

Ciesielski-Carlucci, Chris. Medical student, the University of California, Berkeley. Personal interviews, April 13, 1993, and April 16, 1993.

Ciesielski-Carlucci, Chris, et al. "Interviewing for Medical School: When the Rite Is Wrong." University of California at Berkeley Health and Medical Science Department. Survey conducted at the Annual National Convention of the American Medical Student Association, Miami, March 1993.

Coombs, Robert H., et al. "Stress in the Role Constellation of Female Resident Physicians." *Journal of the American Medical Women's Association* 43(1) (1988):21–27.

Cotton, Paul. "Harassment Hinders Women's Care and Careers." *Journal of the American Medical Association* 267 (1992):778–779, 783.

Denenberg, Laura. Medical student, the University of California at Los Angeles. Personal interview, April 11, 1993.

Dickstein, Leah. Professor of psychiatry and dean for faculty and student advocacy, the University of Louisville School of Medicine. Personal interview, February 25, 1992.

Ducker, Dalia G. "The Professional Context for Women Physicians: Collegial Relations, Role Models, and Mentors." *Journal of the American Medical Women's Association* 43(4) (1988):106–108.

Ehrhart, Julie Kuhn, et al. "Rx for Success: Improving the Climate for Women in Medical Schools and Teaching Hospitals." Project on the Status and Education of Women. Washington, D.C.: Association of American Colleges, May 1990.

Eisenberg, Carola. "Medicine Is No Longer a Man's Profession: Or, When the Men's Club Goes Coed It's Time to Change the Regs" (editorial). *New England Journal of Medicine* 321 (1989):1542–1544.

Friedman, Emily. "Women and Medicine—From Tension to Truce" (editorial). In *Women and Medicine* (special issue). *Western Journal of Medicine* 149 (1988):681–682.

Fugh-Berman, Adriane. "Tales Out of Medical School." *The Nation* (January 20, 1992):1, 54–56.

Grant, Linda. "The Gender Climate of Medical School: Perspectives of Women and Men Students." *Journal of the American Medical Women's Association* 43(4) (1988):109–119.

Grisso, Jeane Anne. University of Pennsylvania School of Medicine. Personal interview, February 18, 1992.

Heins, Marilyn. "II. Medicine and Motherhood" (editorial). *Journal of the American Medical Association* 249 (1983):209–210.

Johnson, Karen. Practicing psychiatrist and assistant clinical professor of psychiatry at the University of California, San Francisco. Personal interview, February 17, 1992.

Komaromy, Miriam, et al. "Sexual Harassment in Medical Training." *New England Journal of Medicine* 328 (1993):322–326.

Lenhart, Sharyn A., et al. "Gender Bias Against and Sexual Harassment of AMWA Members in Massachusetts." *Journal of the American Medical Women's Association* 46(4) (1991):121–125.

Lenhart, Sharyn A. Clinical instructor of psychiatry, Harvard Medical School, Cambridge, Mass., and associate attending psychiatrist, McLean Hospital, Belmont, Mass. Personal interviews, January 23, 1992, and April 16, 1993.

Lenhart, Sharyn A., et al. "Sexual Harassment and Gender Discrimination: a Primer for Women's Physicians." *Journal of the American Medical Women's Association* 46(3) (1991):77–82.

Levinson, Wendy, et al. "Mentors and Role Models for Women in Academic Medicine." *Western Journal of Medicine* 154 (1991):423–426.

Marquart, J.A., et al. "Gender Differences in Medical Student Interviews." Paper presented at the Association of American Medical Colleges' Conference, Innovations in Medical Education, Chicago: November 11–17, 1988.

Martin, Steven C., et al. "Careers of Women Physicians—Choices and Constraints." In *Women and Medicine* (special issue). *Western Journal of Medicine* 149 (1988):758–760.

McDonald, Louise L. "Women Physicians and Organized Medicine." In *Women and Medicine* (special issue). *Western Journal of Medicine* 149 (1988):777–778.

Moulton, Anne. Internist and assistant professor of medicine, Brown University School of Medicine, and associate physician, Rhode Island Hospital, Providence. Personal interview, March 13, 1992.

Moulton, Anne W., et al. "Women's Health Education: What to Do Until We Have the Data." *Society of General Internal Medicine News* 14 (11) (1991):1, 5.

Nadelson, Carol C. "Advancing Through the Medical Hierarchy." *Journal of the American Medical Women's Association* 46(3) (1991):95–99.

Ochberg, Richard L., et al. "Women Physicians and Their Mentors." *Journal of the American Medical Women's Association* 44(4) (1989):123–126.

Ottenheimer, Debra. Medical student, the University of Pennsylvania, Philadelphia. Personal interview, February 19, 1992.

Pressman, Sarah. Medical student, Rush Medical College, Chicago. Personal interview, January 16, 1992.

Pressman, Sarah. "The Numbers Do Not Add Up to Equality" (editorial). *Journal of the American Medical Women's Association* 46(2) (1991):44, 48.

Ramos, Sylvia M., et al. "Women Surgeons: A National Survey." *Journal of the American Medical Women's Association* 44(1) (1989):21–25.

Sinding, Chris. Coordinator of the Women's Health Office, McMaster University Faculty of Health Sciences, Hamilton, Ontario. Personal interview, March 16, 1992.

Wallis, Lila. Clinical professor of medicine, Cornell University Medical College, Ithaca, N.Y., and past president of the American Medical Women's Association. Personal interview, March 10, 1992.

3: BROKEN HEARTS

American Heart Association. "1992 Heart and Stroke Facts." Dallas, Tex., 1991.

American Heart Association. "Silent Epidemic: The Truth About Women and Heart Disease." Dallas, Tex., 1992.

American Medical Association, Department of Public Information. "What Women Don't Know About Heart Disease and Cholesterol Could Hurt Them." Chicago, December 18, 1990.

Anastos, Kathryn, et al. "Hypertension in Women: What Is Really Known?" The Women's Caucus, Working Group on Women's Health of the Society of General Internal Medicine. *Annals of Internal Medicine* 115 (1991):287–293.

Appel, Lawrence J. "Preventing Heart Disease in Women: Another Role for Aspirin?" (editorial). *Journal of the American Medical Association* 266 (1991): 565–566.

Arkus, Bonnie. Founder of the Women's Heart Research Foundation. Personal interview, April 22, 1993.

"Aspirin Appears to Reduce Risk of First Heart Attack in Women." *Heartstyle* 1(4) (1991):1–2.

Ayanian, John Z., et al. "Differences in the Use of Procedures Between Women and Men Hospitalized for Coronary Heart Disease." *New England Journal of*

Medicine 325 (1991):221–225.

Becker, Diane M. "Cardiovascular Disease in Women: The Challenge of the 1990s." *U.S. Pharmacist Cardiovascular Supplement, Special Groups* (March 1991):9–16.

Cole, Thomas G., et al. "Differential Reduction of Plasma Cholesterol by the American Heart Association Phase 3 Diet in Moderately Hypercholesterolemic, Premenopausal Women with Different Body Mass Indexes." *American Journal of Clinical Nutrition* 55 (1992):385–394.

Cotton, Paul. "Examples Abound of Gaps in Medical Knowledge Because of Groups Excluded from Scientific Study." *Journal of the American Medical Association* 263 (1990):1051, 1055.

Crouse, John R., III. "Gender, Lipoproteins, Diet, and Cardiovascular Risk: Sauce for the Goose May Not Be Sauce for Gander." *Lancet* (February 11, 1989):318–320.

Crouse, John R., III. Professor of medicine at the Bowman Gray School of Medicine, Winston-Salem, N.C. Personal interview, February 21, 1992.

Crouse, Linda J. Codirector of the Echocardiographic Laboratory, Saint Luke's Mid America Heart Institute, Kansas City, Mo. Personal interview, February 13, 1992.

Crouse, Linda J., et al. "Exercise Echocardiography as a Screening Test for Coronary Artery Disease and Correlation with Coronary Arteriography." *American Journal of Cardiology* 67 (1991):1213–1218.

Douglas, Pamela S. "Heart Truths: What Women Need to Know." American Heart Association Conference, Iowa, November 3, 1990.

Eaker, Elaine D. Assistant director for science, division of surveillance and epidemiology, Epidemiology Program Office, the National Centers for Disease Control, Atlanta, Ga. Personal interview, February 10, 1992.

Eaker, Elaine D. "Psychosocial Factors in the Epidemiology of Coronary Heart Disease in Women." *Psychiatric Clinics of North America* 12(1) (1989):167–173.

Ginsburg, Helen J. Author of "From the Heart," available from the American Heart Association of Denver, Colorado. Personal interview, April 21, 1993.

Greenland, Philip, et al. "In-Hospital and 1-Year Mortality in 1,524 Women After Myocardial Infarction: Comparison With 4,315 Men." *Circulation* 83 (1991):484–491.

Greenland, Philip. Professor and chairman of the department of community health and preventive medicine, Northwestern University School of Medicine, Chicago. Personal interview, February 7, 1992.

Grundy, S. M., et al. "Comparison of Three Cholesterol Lowering Diets in Normolipidemic Men." *Journal of the American Medical Association* 256 (1986): 2351–2355.

Hypertension Detection and Followup Program Cooperative Group. "Five-Year Findings of the Hypertension Detection and Followup Program. II. Mortality by Race, Sex and Age." *Journal of the American Medical Association* 242 (1979):2572–2577.

Isles, Christopher G., et al. "Relation Between Coronary Risk and Coronary Mortality in Women of the Renfrew and Paisley Survey: Comparison with Men." *Lancet* 339 (1992):702–706.

Kahn, Steven S., et al. "Increased Mortality of Women in Coronary Artery Bypass Surgery: Evidence for Referral Bias." *Annals of Internal Medicine* 112 (1990):561–567.

Kohlmeier, M., et al. "Influences of 'Normal' and 'Prudent' Diets on Biliary and Serum Lipids in Healthy Women." *American Journal of Clinical Nutrition* 42 (1985):1201–1205.

Legato, Marianne. Cardiologist and associate professor of clinical medicine, Columbia University college of Physicians and Surgeons, New York. Personal interview, February 15, 1993.

Legato, Marianne, and Colman, Carol. *The Female Heart: The Truth About Women and Coronary Artery Disease.* New York: Simon & Schuster, 1992.

Lewis, B., et al. "Towards an Improved Lipid-Lowering Diet: Additive Effects of Changes in Nutrient Intake." *Lancet* 2 (1981):1310–1313.

Manson, JoAnn E. "A Prospective Study of Aspirin Use and Primary Prevention of Cardiovascular Disease in Women." *Journal of the American Medical Association* 266 (1991):521–527.

Maynard, Charles, et al. "Underutilization of Thrombolytic Therapy in Eligible Women with Acute Myocardial Infarction." *American Journal of Cardiology* 68 (1991):529–530.

Medical Research Council Working Party. "MRC Trail of Mild Hypertension: Principal Results." *British Medical Journal* 291 (1985):197–204.

"M.I. Management Differs Greatly in Men, Women." *Family Practice News* 22(1) (1992):3, 22.

Pinn, Vivian W. "Commentary: Women, Research, and the National Institutes of Health." *American Journal of Preventive Medicine* 8 (1992):324–327.

Steingart, Richard M., et al. Letter. *New England Journal of Medicine* 326 (1992):571–572.

Steingart, Richard M., et al. "Sex Differences in the Management of Coronary Artery Disease." *New England Journal of Medicine* 325 (1991):226–230.

Tobin, Jonathan N., et al. "Sex Bias in Considering Coronary Bypass Surgery." *Annals of Internal Medicine* 107 (1987):19–25.

Vacek, James L., et al. "Sex-Related Differences in Patients Undergoing Direct Angioplasty for Acute Myocardial Infarction." American College of Cardiology, 41st Annual Scientific Session, Dallas, Tex., April 12–16, 1992.

Welty, Francine K. "Gender Differences in Survival and Recovery Following Cardiovascular Disease Diagnosis and Treatment." Abstract. New England Deaconess Hospital, Cardiology Section, Harvard Medical School, August 30, 1991.

Wenger, Nanette K. "Gender, Coronary Artery Disease, and Coronary Bypass Surgery" (editorial). *Annals of Internal Medicine* 112 (1990):557–558.

Wenger, Nanette K. "Cardiovascular Drugs: The Urgent Need for Studies in Women." *Journal of the American Medical Women's Association* 46(4) (1991):117–120.

Zanni, E. E., et al. "Effect of Egg Cholesterol and Dietary Fats on Plasma Lipids, Lipoproteins, and Apoproteins of Normal Women Consuming Natural Diets." *Journal of Lipid Research* 28 (1987):518–527.

4: BREAST CANCER

American Cancer Society. *Cancer Facts & Figures—1991.* New York: 1991.

Blakeslee, Sandra. "Faulty Math Heightens Fears of Breast Cancer." *New York Times* (March 15, 1992):D1.

Colditz, Graham. Associate professor of medicine, Harvard Medical School. Testimony. Breast Cancer in America: The Status and Promise of Current Research. Hearings convened by the Research Task Force of the Breast Cancer Coalition, Washington, D.C., February 9, 1992.

Davis, Devra Lee. Scholar in residence, National Academy of Sciences. Testimony. Breast Cancer in America: The Status and Promise of Current Research. Hearings convened by the Research Task Force of the Breast Cancer Coalition, Washington, D.C., February 9, 1992.

Dickersin, Kay. Assistant professor, University of Maryland School of Medicine. Testimony. Breast Cancer in America: The Status and Promise of Current Research. Hearings convened by the Research Task Force of the Breast Cancer Coalition, Washington, D.C., February 9, 1992.

FitzGerald, Susan. "Study Asks: Can Drug Prevent Breast Cancer." *Philadelphia Inquirer,* (April 30, 1992):A1, A16.

FitzGerald, Susan, and Vrazo, Fawn. "Study: No Benefit to Mammograms Under 50." *Philadelphia Inquirer* (May 5, 1992):A3.

Henderson, Maureen. Head, Cancer Prevention Research Program, and professor of epidemiology and medicine, Fred Hutchinson Cancer Research Center, Seattle, Wash. Personal interview, February 9, 1992.

Hendrick, R. Edward. "What Primary Care Physicians Should Know About Radiation Exposure, Image Quality, and Accreditation of Mammography Providers." *Women's Health Issues* 1 (1991):79–85.

Holmberg, Lars. Associate professor of surgery, Uppsala, Sweden, and visiting scientist, Centers for Disease Control. Testimony. Breast Cancer in America: The Status and Promise of Current Research. Hearings convened by the Research Task Force of the Breast Cancer Coalition, Washington, D.C., February 9, 1992.

Jenks, Susan. "Cancer Experts Set Research Agenda for Women's Health in the 1990s." *Journal of the National Cancer Institute* 83 (1991):1443–1444.

Kushner, Harvey. Testimony. Breast Cancer in America: The Status and Promise of Current Research. Hearings convened by the Research Task Force of the Breast Cancer Coalition. Washington, D.C., February 9, 1992.

Lippman, Marc. Director, Lombardi Cancer Center, Georgetown University Medical Center, Washington, D.C. Testimony. Breast Cancer in America: The Status and Promise of Current Research. Hearings convened by the Research Task Force of the Breast Cancer Coalition, Washington, D.C., February 9, 1992.

Love, Susan M. Testimony. Breast Cancer in America: The Status and Promise of Current Research. Hearings convened by the Research Task Force of the Breast Cancer Coalition, Washington, D.C., February 9, 1992.

Love, Susan M. Director, University of California at Los Angeles Breast Clinic. Personal interview, May 10, 1991.

Love, Susan M., with Lindsey, Karen. *Dr. Susan Love's Breast Book.* Reading, Mass.: Addison-Wesley, 1990.

Nayfield, Susan G., et al. "Potential Role of Tamoxifen in Prevention of Breast Cancer." *Journal of the National Cancer Institute* 83 (1991):1450–1458.

Osuch, Janet Rose. "Use of Legislation to Assure the Quality of Mammography." *Journal of the American Medical Women's Association* 46 (1991):114–116.

Pearson, Cynthia. Executive director, National Women's Health Network, Washington, D.C. Personal interview, February 27, 1992.

Powell, Roger. Program director, Diagnostic Imaging Research Branch, National Cancer Institute, Rockville, Md. Personal interview. February 9, 1992.

Romans, Martha C. "Report of the Jacobs Institute Workshop on Screening Mammography." *Women's Health Issues* 1 (1991):63–67.

Romans, Martha C., et al. "Utilization of Screening Mammography—1990." *Women's Health Issues* 1 (1991):68–73.

Roser, Mary Ann. "Drawing Attention to Breast Cancer." *Philadelphia Inquirer* (October 9, 1991):A4.

Sager, Ruth. Chief, Division of Cancer Genetics, Dana-Farber Cancer Institute, Boston, Mass. Testimony. Breast Cancer in America: The Status and Promise of Current Research. Hearings convened by the Research Task Force of the Breast Cancer Coalition. Washington, D.C., February 9, 1992.

Shellenbaugh, Joanne. American Cancer Society. Personal interview, January 22, 1992.

U.S. Congress. *Hearings before the Subcommittee on Health and the Environment of the Committee on Energy and Commerce House of Representatives,* 101st Cong., Serial 101-191. Washington, D.C.: U.S. Government Printing Office, 1991.

U.S. General Accounting Office. *Report to the Chairman, Subcommittee on Human Resources and Intergovernmental Relations, Committee on Government Operations, U.S. House of Representatives: Breast Cancer, 1971–91, Prevention, Treatment and Research.* Washington, D.C., December 1991.

Wallis, Claudia. "A Puzzling Plague." *Time* (January 14, 1991):48–55.

5: WOMEN WITH AIDS

Altman, Lawrence K. "Women Worldwide Nearing Higher Rate for AIDS Than Men." *New York Times* (July 21, 1992):C3.

American Medical Women's Association. "AIDS in Women and Children." *Journal of the American Medical Women's Association* 44 (1989):10–11.

Banzhaf, Marian. Director, New Jersey Women and AIDS Network, New Brunswick, N.J. Personal interviews, February 19, 1992; February 26, 1992; and April 28, 1993.

Blendon, Robert J., et al. "Public Opinion and AIDS: Lessons for the Second

Decade." *Journal of the American Medical Association* 267 (1992):981–986.

Campbell, Carole A. Professor of sociology, California State University, Long Beach. Personal interview, February 12, 1992.

Campbell, Carole A. "Prostitution, AIDS and Preventive Health Behavior." *Social Sciences and Medicine* 32 (1991):1367–1378.

Campbell, Carole A. "Women and AIDS." *Social Sciences and Medicine* 30 (1990):407–415.

Carpenter, Charles. "Sexually Transmitted Diseases and AIDS." Workshop. First Annual Congress on Women's Health, Washington, D.C., June 4, 1993.

Centers for Disease Control. "AIDS in Women—United States." *Morbidity and Mortality Weekly Report* 39 (1990):845–846.

Centers for Disease Control. "Review of Draft for Revision of HIV Infection Classification System and Expansion of AIDS Surveillance Case Definition." Atlanta, Ga., November 15, 1991.

Chu, Susan Y., et al. "Impact of the Human Immunodeficiency Virus Epidemic on Mortality in Women of Reproductive Age, United States." *Journal of the American Medical Association* 265 (1990):225–229.

Cohen, Mardge. Director, Women and Children with HIV Clinic, Cook County Hospital, Chicago. Personal interview, February 28, 1993.

Cotton, Deborah. Assistant professor of health policy and management at the Harvard School of Public Health, deputy project director for the Institute of Medicine's Committee on a National Strategy for AIDS, and investigator for the Harvard AIDS Clinical Trials Unit, Cambridge, Mass. Personal interview, June 18, 1992.

Denson, Louise. Personal interview. May 18, 1993.

Easterbrook, Philippa, et al. "Racial and Ethnic Differences in Outcome in Zidovudine-Treated Patients With Advanced HIV Disease." *Journal of the American Medical Association* 266 (1991):2713–2718.

Ellerbrock, Tedd V., et al. "Epidemiology of Women with AIDS in the United States, 1981 Through 1990: A Comparison with Heterosexual Men with AIDS." *Journal of the American Medical Association* 265 (1991):2971–2975.

Ellerbrock, Tedd V., and Rogers, Martha F. "Epidemiology of Human Immunodeficiency Virus Infection in Women in the United States." *Obstetrics and Gynecology Clinics of North America* 17(1990):523–543.

Folkers, Greg. "AZT Effective in Minorities and Women, New Analysis Shows." *Dateline:NIAID* (January 1992):7–8.

Gwinn, Marta, et al. "Prevalence of HIV Infection in Childbearing Women in the United States." *Journal of the American Medical Association* 265 (1991):1704–1708.

Hilts, Philip J. "AIDS Definition Excludes Women, Congress Is Told." *The New York Times* (June 7, 1991).

"HIV/AIDS." *Health and Sexuality* (Summer 1991):11.

Johns Hopkins School of Public Health Public Affairs Department. "Proposed AIDS Definition Unreliable, Public Health Study Says." Baltimore, July 15, 1992.

King, Donna. " 'Prostitutes as Pariah in the Age of AIDS': A Content Analysis of

Coverage of Women Prostitutes in *The New York Times* and in *The Washington Post* September 1985–April 1988." *Women and Health* 16 (1990): 155–176.

Lagakos, Stephen, et al. "Effects of Zidovudine Therapy in Minority and Other Subpopulations with Early HIV Infection." *Journal of the American Medical Association* 266 (1991):2709–2712.

Masur, Henry, et al. "Opportunistic Infection in Previously Healthy Women." *Annals of Internal Medicine* 97 (1982):533–538.

McBride, Gail. "Testing Drugs on Babies." *Newsday* (January 11, 1989):5.

McGoldrick, Kathryn E. "AIDS: The First Tumultuous Decade" (editorial). *Journal of the American Medical Women's Association.* 46 (1991):138, 149.

Minkhoff, Howard. American Medical Association media briefing: Toward Better Mother and Child Health: Issues in Contraception, Conception and Early Infant Development. New York, March 11, 1992.

Minkhoff, Howard L., and DeHovitz, Jack A. "Care of Women Infected with the Human Immunodeficiency Virus." *Journal of the American Medical Association* 266 (1991):2253–2258.

Mitchell, Janet L., et al. "HIV and Women: Current Controversies and Clinical Relevance." *Journal of Women's Health* 1 (1992):35–39.

National Institute of Allergy and Infectious Diseases. "ACTG Protocol 076—Questions and Answers." Bethesda, Md., March 8, 1991.

National Institute of Allergy and Infectious Diseases. "Study of AZT in HIV-Infected Pregnant Women and Their Offspring to Begin." Bethesda, Md., March 8, 1991.

National Women's Health Network. "Women, AIDS and Public Health Policies: A National Women's Health Network Report." Washington, D.C., 1990.

Navarro, Mireya. "AIDS Definition Is Widened to Include Blood Cell Count." *The New York Times* (August 8, 1991):D21.

New Jersey Women and AIDS Network. "CDC Announces Change in AIDS Case Definition But Still Ignores Women-Specific Illnesses." *NJWAN News* (Fall 1991):1–2.

Padian, Nancy S., et al. "Female-to-Male Transmission of Human Immunodeficiency Virus." *Journal of the American Medical Association* 266 (1991): 1664–1667.

Selik, Richard M., et al. "Epidemiology of AIDS and HIV Infection in Women in the United States." *Clinical Practice of Gynecology* 1 (1989):33–42.

Shuman, Paula. "Sexually Transmitted Diseases and AIDS." Workshop. First Annual Congress on Women's Health, June 4, 1993.

Sofield, Karen. Personal interview, May 19, 1993.

Somerville, Margaret. Director, McGill University Centre for Medicine, Ethics and the Law, Montreal. Personal interview, February 12, 1992.

Sperling, Rhoda S., et al. "Treatment Options for Human Immunodeficiency Virus-Infected Pregnant Women." *Obstetrics and Gynecology* 79 (1992): 443–448.

Staver, Sari. "Officials Pledge to Target Women for HIV Studies." *American Medical News* (March 4, 1991):15–16.

Staver, Sari. "Study Confirms Value of Early AZT Use." *American Medical News* (March 4, 1991):3, 16–17.

Stein, Michael, et al. "Differences in Access to Ziduvodine (AZT) Among Symptomatic HIV-infected Persons." *Journal of General Internal Medicine* 6 (1991):35–40.

Torres, Vivian. Personal interview, May 25, 1993.

Welch, William M. "Proposed AIDS Funding Is Questioned." Associated Press (February 25, 1992).

Whitlow, Joan. "UMDNJ Tests AZT in Pregnant Women to Protect Fetuses from AIDS." *Star Ledger* (March 16, 1991): 4.

Wofesy, Constance B. "Women and the Acquired Immunodeficiency Syndrome: An Interview." *Western Journal of Medicine* 149 (1988):687–690.

6: THE AGING WOMAN

"AMWA Position Statement on Osteoporosis." *Journal of the American Medical Women's Association* 45 (May–June 1990):75–79.

Avorn, Jerry. Associate professor of social medicine, Harvard University Medical School, Cambridge, Mass. Personal interview, March 16, 1992.

Barrett-Connor, Elizabeth. "Postmenopausal Estrogen and Prevention Bias." *Annals of Internal Medicine* 115 (September 15, 1991):455–456.

Barrett-Connor, Elizabeth, and Laakso, Markku. "Ischemic Heart Disease Risk in Postmenopausal Women: Effects of Estrogen Use on Glucose and Insulin Levels." *Arteriosclerosis* 10 (July–August 1990):531–534.

Burklow, John. "Doctors Concerned about Age Bias in Cancer Treatment." *Journal of the National Cancer Institute* 84 (March 18, 1992).

Carbone, Paul. Director, University of Wisconsin Comprehensive Cancer Center, Madison. Personal interview, April 28, 1993.

Cassel, Christine K., and Neugarten, Bernice L. "A Forecast of Women's Health and Longevity: Implications for an Aging America." *Western Journal of Medicine* 149 (December 1988):712–717.

"The Choices for Treating Osteoporosis." *The Johns Hopkins Medical Letter: Health After 50* 4 (April 1992):6–7.

Col, Nananda. Harvard University Medical School, Cambridge, Mass. Personal interview, March 16, 1992.

Colditz, Graham A., et al. "Prospective Study of Estrogen Replacement Therapy and Risk of Breast Cancer in Postmenopausal Women." *Journal of the American Medical Association* 264 (November 28, 1990):2648–2653.

Cotton, Paul. "Is There Still Too Much Extrapolation from Data on Middle-Aged White Men?" *Journal of the American Medical Association* 263 (February 23, 1990):1049–1050.

Egeland, Grace M., et al. "Postmenopausal Determinants of Menopausal Estrogen Use." *Preventive Medicine* 20 (1991):343–349.

Ettinger, Bruce. "A Practical Guide to Preventing Osteoporosis." *Western Journal of Medicine* 149 (December 1988):691–695.

Fausto-Sterling, Ann. *Myths of Gender: Biological Theories about Women and Men.* New York: Basic Books, 1985.

Fried, Linda. Director, Johns Hopkins Functional Status Laboratory; assistant professor of medicine, Johns Hopkins University; and director of research, Women's Aging Study, Baltimore. Personal interview, March 30, 1992.

Goldman, Lee, and Tosteson, Anna N. A. "Uncertainty About Postmenopausal Estrogen—Time for Action, Not Debate." *New England Journal of Medicine* 325 (September 12, 1991):800–802.

Greenfield, Sheldon, et al. "Patterns of Care Related to Age of Breast Cancer Patients." *Journal of the American Medical Association* 257 (May 22–29, 1987): 2766–2770.

Henderson, Brian E., et al. "Decreased Mortality in Users of Estrogen Replacement Therapy." *Archives of Internal Medicine* 151 (January 1991):75–78.

Kaplan, Barbara. Associate executive director, National Osteoporosis Foundation, Washington, D.C. Personal interview, April 2, 1992.

Kaufman, David W., et al. "Estrogen Replacement Therapy and the Risk of Breast Cancer: Results from the Case-Control Surveillance Study." *American Journal of Epidemiology* 134 (1991):1375–1385.

Kauvert, Patricia. University of Manitoba. Personal interview, March 16, 1992.

Leary, Warren. "U.S. Issues Guidelines on Bladder Problems." *New York Times* (March 24, 1992).

Lock, Margaret. "Contested Meanings of the Menopause." *Lancet* 337 (May 25, 1991):1270–1272.

Matthews, Karen A., et al. "Menopause and Risk Factors for Coronary Heart Disease." *New England Journal of Medicine* 321 (September 7, 1989):641–646.

"Menopause Gets an Emotional Reprieve." *Science News* 138 (July 7, 1990):12.

Miller, Valery T., et al. "ERT: Weighing the Risks and Benefits." *Patient Care* 24 (June 15, 1990):30–48.

National Osteoporosis Foundation. "Gallup Survey Finds Women Underestimate Severity, Consequences of Osteoporosis." Washington D.C.: News release, July 18, 1991.

The Office of Technology Assessment, Congressional Board of the 102d Cong. "The Menopause, Hormone Therapy, and Women's Health." Background paper. May 1992.

"Osteoporosis at the End of the Century" (editorial). *Western Journal of Medicine* 154 (January 1991):106–107.

Palmer, Julie R., et al. "Breast Cancer Risk after Estrogen Replacement Therapy: Results from the Toronto Breast Cancer Study." *American Journal of Epidemiology* 134 (1991):1386–1395.

Peck, Peggy. "Estrogen Benefit Challenged." *Medical Tribune* 32 (October 13, 1991).

Schiff, Isaac. "Treatment Issues in the Menopausal Woman." Paper presented at the First Annual Congress on Women's Health. Washington, D.C., June 4, 1993.

Stampfer, Meir J., et al. "Postmenopausal Estrogen Therapy and Cardiovascular

Disease—Ten-Year Follow-up from the Nurses' Health Study." *New England Journal of Medicine* 325 (September 12, 1991):756–762.

Steinberg, Karen K., et al. "A Meta-analysis of the Effect of Estrogen Replacement Therapy on the Risk of Breast Cancer." *Journal of the American Medical Association* 265 (April 17, 1991):1965–1990.

Strickland, Bonnie R. Professor of psychology, the University of Massachusetts, Amherst. Personal interview, March 25, 1992.

U.S. Department of Health and Human Services. Washington, D.C.: News release, August 23, 1991.

"Use of Estrogen Replacement in All Older Women Is Questioned." *Family Practice News* 22 (January 1, 1992).

Wallis, Lila. "Controversies in Preventing and Treating Osteoporosis." *Contemporary Internal Medicine* 2 (May 1990):56–73.

7: MIND GAMES

Barnhouse, Ruth Tiffany. Letter to Allen Francis, September, 21, 1992.

Blumenthal, Susan. "Depression in Women: Diagnosis and Treatment Issues." Paper presented at the First Annual Congress on Women's Health, Washington, D.C., June 3, 1993.

Bohan, Janis S. "Contextual History: A Framework for Replacing Women in the History of Psychology." *Psychology of Women Quarterly* 14 (1990):213–227.

Bohan, Janis S. Professor of psychology, Metropolitan State College, Denver, Colo. Personal interview, February 19, 1992.

Braude, Marjorie. Chief of psychiatry, Westwood Hospital, Los Angeles. Personal interview, February 19, 1992.

Braude, Marjorie. "Update: DSM-III Diagnosis Debate." *Journal of the American Medical Women's Association* 43(1) (1988):30.

Broverman, Inge K., et al. "Sex-Role Stereotypes and Clinical Judgments of Mental Health." *Journal of Consulting and Clinical Psychology* 34(1) (1970):1–7.

Brown, Laura S. Clinical psychologist and associate professor of psychology, the University of Washington, Seattle. Personal interview, February 29, 1992.

Brown, Laura S. "Diagnosis and Dialogue" (discussion). *Canadian Psychology* 32(2) (1991):142–144.

Brown, Laura S. "Plus Ça Change . . . or, Who Writes the Scripts for These Guys Anyway?" *Feminism and Psychology* 1 (1991):89–92.

Brown, Laura S. "The Potential for Misdiagnosis: Some Thoughts on the DSM-III-R." Unpublished paper. Seattle, Wash., 1987.

Brown, Laura S. "Taking Account of Gender in the Clinical Assessment Interview." *Professional Psychology: Research and Practice* 21 (1990):12–17.

Caplan, Paula J. Clinical and research psychologist and professor of applied psychology, the Ontario Institute for Studies in Education, Toronto, Ontario. Personal interview, March 6, 1992.

Caplan, Paula J. "The Dangers of Self-Defeating Personality Disorder as a Category." A position paper prepared for the ICD-10 Committee and the National Institute of Mental Health. Washington, D.C., 1987.

Caplan, Paula J. "Gender Issues in Diagnosis of Mental Disorder." Paper presented at the Gender, Science and Medicine Conference, University of Toronto, November 1988.

Caplan, Paula J. "How *Do* They Decide Who Is Normal? The Bizarre, but True, Tale of the *DSM* Process." *Canadian Psychology* 32(2) (1991):162–170.

Caplan, Paula J. *The Myth of Women's Masochism.* New York: Signet, 1987. From the chapter "Afterword: A Warning."

Caplan, Paula J. "Response to the DSM Wizard" (discussion). *Canadian Psychology* 32(2) (1991):174–175.

Caplan, Paula J., et al. "Should 'Premenstrual Syndrome' Be Called a Psychiatric Abnormality?" *Feminism and Psychology* 2(1) (1992):27–44.

Denmark, Florence, et al. "Guidelines for Avoiding Sexism in Psychological Research: A Report of the Ad Hoc Committee on Nonsexist Research." *American Psychologist* (July 1988):582–585.

Diagnostic and Statistical Manual of Mental Disorders, 3d ed., revised. Washington, D.C.: American Psychiatric Association, 1987.

Dye, Ellen, et al. "Psychotherapists' Knowledge About and Attitudes Toward Assault Victim Clients." *Psychology of Women Quarterly* 14 (1990):191–212.

Fee, Elizabeth. "Manmade Medicine and Women's Health: The Biopolitics of Sex/Gender and Racial Ethnicity." Paper presented at the Johns Hopkins School of Public Health. Symposium on Women's Health: The New View, April 30, 1993.

Frances, Allen, et al. "DSM-IV: Toward a More Empirical Diagnostic System" (discussion). *Canadian Psychology* 32(2) (1991):171–173.

Gallant, Sheryle J. (Alagna), et al. "On a Premenstrual Psychiatric Diagnosis: What's in a Name?" *Professional Psychology: Research and Practice* 19 (1988): 271–278.

Guinan, Mary E. "PMS or Perifollicular Phase Euphoria?" (editorial). *Journal of the American Medical Women's Association* 43(3) (1988):91–92.

Hamilton, Jean A. "Feminist Theory and Health Psychology: Tools for an Egalitarian, Woman-Centered Approach to Women's Health." *Journal of Women's Health* 2(1) (1993):49–54.

Hamilton, Jean A. Professor of social and health sciences and women's studies, Duke University, Durham, N.C. Personal interview, February 24, 1992.

Hamilton, Jean A., et al. "Premenstrual Dysphoric Disorder in DSM-II-R Will Stigmatize Women." Paper presented at the American Psychiatric Association Annual Meeting, Washington, D.C., May 1986.

Hamilton, Jean A., et al. "Problematic Aspects of Diagnosing Premenstrual Phase Dysphoria: Recommendations for Psychological Research and Practice." *Professional Psychology: Research and Practice* 21(1) (1990):60–68.

Harrison, Michelle. "Women's Health: A Medical Specialty?" Paper presented at the First Annual Congress on Women's Health, Washington, D.C., June 3, 1993.

Herman, Judith. Letter to John Gunderson. September 18, 1992.

Jensvold, Margaret F. Letter to Allen Francis. April 11, 1993.

Jensvold, Margaret F. Practicing psychiatrist and director of the Institute for Research on Women's Health, Washington, D.C. Personal interview, May 2, 1993.

Jensvold, Margaret F. Written testimony. Recruitment and Retention of Women in Clinical Studies, the National Institutes of Health Public Hearings, Bethesda, Md., submitted March 26, 1993.

Jensvold, Margaret F. "Workplace Sexual Harassment: The Uses of and Misuse and Abuse of Psychiatry." *Psychiatric Annals* (in press).

Johnson, Karen. "The Making of a Woman's Psychiatrist: Residency Training and Clinical Practice from a Feminist Biopsychosocial Perspective." *Psychiatric Annals* (in press).

Johnson, Karen. Practicing psychiatrist and assistant clinical professor of psychiatry, the University of California, San Francisco. Personal interview, April 28, 1993.

Landrine, Hope. "The Politics of Personality Disorder." *Psychology of Women Quarterly* 13 (1989):325–339.

McGrath, Ellen, et al., eds. *Women and Depression: Risk Factors and Treatment Issues.* Final report of the American Psychological Association's National Task Force on Women and Depression. Washington, D.C.: 1990.

Pantony, Kaye-Lee, et al. "Delusional Dominating Personality Disorder: A Modest Proposal for Identifying Some Consequences of Rigid Masculine Socialization." *Canadian Psychology* 32(2) (1991):120–133.

Pantony, Kaye-Lee, et al. "Response to Commentators" (editorial). *Canadian Psychology* 32(2) (1991):161.

Russo, Nancy Felipe, ed. *A Women's Mental Health Agenda.* Washington, D.C.: American Psychological Association, 1985.

Sanders, D., et al. "Mood, Sexuality, Hormones, and the Menstrual Cycle." *Psychosomatic Medicine* 45 (1983):487–503.

Solomon, Alisa. "Snake Pit." *Mirabella* (April 1993):140–144.

Waisberg, Jodie, et al. "Gender Role Nonconformity and Perception of Mental Illness." *Women & Health* 14(1) (1988):3–16.

Wellesley College Center for Research on Women. *How Schools Shortchange Girls.* Commissioned by the American Association of University Women Educational Foundation, Washington, D.C.: 1992.

8: VIOLENCE

The American College of Obstetricians and Gynecologists. "Physicians Urged to Join Fight Against Domestic Violence." Washington, D.C.: News release, April 29, 1992.

Berrios, Daniel C., and Grady, Deborah. "Domestic Violence: Risk Factors and Outcomes." *Western Journal of Medicine* 155 (August 1991):133–135.

Bowker, Lee H., and Maurer, Lorie. "The Medical Treatment of Battered Wives." *Women & Health* 12 (1987):25–45.

Caputi, Jane, and Russell, Diana E. H. " 'Femicide': Speaking the Unspeakable." *Ms.* (September–October 1990):34–37.

Carmen (Hilberman), Elaine, et al. "Victims of Violence and Psychiatric Illness." *American Journal of Psychiatry* 141 (1984):378–383.

Committee on the Judiciary, U.S. Senate. "Violence Against Women: The Increase of Rape in America 1990." March 21, 1991.

Dye, Ellen, et al. "Psychotherapists' Knowledge About and Attitude Toward Assault Victim Clients." *Psychology of Women Quarterly* 14 (1990):191–212.

Hadley, Susan. Director, WomanKind, Fairview Southdale Hospital, Edina, Minn. Personal interview, January 21, 1992.

Herman, Judith Lewis. "Complex PTSD: A Sundrome in Survivors of Prolonged and Repeated Trauma." Unpublished manuscript. 1992.

Herman, Judith Lewis. Personal interview, February 10, 1992.

Hilberman, Elaine. "Overview: The 'Wife-Beater's Wife' Reconsidered." *American Journal of Psychiatry* 137 (1980):1336–1347.

Jacobson, Andrea, and Richardson, Bonnie. "Assault Experiences of 100 Psychiatric Inpatients: Evidence of the Need for Routine Inquiry." *American Journal of Psychiatry* 144 (July 1987):908–913.

Koss, Mary, and Heslet, Lynette. "Medical Consequences of Violence Against Women." Unpublished manuscript, 1990.

Koss, Mary, et al. "Criminal Victimization Among Primary Care Medical Patients: Prevalence, Incidence and Physician Usage." *Behavioral Sciences and the Law* 9 (1991):85–96.

Koss, Mary, et al. "Deleterious Effects of Criminal Victimization on Women's Health and Medical Utilization." *Archives of Internal Medicine* 151 (February 1991):342–347.

Martin, Patricia Yancey, and DiNitto, Diana M. "The Rape Exam: Beyond the Hospital Emergency Room." *Women and Health* 12 (1987):5–27.

Martins, Rui, et al. "Wife Abuse: Are We Detecting It?" *Journal of Women's Health* 1(1992):77–80.

McCormick, Brian. "Doctors Urged to Act in Crisis of Violence." *American Medical News* (March 4, 1991):34.

McLeer, Susan V., et al. "Education Is Not Enough: A Systems Failure in Protecting Battered Women." *Annals of Emergency Medicine* 18 (June 6, 1989): 651–653.

Mehta, Paulette, and Dandrea, Loretta A. "The Battered Woman." *American Family Physician* 37 (January 1988):193–199.

National Victim Center and Crime Victims Research and Treatment Center. "Rape in America—A Report to the Nation." Forth Worth, Tex.: April 23, 1992.

Randall, Teri. "Domestic Violence Begets Other Problems of Which Physicians Must Be Aware." *Journal of the American Medical Association* 264 (August 22–29, 1990):940–944.

Randall, Teri. "Hospital-Wide Program Identifies Battered Women; Offers Assistance." *Journal of the American Medical Association* 266 (September 4, 1991):1177–1179.

Warshaw, Carole. Primary Care Internal Medicine, Cook County Hospital,

Chicago. Personal interview, February 21, 1992.

Warshaw, Carole, and Poirer, Suzanne. "Hidden Stories of Women." *Second Opinion* (October 1991):48–61.

Wartel, Stephen G. "Clinical Considerations for Adults Abused as Children." *Families in Society: The Journal of Contemporary Human Services* 72 (March 1991):157–163.

9: "FALLEN WOMEN"

"Alcohol and Women." *Alcohol Alert* 10, October 1990:1–4.

Blume, Sheila. "Alcohol and Substance Abuse in Women." Paper presented at the first Annual Congress on Women's Health, Washington, D.C., June 3, 1993.

Blume, Sheila B., "Alcoholism and Women's Health." Proceedings of the National Conference on Women's Health, Bethesda, Md., June 17–18, 1986. *Public Health Reports: Journal of the U.S. Public Health Service* (suppl.) (July–August 1987):34–48.

Blume, Sheila B. "Women, Alcohol, and Drugs." In Norman S. Miller, ed., *Comprehensive Handbook of Drug and Alcohol Addiction*. New York: Dekker, 1991.

Conte, Hope R., et al. "Sex Differences in Personality Traits and Coping Styles of Hospitalized Alcoholics." *Journal of Studies on Alcoholism* 52(1) (1991):26–32.

Delbanco, Thomas. "Patients Who Drink Too Much: Where Are Their Doctors?" (editorial). *Journal of the American Medical Association* 267 (1992):702–703.

Frezza, Mario, et al. "High Blood Alcohol Levels in Women: The Role of Decreased Gastric Alcohol Dehydrogenase Activity and First-Pass Metabolism." *New England Journal of Medicine* 322 (1990):95–99.

Gaunt, Jane. Certified addictions counselor and clinical supervisor of the women's unit, the Betty Ford Center, Rancho Mirage, Calif. Personal interview, September 30, 1991.

Hughes, Tonda L. Assistant professor, the department of psychiatric nursing, the University of Illinois, Chicago. Personal interview, February 17, 1992.

Hughes, Tonda L. "Evaluating Research on Chemical Dependency Among Women: A Women's Health Perspective." *Family and Community Health* 13(3) (1990):35–46.

Klassen, A. D., and Wisnack, S. C. "Sexual Experiences and Drinking Among Women in a U.S. National Survey." *Archives of Sexual Behavior* 15 (1986): 363–392.

Matteo, Sherri. "The Risk of Multiple Addictions: Guidelines for Assessing a Woman's Alcohol and Drug Use." *Western Journal of Medicine* 149 (1988):741–745.

Miller, B. A., and Downs, W. R. "Conflict and Violence Among Alcoholic Women as Compared to a Random Household Sample." Paper presented at the 38th Annual Meeting of the American Society of Criminology, Atlanta, Ga.

National Council on Alcoholism and Drug Dependence, Inc., "NCADD Fact Sheet: Alcoholism, Other Drug Addictions and Related Problems Among Women." New York, June 1990.

Reed, Beth Glover. "Developing Women-Sensitive Drug Dependence Treatment

Services: Why So Difficult?" *Journal of Psychoactive Drugs* 19(2) (1987): 151–164.

Schlesinger, Susanna, et al. "Self-Esteem and Purpose in Life: A Comparative Study of Women Alcoholics." *Journal of Alcohol and Drug Education* 36 (1) (1990):127–141.

Sherlock, Sheila. "Liver Disease in Women: Alcohol, Autoimmunity, and Gallstones." *Western Journal of Medicine* 149 (1988):683–686.

Stokes, Emma J. "Alcohol Abuse Screening: What to Ask Your Female Patient." *The Female Patient* 14(12) (1989):17–24.

Trimpey, Lois. Associate director, Rational Recovery Systems, Lotus, Calif. Personal interview, April 29, 1993.

Unger, Kathleen Bell. "Chemical Dependency in Women: Meeting the Challenges of Accurate Diagnosis and Effective Treatment." *Western Journal of Medicine* 149 (1988):746–750.

Vannicelli, Marsha. Associate professor, Harvard Medical School, Cambridge, Mass., and director of the Appleton Outpatient Clinic, McLean Hospital, Boston. Personal interview, March 16, 1992.

Vannicelli, Marsha. "Barriers to Treatment of Alcoholic Women." *Substance and Alcohol Actions/Misuse* 5 (1984):29–37.

Vannicelli, Marsha. "Effect of Sex Bias on Women's Studies on Alcoholism." *Alcoholism: Clinical and Experimental Research* 8(3) (1984):334–336.

Vannicelli, Marsha. "Treatment Considerations." In *Women and Alcohol: Health Related Issues.* National Institute on Alcohol Abuse and Alcoholism, Research Monograph No. 16. Department of Health and Human Services publication ADM 86-1,139. Washington, D.C.: U.S. Government Printing Office, 1984.

Vannicelli, Marsha. "Treatment Outcome of Alcoholic Women: The State of the Art in Relation to Sex Bias and Expectancy Effects." In Sharon C. Wilsnack and Linda J. Beckman, eds., *Alcohol Problems in Women.* pp. 369–412. New York: Guilford Press, 1984.

Walsh, Diana Chapman, et al. "The Impact of a Physician's Warning on Recovery After Alcoholism Treatment." *Journal of the American Medical Association* 267 (1992):663–667.

10: POOR WOMEN, POOR HEALTH

Allstetter, Billy. "Compulsory Contraception: Does the Punishment Fit the Crime?" *American Health* (May 1991):32–33.

American Heart Association, Department of Public Relations. "Strokes Hit African-Americans Harder, Two New Studies Show." Dallas, Tex.: December 13, 1991.

American Medical Association, Public Relations Department. "Poor and Elderly More Likely to Use Hospital Emergency Room and Resources." Chicago: October 22, 1991.

American Medical Association, Public Relations Department. "Public Hospital Patients Forgo Care While Waiting Too Long in the Emergency Room." August 27, 1991.

Bal, Dileep G. "Cancer in African Americans" (guest editorial). *Ca-A Cancer Journal for Clinicians* 42 (1992):5–6.

Barbara Boggs Sigmund Symposium on Women and Poverty. The Deadly Connection: Women, Health Care and Poverty. Princeton University, Princeton, N.J., March 27, 1992.

Baquet, Claudia R., et al. "Socioeconomic Factors and Cancer Incidence Among Blacks and Whites." *Journal of the National Cancer Institute* 83 (1991):551–556.

Blendon, Robert J., et al. "Access to Medical Care for Black and White Americans: A Matter of Continuing Concern." *Journal of the American Medical Association* 261 (1989):278–281.

Braveman, Paula, et al. "Women Without Health Insurance: Links Between Access, Poverty, Ethnicity and Health." *Western Journal of Medicine* 149 (1988):708–711.

Center on Budget and Policy Priorities. "Limited Access: Health Care for the Rural Poor." Washington, D.C., March 1991.

Center on Budget and Policy Priorities, Center for the Study of the States. "The States and the Poor: How Budget Decisions in 1991 Affected Low Income People." Washington, D.C./Albany, N.Y., December 1991.

Cousins, Olivia. Chairperson, board of directors, National Women's Health Network, Washington, D.C. Personal interview, March 27, 1992.

Curry, Mary Ann. "Nonfinancial Barriers to Prenatal Care." *Women & Health* 15 (1989):85–99.

Diehr, Paula, et al. "Treatment Modality and Quality Differences for Black and White Breast-Cancer Patients Treated in Community Hospitals." *Medical Care* 27 (1989):942–954.

El-Sadr, Wafaa, and Capps, Linnea. "The Challenge of Minority Recruitment in Clinical Trials for AIDS." *Journal of the American Medical Association* 267 (1992):954–957.

Fedele, Helene, Director, the Women's Center, Memorial Hospital Community Health Center, Mount Holly, N.J. Personal interview, May 10, 1993.

Freeman, Harold P. "Cancer in the Socioeconomically Disadvantaged." *Ca-A Cancer Journal for Clinicians* 39 (1989):263–295.

Freeman, Harold P. "Race, Poverty and Cancer." *Journal of the National Cancer Institute* 83 (1991):526–527.

Friedman, Emily. "The Uninsured: From Dilemma to Crisis." *Journal of the American Medical Association* 265 (1991):2491–2495.

Gaines, Jackie. "Healthcare for the Homeless." Presentation at the Johns Hopkins School of Public Health Symposium on Women's Health: The New View, Baltimore, April 30, 1993.

Giachello, Aida. Assistant professor, Jane Addams College of Social Work, University of Illinois, Chicago. Personal interview, March 31, 1992.

Hand, Roger, et al. "Hospital Variables Associated with Quality of Care for Breast Cancer Patients." *Journal of the American Medical Association* 266 (1991): 3429–3432.

Jackson, Kayla. Project specialist, National Council of Negro Women, Washington, D.C. Personal interview, March 10, 1992.

Johns Hopkins School of Public Health, Office of Public Affairs. "Breast Cancer Has Worse Outcomes for Poorer Women." News release, March 15, 1992.

McBarnette, Lorna. "Women and Poverty: The Effects on Reproductive Status." *Women & Health* 14 (1988):55–81.

McCord, Colin, and Freeman, Harold P. "Excess Mortality in Harlem." *New England Journal of Medicine* 322 (1990):173–177.

Muller, Charlotte. "Medicaid: The Lower Tier of Health Care for Women." *Women & Health* 14 (1988):81–103.

National Council of Negro Women and Communications Consortium Media Center. "Women of Color Reproductive Health Poll." Washington, D.C.: August 30, 1991.

Sack, Kevin. "New, and Volatile, Politics of Welfare." *New York Times* (March 15, 1992):25.

Svensson, C. K. "Representation of American Blacks in Clinical Trials of New Drugs." *Journal of the American Medical Association* 261 (1989):263–265.

Tavani, Cleonice. "Report on a Seminar on Financing and Service Delivery Issues in Caring for the Medically Underserved." *Public Health Reports* 106 (1991): 19–25.

U.S. Congress. *Hearings before the Subcommittee on Health and the Environment of the Committee on Energy and Commerce House of Representatives.* 101st Cong., Serial 101-141. Washington, D.C., U.S. Government Printing Office, 1990.

Yergan, John, et al. "Relationship Between Patient Race and the Intensity of Hospital Services." *Medical Care* 25 (1987):592–603.

Zambrana, Ruth E. "A Research Agenda on Issues Affecting Poor and Minority Women: A Model for Understanding Their Health Needs." *Women & Health* 14 (1988):137–153.

11: MATERNAL VERSUS FETAL RIGHTS

The American College of Obstetricians and Gynecologists. "Patient Choice: Maternal-Fetal Conflict." Committee Opinion from the Committee on Ethics. *Women's Health Issues* 1 (1990):13–15.

"AMWA Signs Amicus Brief." *Journal of the American Medical Women's Association* 45 (March/April 1990):38–39.

Bonavoglia, Angela. "The Ordeal of Pamela Rae Stewart." *Ms.* (July–August 1987):94–95, 196–204.

Chasnoff, Ira. Associate professor of pediatrics and psychiatry, Northwestern University, Chicago, and president, National Association for Perinatal Addiction Research and Education. "American Medical Association Media Briefing: Toward Better Mother and Child Health—Issues in Contraception, Conception and Early Infant Development." Presentation and personal communication, New York, March 11, 1992.

Chasnoff, Ira. "Drug Use in Pregnancy: Parameters of Risk." *The Pediatric Clinics of North America* 35 (1988):1403–1412.

Chasnoff, Ira, et al. "The Prevalence of Illicit-Drug or Alcohol Use During Pregnancy and Discrepancies in Mandatory Reporting in Pinellas County,

Florida." *New England Journal of Medicine* 322 (April 26, 1990):1202–1206.

Eagan, Andrea Boroff. "Who Decides for Women?" *American Health* (September 1990):42–43.

Elmer-Dewitt, Philip. "Why Isn't Our Birth Control Better?" *Time* (August 12, 1991).

Gest, Ted. "The Pregnancy Police, on Patrol." *U.S. News & World Report* (February 6, 1989):50.

Greenhouse, Linda. "Hospital Sets Policy on Pregnant Patients' Rights." *New York Times* (November 29, 1990):1, 18.

Hilts, Philip J. "Birth Control Backlash." *New York Times Magazine* (December 16, 1990):4, 55, 70, 72, 74.

Jonsen, Albert R. "Women's Choices—The Ethics of Maternity." *Western Journal of Medicine* 149 (December 1988):726–728.

Kolder, Veronika E. B., et al. "Court-Ordered Obstetrical Interventions." *New England Journal of Medicine* 316 (May 7, 1987):1192–1196.

Lewin, Tamar. "Courts Acting to Force Care of the Unborn." *New York Times* (November 23, 1987):1.

Lewin, Tamar. "Drug Verdict Over Infants Is Voided." *New York Times* (July 24, 1992):B7.

Macklin, Ruth. "Maternal–Fetal Conflict: An Ethical Analysis." *Women's Health Issues* 1 (1990):28–30.

Macklin, Ruth. Professor, department of epidemiology and social medicine, Albert Einstein College of Medicine, the Bronx, New York. Personal interview, February 20, 1992.

Mandelbaum, Sara. Attorney, Women's Rights Project of the American Civil Liberties Union, New York. Personal interview, May 4, 1993.

Marshall, Alison B. Attorney, Miller, Canfield, Paddock and Stone, Washington, D.C., and general counsel, National Association for Perinatal Addiction Research and Education. Personal interview, February 24, 1992.

Mastroianni, Luigi, Jr. Director of the Division of Human Reproduction, University of Pennsylvania, Philadelphia. Personal interview, February 10, 1992.

Mastroianni, Luigi, Jr., et al. "Special Report: Development of Contraceptives— Obstacles and Opportunities." *New England Journal of Medicine* 322 (February 15, 1990):482–484.

Mayes, Linda C., et al. "The Problem of Prenatal Cocaine Exposure: A Rush to Judgment" (commentary). *Journal of the American Medical Association* 267 (January 15, 1992):406–408.

McFarlane, Judith. "Battering During Pregnancy: Tip of an Iceberg Revealed." *Women and Health* 15 (1989):69–83.

Moss, Kary L. "Substance Dependency During Pregnancy: The Limits of the Law." *Women's Health Issues* 1 (1991):120–126.

National Council on Alcoholism and Drug Dependence, Inc. "NCADD Fact Sheet: Alcohol-Related Birth Defects." New York: 1990.

National Institute on Alcohol Abuse and Alcoholism. "Fetal Alcohol Syndrome." *Alcohol Alert* 13 (July 1991):1–4.

Nelson, Lawrence J., and Milliken, Nancy. "Compelled Medical Treatment of

Pregnant Women: Life, Liberty and Law in Conflict." *Journal of the American Medical Association* 259 (February 19, 1988):1060–1066.

Newberger, Eli H., et al. "Abuse of Pregnant Women and Adverse Birth Outcome: Current Knowledge and Implications for Practice" (commentary). *Journal of the American Medical Association* 267 (May 6, 1992):2370–2372.

Paterno, Vicki. University of California School of Medicine, Los Angeles. Personal interview, February 11, 1992.

Planned Parenthood Federation of America, Inc. "New Birth Control Conferences Report." New York: 1991.

Regelson, William, et al. "Beyond 'Abortion': RU-486 and the Needs of the Crisis Constituency" (commentary). *Journal of the American Medical Association* 8 (August 22/29, 1990):1026–1027.

Regelson, William. Oncologist, Medical College of Virginia, Richmond. Personal interview, February 11, 1992.

Rosenfield, Allen. Dean, Columbia University School of Public Health. "Reproductive Rights in Perspective." Presentation given at the First Annual Congress on Women's Health, Washington, D.C., June 3, 1993.

Ruben, David. "Motherhood on Trial." *Parenting* (June/July 1990):74–159.

Ryan, Kenneth J. "Erosion of the Rights of Pregnant Women: In the Interest of Fetal Well-Being." *Women's Health Issues* 1 (1990):21–24.

Silver, Lynn, and Wolfe, Sidney M. *Unnecessary Cesarean Sections: How to Cure a National Epidemic.* Washington, D.C.: Public Citizen Health Research Group, 1989.

Toner, Robin. "Clinton Would End Ban of Aid to Poor Seeking Abortions." *New York Times* (March 30, 1993):A1.

Zelon, Laurie. Personal interview, February 17, 1992.

12: SEX IN THE OFFICE

Bouhoutsos, J., et al. "Sexual Intimacy Between Psychotherapists and Patients." *Professional Psychologist* 14(2) (1983):185–196.

College of Physicians and Surgeons of Ontario. "Final Report of the Task Force on Sexual Abuse of Patients." November 25, 1991.

Council on Ethical and Judicial Affairs, American Medical Association. "Sexual Misconduct in the Practice of Medicine." *Journal of the American Medical Association* 266 (1991):2741–2745.

Ethical Treatment in Health Care. "The Aftermath of Sexual Abuse by a Health or Mental Health Professional." Weston, Mass., 1991.

Gartrell, Nanette. Associate clinical professor of psychiatry, the University of California, San Francisco. Personal interview, February 8, 1992.

Gartrell, Nanette K., et al. "Institutional Resistance to Self-Study: a Case Report." In Ann W. Burgess and Carol R. Hartman, eds. *Sexual Exploitation of Patients by Health Professionals.* New York: Praeger, 1986.

Gartrell, Nanette, et al. "Management and Rehabilitation of Sexually Exploitative Therapist." *Hospital and Community Psychiatry* 39 (1988):1070–1074.

Gartrell, Nanette, et al. "Physician–Patient Sexual Contact: Prevalence and Problems." *Western Journal of Medicine* 157(2) (1992):139–143.

Gartrell, Nanette, et al. "Psychiatrist–Patient Sexual Contact: Results of a National Survey. I. Prevalence." *American Journal of Psychiatry* 143 (1986):1126–1131.

Gartrell, Nanette, et al. "Reporting Practices of Psychiatrists Who Knew of Sexual Misconduct by Colleagues." *American Journal of Orthopsychiatry* 57(2) (1987):287–295.

Herman, Judith, et al. "Psychiatrist–Patient Sexual Contact: Results of a National Survey. II. Psychiatrists' Attitudes." *American Journal of Psychiatry* 144(2) (1987):164–169.

Public Broadcasting System. My Doctor, My Lover. *Frontline.* November 12, 1991, and May 12, 1993. Transcript from Journal Graphics, Inc., 1535 Grant St., Denver, Colo. 80203.

Schoener, Gary. Licensed psychologist and executive director, the Walk-In Counseling Center, Minneapolis, Minn. Personal interview, January 15, 1992.

Sostek, Gale. President of Ethical Treatment in Health Care, Weston, Mass. Personal interview, February 24, 1992.

Therapy Exploitation Link Line, P.O. Box 115, Waban, Mass. 02168, (617) 964-TELL.

13: THE VISIBLE WOMAN

Congressional Caucus for Women's Issues. "Women's Health Equity Act Update." Washington, D.C., November 1992.

Cotton, Paul. "Women's Health Initiative Leads Way as Research Begins to Fill Gender Gaps." *Journal of the American Medical Association* 267 (January 22–29, 1992):469–473.

Davis, Flora. *Moving the Mountain: The Women's Movement in America Since 1960.* New York: Touchstone, 1991.

Hamilton, Jean A. "Biases in Women's Health Research." Unpublished manuscript: 1992.

Hamilton, Jean A. "Medical Research: The Forgotten 51%." In *1992 Medical and Health Annual.* Chicago: Encyclopedia Britannica, 1992.

Hamilton, Jean A. "Women's Health Research: Public Policy Issues." Paper presented at the Second Annual Syntex Women's Health Roundtable, Washington, D.C., February 7–9, 1992.

Harrison, Michelle. "Women's Health: A Medical Specialty?" Presentation at the First Annual Congress on Women's Health, Washington, D.C., June 3, 1993.

Haseltine, Florence. Director, Society for the Advancement of Women's Health Research, Washington D.C., and director, Center for Population Research, National Institutes of Health, Bethesda, Md. Personal interview. May 12, 1992.

Healy, Bernadine. "Women's Health, Public Welfare" (editorial). *Journal of the American Medical Association* 266 (1991):566–568.

Johnson, Karen. "Women's Health: A Medical Specialty?" Presentation at the First Annual Congress on Women's Health, Washington, D.C., June 3, 1993.

National Women's Health Network. "Research to Improve Women's Health: An

Agenda for Equity." Washington, D.C., December 1991.

Ratner, Vicki. President, Interstitial Cystitis Foundation. Personal interview, June 3, 1993.

Ratner, Vicki. "Patients, Politics and the Perils of Healthcare Policy: Interstitial Cystitis and Other Women's Ills." Presentation at the First Annual Congress on Women's Health, Washington, D.C., June 3, 1993.

Schroeder, Patricia. U.S. Congresswoman and cochair of the Congressional Caucus for Women's Issues, Washington, D.C. Personal interview, May 11, 1992.

Society for the Advancement of Women's Health Research. "Toward a Women's Health Research Agenda: Findings from the Autumn Roundtables." Chicago, November 5, 1991.

Society for the Advancement of Women's Health Research. "Women's Health Research: Prescription for Change." Annual Report. Chicago, January 1991.

Wallis, Lila. "Women's Health: A Medical Specialty?" Presentation at the First Annual Congress on Women's Health, Washington, D.C., June 3, 1993.

INDEX